STARS
—AND—
PLANETS

DORLING KINDERSLEY
—**HANDBOOKS**—

STARS
—AND—
PLANETS

IAN RIDPATH

Editorial Consultant
IAIN NICOLSON

Star charts by
ROYAL GREENWICH OBSERVATORY

A Dorling Kindersley Book

LONDON, NEW YORK, MUNICH,
MELBOURNE and DELHI

Important Notice
Observing the Sun through any kind of optical instrument can cause blindness.
The author and publishers cannot accept any responsibility for readers who
ignore this advice.

Project Editor Peter Frances
Project Designer Helen Taylor
DTP Designer Rob Campbell
Picture Research Angela Anderson, Robin Scagell
Production Controllers Michelle Thomas, Alison Jones
Managing Editor Jonathan Metcalf
Managing Art Editors Peter Cross, Steve Knowlden

— ♠ —

First published in Great Britain in 1998
by Dorling Kindersley Limited
80 Strand, London WC2R 0RL
Reprinted with corrections in 2000, 2002

A Penguin Company

12   14   16   18   20   19   17   15   13

Copyright © 1998, 2000, 2002
Dorling Kindersley Limited, London
Text copyright © 1998, 2000, 2002 Ian Ridpath

A CIP catalogue record for this book is available
from the British Library

ISBN 0-7513-2712-3

— ♠ —

Text film output by The Right Type, Great Britain
Reproduced by Colourscan, Singapore
Printed and bound by South China Printing Company, China

see our complete catalogue at
www.dk.com

CONTENTS

AUTHOR'S INTRODUCTION

As the Sun sets and the sky darkens, the marvels of the night sky come into view: planets in our Solar System; stars, star clusters, and nebulae in our Galaxy; and other galaxies, unimaginably distant. Examples of all these objects can be seen with the naked eye, while binoculars or a small telescope reveal many more. This book shows you where and how to find them.

ASTRONOMY IS USUALLY regarded as the oldest of the sciences – yet, with the continuing development of space probes to the planets and orbiting telescopes, it is also among the most modern.

ANCIENT ASTRONOMY

Serious study of the sky began thousands of years ago in the Middle East and, at least in the ancient world, reached a pinnacle with the Greeks 2,000 years ago. At that time, the stars and planets were still mysterious lights in the sky, and the Earth was thought to be at the centre of the Universe. This view was not seriously challenged until the 16th century, when Nicolaus Copernicus, a Polish astronomer, proposed that the Earth is simply a planet and that all planets orbit the Sun. His revolutionary view was confirmed in the following century by the Italian Galileo Galilei, using the newly invented telescope. Johannes Kepler, a German mathematician, worked out that planets orbit on elliptical paths, and the Englishman Isaac Newton explained the gravitational forces governing all orbital motions.

THE FARNESE ATLAS
The celestial globe held here by Atlas shows the constellations known to the ancient Greeks.

MODERN ASTRONOMY

From Newton's time in the 17th century onwards, it was recognized that the stars are other suns, but only in the 20th century, with the work of the American astronomer Edwin Hubble, did it become clear that our Galaxy of stars is only one among countless others, and that the Universe as a whole is expanding, as though from a massive explosion billions of years ago. And only with the development of nuclear physics has it become clear how the stars generate the energy that makes them shine.

SKYWATCHING

For all its modern advances, astronomy remains a branch of science where amateurs can make a real contribution, often with modest equipment – for example, monitoring changes in the brightness of variable stars, logging meteor showers, following storms in the atmospheres of Mars, Jupiter, and Saturn – and, if you're lucky, discovering an exploding star (a nova) or a comet. Perhaps one of the readers of this book will go on to make such a discovery.

HOW THIS BOOK WORKS

THIS BOOK IS divided into four parts: a general introduction to astronomy; a detailed guide to the Solar System; an alphabetical catalogue of the constellations; and a month-by- month companion to the night sky. Sample pages from the three main sections (excluding the Introduction) are shown below. Further explanation appears at the start of each section.

THE SOLAR SYSTEM, PP.25–62

This section contains descriptions of the nine planets, the Sun and Moon, and the more significant smaller bodies. It also includes advice on how and where to find them.

THE CONSTELLATIONS, PP.63–141

Entries on the 88 constellations are arranged alphabetically by name. Collectively, the charts in this section form a complete atlas of the sky. The text describes the origins of the constellations and selected features of interest.

MONTHLY SKY GUIDE, PP.142–215

An introduction to each month, with easy-to-use charts and descriptions of what to look out for, is followed by more detailed charts of the night sky as seen from northern and southern latitudes.

INTRODUCTION TO THE MONTH

KEY TO SYMBOLS

GREEK ALPHABET
Greek letters form part of the names of certain stars and appear on some of the charts in this book.

α alpha	ι iota	ρ rho	
β beta	κ kappa	σ sigma	
γ gamma	λ lambda	τ tau	
δ delta	μ mu	υ upsilon	
ε epsilon	ν nu	φ phi	
ζ zeta	ξ xi	χ chi	
η eta	ο omicron	ψ psi	
θ theta	π pi	ω omega	

DEEP-SKY OBJECTS
These symbols appear in red on the constellation and whole-sky charts.

- Galaxy
- Globular cluster
- Open cluster
- Diffuse nebula
- Planetary nebula
- X-ray and radio sources

OBSERVATION SYMBOLS
These symbols indicate the type of instrument needed to observe features described in the Constellations section.

- Naked eye
- Binoculars
- Telescope
- Not observable with amateur equipment

THE UNIVERSE

THE UNIVERSE is everything that exists – all matter, space, and time. It extends as far as the largest telescopes can see, at least 10 billion light-years in all directions around us. The Universe is thought to have formed in a gigantic explosion, called the Big Bang, about 13 to 14 billion years ago and is still expanding. Within the Universe, matter is held together by gravity in structures of varying size.

OUR GALAXY

Most of the visible matter in the Universe is grouped in huge aggregations of stars, gas, and dust called galaxies. Our nearest star, the Sun, is an insignificant star in a galaxy of at least 100,000 million others (usually known as "the Galaxy"). Although it is difficult to tell from our position inside it, the Galaxy is thought to be spiral in shape. There is some evidence indicating that there is a bar of material across the centre. The Galaxy is about 100,000 light-years in diameter, and we are located about two-thirds of the way from the center to the rim, in one of its spiral arms. The stars that we see in the sky are all part of the Galaxy. Those nearest to us appear in all directions in the sky, and form the constellations (see p.18). Since the Galaxy is flattened in shape, more distant stars mass into a hazy band known as the Milky Way.

△ THE MILKY WAY

The Milky Way, a pale band that can be seen arching across the sky on dark nights, consists of innumerable distant stars within our Galaxy. In this view of the Milky Way, looking towards the centre of the Galaxy, apparent gaps are caused by clouds of dark dust that lie in the spiral arms, obscuring the light from stars behind.

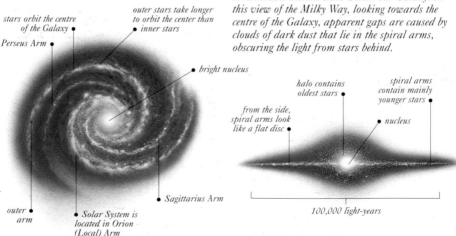

stars orbit the centre of the Galaxy

outer stars take longer to orbit the center than inner stars

Perseus Arm

bright nucleus

halo contains oldest stars

spiral arms contain mainly younger stars

from the side, spiral arms look like a flat disc

nucleus

outer arm

Solar System is located in Orion (Local) Arm

Sagittarius Arm

OVERHEAD VIEW OF OUR GALAXY

100,000 light-years

SIDE VIEW OF OUR GALAXY

OTHER GALAXIES

The Universe contains countless galaxies, some of which we can see from the Earth. Galaxies are divided into spirals, barred spirals, ellipticals, and irregulars. Spirals have arms which consist of relatively young stars, gas clouds, and dust, and which curve out from a central bulge of old stars. In barred spirals, the arms extend from the ends of a central bar. Elliptical galaxies, consisting of old stars, have no arms and very little gas or dust. Irregular galaxies have no regular shape or structure. The largest galaxies are ellipticals, with more than ten times the mass of our Galaxy; some giant ellipticals may have formed by the merger of smaller galaxies. Far off in the Universe are objects called quasars that emit as much energy as a galaxy from an area not much larger than the Solar System. Quasars, and their less luminous relatives, known as Seyfert galaxies and BL Lacertae objects, are thought to be galaxies with massive black holes at their centres.

SPIRAL GALAXY
This galaxy, M83, appears "face-on" to us, so that we see its nucleus and curving arms.

BARRED SPIRAL GALAXY
In a barred spiral, such as NGC 1365, a bar of stars and gas lies across the nucleus.

ELLIPTICAL GALAXY
Elliptical galaxies range from dwarfs to giants. M87 is an example of a giant elliptical.

GROUPS OF GALAXIES

Galaxies usually occur in groups known as clusters. Our Galaxy is the second largest in a relatively small family of about 30 galaxies called the Local Group, about 3 million light years across. The Group's largest member is the Andromeda Galaxy, a spiral galaxy more than 2 million light years away and the most distant object visible to the naked eye. Some clusters have thousands of members, as does the Virgo Cluster, the nearest large cluster to us, about 50 million light years away. Its brightest members can be seen with the size of telescope used by amateur astronomers.

THE LOCAL GROUP

IC 10 (dwarf irregular galaxy)

Leo A (dwarf irregular galaxy)

Andromeda Galaxy   M33

Milky Way

Large Magellanic Cloud
Small Magellanic Cloud

WHAT IS A STAR?

STARS ARE BALLS of gas that release energy produced by nuclear reactions within their cores. Most stars are similar to the Sun, our nearest star, but because they are so far away they appear to us as mere points of light. Throughout the Galaxy, stars are forming, evolving, and being destroyed. By studying a range of stars, astronomers have been able to build a picture of how stars change over time, and hence understand more about the past and probable future of the Sun.

STAR FORMATION

Stars form in huge clouds of gas and dust in space called nebulae, in a process that is continuing today. The nebula shrinks under the inward pull of its own gravity, forming an embryonic star known as a protostar. Eventually, the density and temperature of the gas at the protostar's centre become high enough for nuclear reactions to begin. The object "switches on" to become a true star, generating its own heat and light. The star is then said to be on the main sequence. How long it stays like this and what happens next depend on the star's mass.

STAR FORMATION

dense area in nebula begins to contract

contraction causes temperature of protostar to rise to about 15 million °C (27 million °F)

star emits heat and light produced by nuclear fusion

200,000 BILLION KM
NEBULA

100 MILLION KM
PROTOSTAR

1 MILLION KM
MAIN-SEQUENCE STAR

NEBULAE

Nebulae are clouds of gas and dust within galaxies. Bright diffuse nebulae are areas of hydrogen gas where new stars are being formed. Two types of nebula are linked with the late stages of star development: planetary nebulae are shells of gas thrown off by red giant stars, while supernova remnants are the twisted wreckage of exploded massive stars. Some nebulae are dark because they contain no stars to illuminate them, and are visible only when silhouetted against a brighter background.

GREAT ORION NEBULA
(BRIGHT DIFFUSE NEBULA)

VELA SUPERNOVA REMNANT
(SUPERNOVA REMNANT)

CAT'S EYE NEBULA
(PLANETARY NEBULA)

MASSIVE STARS

A main-sequence star with a mass of more than about 10 Suns experiences a spectacular end. It swells into a red supergiant with cooling, expanding outer layers. Eventually its core collapses, causing a huge explosion known as a supernova. For a few weeks, the supernova shines as brightly as an entire galaxy. While the outer layers of the star are scattered in space, the fate of the core again depends on its mass. A core of relatively low mass will be crushed into a tiny, superdense neutron star. If the core has a mass of more than about two Suns, its own gravity will squash it further, into a black hole.

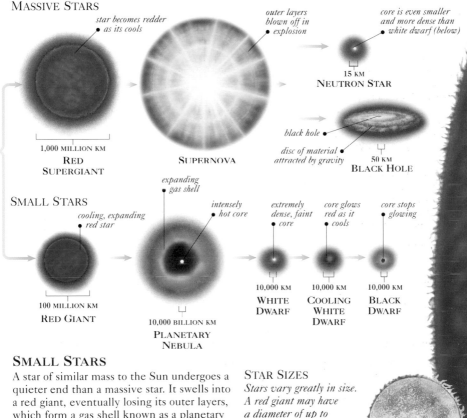

MASSIVE STARS

star becomes redder as its cools

1,000 MILLION KM
RED SUPERGIANT

SUPERNOVA

outer layers blown off in explosion

15 KM
NEUTRON STAR

core is even smaller and more dense than white dwarf (below)

black hole
disc of material attracted by gravity

50 KM
BLACK HOLE

SMALL STARS

cooling, expanding red star

expanding gas shell

intensely hot core

100 MILLION KM
RED GIANT

10,000 BILLION KM
PLANETARY NEBULA

extremely dense, faint core

core glows red as it cools

core stops glowing

10,000 KM
WHITE DWARF

10,000 KM
COOLING WHITE DWARF

10,000 KM
BLACK DWARF

SMALL STARS

A star of similar mass to the Sun undergoes a quieter end than a massive star. It swells into a red giant, eventually losing its outer layers, which form a gas shell known as a planetary nebula (because of its resemblance to the disc of a distant planet). The core is exposed as a hot white dwarf that cools and fades over billions of years. On ceasing to emit light, it will become a black dwarf. The least massive stars, red dwarfs with only about one-tenth the Sun's mass, can last for 100 billion years or more, whereas the most massive stars burn out after only about a million years. The Sun, which formed about 5,000 million years ago, is about halfway through its life-cycle.

STAR SIZES
Stars vary greatly in size. A red giant may have a diameter of up to 150 million km (100 million miles). The Sun (a main-sequence star) is 1.39 million km (865,000 miles) in diameter, while a white dwarf, the size of which is exaggerated on this diagram, is typically only 10,000 km (6,000 miles) across.

white dwarf
main-sequence star
red giant

STAR FAMILIES AND VARIABLE STARS

STARS ARE not always the simple, unchanging points of light that they may at first appear to be. Many of them occur in families of two or three, or sometimes in much larger groupings.

Others vary in brightness in cycles that last days, months, or years. Examples of double and multiple stars, star clusters, and variable stars can be seen with small instruments or even the naked eye.

DOUBLE AND MULTIPLE STARS

When seen with binoculars or a telescope, many stars turn out to have one or more companions. Sometimes the companion stars are unrelated objects in the foreground or background, in which case the pair form what is called an optical double. But in most cases, the stars lie close together in space, forming a pairing known as a binary. Linked by gravity, the members of a binary orbit around each other, although it usually takes many years to detect any motion, and in the case of multiple stars the orbital motions can be very complex. Separating the components of double stars is a popular activity among amateur astronomers. The closer together the stars are as seen from Earth, the larger the aperture of telescope needed to divide

ALBIREO
A colour contrast of orange and blue makes this a particularly attractive double star for users of small telescopes.

(or "split") them. When the stars are very unequal in brightness, the fainter star (the secondary) can be difficult to see because of the glare from the brighter one (the primary). Some doubles, called spectroscopic binaries, have components that are too close together to be separated through an optical telescope. Only by studying the spectra of light from these stars are professional astronomers able to establish that they are double.

OPTICAL DOUBLE STARS
Two stars that lie in the same line of sight but are at different distances from us are known as an optical double. Double stars of this type are less common than genuine binaries. In fact, more than three-quarters of all stars are linked to one or more companions by gravity.

STARS LINKED BY GRAVITY

EQUAL MASS
In a binary star with members of equal mass, the stars orbit around a centre of mass midway between them.

UNEQUAL MASS
When one member of a binary is more massive than the other, the centre of mass lies closer to the heavier star.

A MULTIPLE STAR
Here, four stars of equal mass form two pairs orbiting a centre of mass. Multiple star orbits are usually highly elliptical.

STAR CLUSTERS

Rather than originating singly, most stars form as part of a group or cluster, of which there are two distinct types. Open clusters, the more common type, have no specific shape, being scattered collections of dozens to hundreds of relatively young stars lying in the spiral arms of our Galaxy. Globular clusters, which lie in a halo around our Galaxy, are spherical or slightly elliptical in shape and contain large numbers of very old stars.

OMEGA CENTAURI ▷
(GLOBULAR CLUSTER)

△ THE PLEIADES
(OPEN CLUSTER)

VARIABLE STARS

A variable star is one that varies in brightness over time. Nearly 20 per cent of such stars are eclipsing binaries – very close pairs in which one star periodically passes in front of the other, causing a drop in the total amount of light reaching the Earth. The most famous eclipsing binary is a star called Algol (in the constellation Perseus). But most stars that vary in brightness do so because they pulsate in size. The most common of these are red giants and supergiants called Mira stars, after their prototype, Mira (in Cetus). Such stars vary by up to 25,000 times in cycles lasting 3 months to 3 years. Many other red giants and supergiants also pulsate, but with less regularity and smaller changes in output than Mira stars. Relatively rare, but important, are Cepheid variables, named after Delta Cephei (in Cepheus). The pulsation period of these yellow supergiant stars is directly related to their luminosity, so by timing a star's variations astronomers can work out its actual brightness. Since the brightness of a star in our sky depends on its distance from us, such stars act as valuable "standard candles" for measuring distances in space.

BRIGHTNESS OF ALGOL AND DELTA CEPHEI

These graphs show how the apparent brightness (or magnitude) of these two stars varies over time. While the curve for Delta Cephei is relatively smooth, the brightness of Algol falls dramatically when the primary is eclipsed by its fainter partner.

DELTA CEPHEI

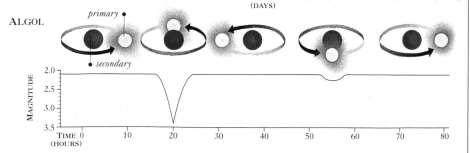

THE SOLAR SYSTEM

THE HUB of the Solar System is the Sun. Around it orbit nine planets and their moons, along with a swarm of asteroids (also known as minor planets) and smaller pieces of debris. The Sun contains about 99.9 per cent of the Solar System's total mass, and all the objects in the system are held in place by its gravity. At the edge of the Solar System is a cloud of comets that extends roughly halfway to the nearest star, a distance of about 2 light years.

THE SUN AND PLANETS

The Solar System is orbiting the centre of the Galaxy. At the same time, the planets are in orbit around the Sun, all moving anti-clockwise as viewed from over the Sun's north pole. Each planet also spins on its own axis of rotation. The four innermost planets – Mercury, Venus, Earth, and Mars – are small, rocky bodies, sometimes known as the terrestrial planets. Beyond Mars is the asteroid belt and then the gas giants: Jupiter, Saturn, Uranus, and Neptune, so-called because they are much larger than the Earth and consist mostly of hydrogen and helium. All four have ring systems and numerous moons. Pluto is a small, frozen oddity, which for part of its orbit is closer to the Sun than Neptune is. The planets are thought to have formed from a disc of gas and dust around the newly formed Sun about 4.6 billion years ago. Astronomers have found evidence that planets exist around other stars, too.

ORBITS OF THE INNER PLANETS ▷

The Earth is the largest of the four rocky inner planets. Mercury and Venus, which orbit between the Sun and Earth, are known as inferior planets.

THE PLANETS IN SCALE

OBSERVING THE PLANETS

The orbits of the Earth and other planets are in much the same plane. As a result, the planets stay close to an imaginary line called the ecliptic (see p.16) that represents the Sun's apparent path across the sky over the course of a year. Inferior planets (Mercury and Venus) are always close to the Sun in the sky, appearing before dawn or after sunset, but never in a truly dark sky. Five planets – Mercury, Venus, Mars, Jupiter, and Saturn – are bright enough to be seen with the naked eye. They can be identified by watching their movement from night to night against the backdrop of seemingly fixed stars, noting how they disturb the shapes of the constellations. The outermost planets are harder to see: Uranus and Neptune can be found with binoculars, but Pluto can be seen only with a telescope.

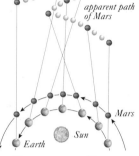

apparent path of Mars

Saturn

Neptune

asteroid belt

Jupiter

Mars

Earth   *Sun*

RETROGRADE MARS

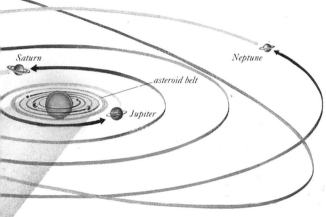

△ ORBITS OF THE OUTER PLANETS
The six planets beyond the Earth are referred to as superior planets. Like all planets, their orbits take longer to complete the further they are from the Sun.

RETROGRADE MOTION
Relative to the stars, the planets seem to move across the Earth's sky from west to east. But when the Earth, which is travelling more quickly on its inside track around the Sun, overtakes a superior planet, the planet seems to execute a backward loop in the sky. Known as retrograde motion, this effect is most obvious in the motion of Mars.

OPPOSITION AND CONJUNCTION

The ease with which most planets can be seen depends on their position in relation to the Sun and Earth. The angle between the Sun and a planet, as seen from the Earth, is known as elongation. At their greatest eastern and western elongations, inferior planets lie in the evening and morning skies respectively. At conjunction (when elongation is zero), a planet is lost in the Sun's glare. A superior planet can lie opposite the Sun in the sky, a position called opposition; at this time, it looks largest, is visible all night, and at midnight lies due south from northern latitudes and due north from southern latitudes.

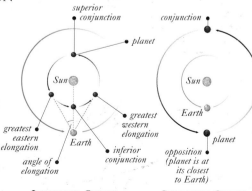

superior conjunction

planet

conjunction

Sun

Sun

Earth

greatest eastern elongation

greatest western elongation

Earth

planet

angle of elongation

inferior conjunction

opposition (planet is at its closest to Earth)

INFERIOR ORBIT

SUPERIOR ORBIT

THE CELESTIAL SPHERE

ALL CELESTIAL OBJECTS appear to be attached to an invisible sphere of infinite size centred on the Earth. Known as the celestial sphere, this seems to spin around the Earth once a day, although it is actually the Earth that is rotating. The portion of the celestial sphere seen from the Earth depends on the observer's latitude, the time of night, and the time of year.

THE CELESTIAL SPHERE

There are various important points and lines on the celestial sphere, similar to those on the Earth's globe. Directly over the Earth's poles lie the celestial poles, around which the sphere appears to turn each day. The celestial equator is a circle on the celestial sphere above the Earth's equator. Another circle, known as the ecliptic, represents the Sun's apparent path around the sphere each year. Of course, the Sun's motion is actually due to the Earth orbiting the Sun; hence the ecliptic is really the plane of the Earth's orbit projected on to the celestial sphere. Because the Earth's axis is tilted at 23.5 degrees, the celestial equator is tilted at the same angle to the ecliptic.

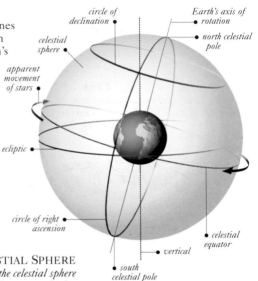

circle of declination •

Earth's axis of rotation

celestial sphere •

north celestial pole

apparent movement of stars •

ecliptic •

circle of right ascension •

vertical

celestial equator

south celestial pole

THE CELESTIAL SPHERE
Viewed from the Earth's north pole, the celestial sphere appears to turn anti-clockwise, with the stars and other objects moving parallel to the celestial equator.

LATITUDE

How much of the celestial sphere we can see depends on our latitude. From either pole, only half the sky can ever be seen; on any night, objects circle the celestial pole but do not rise or set (they are circumpolar). At the equator, the whole celestial sphere can be seen in a year; the celestial poles lie on the horizons to the north and south, and all objects rise and set. At mid-latitudes, all of one celestial hemisphere is visible over a year, plus part of the other one. Only some objects are circumpolar.

APPARENT MOTION

Seen from various locations on the surface of the globe, celestial objects appear to move differently.

90°

NORTH POLE (90°N)
All objects move without rising or setting.

MID-LATITUDE (45°N)
Some objects rise and set; others are circumpolar.

EQUATOR (0°)
All celestial objects rise and set.

TIME OF NIGHT AND TIME OF YEAR

As the Earth spins, the stars seem to move across the sky; hence our view of the sky changes as the night progresses. The celestial sphere turns once in the time it takes the Earth to spin on its axis relative to the stars – 23 hours 56 minutes. But the time between successive noons (a mean-time day) is longer, 24 hours, since the Earth is also orbiting the Sun. This means a star will rise four minutes earlier each night, as measured in mean time. The Earth's orbit of the Sun also means that a star near the celestial equator that is in the night sky (and hence visible) at one time of year will be in the daytime sky (and hence invisible) six months later.

TIME OF NIGHT ▷
In this picture, taken with a long exposure, the images of the stars have been drawn into curving lines round the north celestial pole by the Earth's rotation.

constellations of the zodiac •   • *ecliptic*

Sun

Earth

THE ZODIAC

During one year, the Sun passes in front of a band of constellations (see p.18) along the ecliptic. Collectively known as the zodiac, they form an area in which the planets are always to be seen. The dates when the Sun is in each constellation no longer accord with the dates attached to the astrological house of the same name.

THE ECLIPTIC AND THE ZODIAC
As the Earth moves around the Sun, the Sun appears to move against the background of stars.

CELESTIAL COORDINATES

Positions of objects on the celestial sphere are measured in coordinates called right ascension (RA) and declination (dec.). Right ascension is the equivalent of longitude on the Earth. It is measured in hours, anti-clockwise around the celestial equator, starting at the point where the Sun moves northwards across the equator each year (the vernal equinox). Declination, the equivalent of latitude on the Earth, is measured from 0 degrees at the celestial equator to 90 degrees at the celestial poles.

90°
60°
30°

star's position is 2h +45°

one hour of right ascension equals 15 degrees of rotation •   —12h

declination is measured in degrees

6h

declination of star is +45° •

right ascension of star is 2 hours

18h

celestial equator •

0h   • *vernal equinox*

STAR NAMES AND CONVENTIONS

THE SKY is divided into 88 interlocking areas known as constellations, whose boundaries were defined by the International Astronomical Union in 1930. Within these areas, astronomers use an agreed system of names, letters, and numbers to identify celestial objects.

star forming part of constellation pattern

linking line

THE CONSTELLATIONS

In his book *The Almagest* (c. AD 150), the Greek astronomer Ptolemy listed 48 constellations, many of them depicting characters or creatures from Greek myth. Others were added later, making the modern total of 88. Many of the more recent constellations lie in the far southern sky that was below the horizon of the Greeks and depict scientific or technical instruments or exotic animals. On star charts, some of the stars in a constellation may be joined by lines to form a pattern that symbolizes the object after which the constellation is named. However, the resemblance to the real object is usually slight, and the way the linking lines are arranged varies between charts. Constellations are often referred to by a set of standard three-letter abbreviations – for example, Sagittarius is abbreviated to Sgr, Ursa Major to UMa.

CONSTELLATIONS AROUND
THE SOUTH CELESTIAL POLE

constellation boundary

abbreviated constellation name

MAGNITUDE

The brightness of an object in the night sky is called its apparent magnitude, and depends on both its actual luminosity and its distance from the Earth. Astronomers use a numerical scale to describe the magnitude of celestial objects. Bright stars are given low or negative numbers, while faint objects are given high numbers. Under good conditions, it is possible to see stars down to about magnitude 6 with the naked eye, while binoculars or a telescope are needed to see objects with higher values. The scale is logarithmic, so a star of magnitude 1 is 100 times brighter than a star of magnitude 6.

APPARENT MAGNITUDE

Betelgeuse is nearly 10,000 times brighter than the Sun, yet it looks fainter than Sirius, which is only 20 times brighter than the Sun, because it is 50 times further away.

• Sun

Sirius (8.6 light years
• from the Sun)

Betelgeuse (430 •
light years from
the Sun)

DISTANCE IN LIGHT YEARS

0 1 2 3 4 5 6 7 8 9 10   100   200   300   400   500

STAR NAMES

There is no single system used to assign names to stars. Instead, several different schemes are used to name the various stars in a constellation. A large number of stars are referred to by letters or numbers, linked to the (Latin) genitive case of the name of the constellation; the brightest stars are given Greek letters, called Bayer letters, which are assigned alphabetically in roughly the order of brightness – hence the brightest star in Cygnus is named Alpha (α) Cygni. Most naked-eye stars have Flamsteed numbers (e.g. 61

Cygni), which run in order of right ascension. Some stars not in the Flamsteed catalogue are identified by upper- and lower-case letters, especially in southern constellations. A separate lettering system, starting with the capital letter R, is used for certain variable stars (e.g. T Cygni). Some bright stars also have common names derived from Latin, Greek, or Arabic – e.g. Deneb (Arabic). Deep-sky objects (such as nebulae, clusters, and galaxies) are given numbers preceded by the letters M, NGC, or IC , taken from the Messier, New General, or Index catalogues.

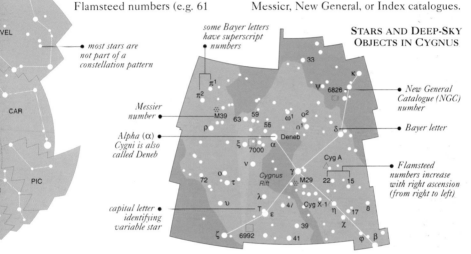

STARS AND DEEP-SKY OBJECTS IN CYGNUS

some Bayer letters have superscript numbers

most stars are not part of a constellation pattern

New General Catalogue (NGC) number

Messier number

Bayer letter

Alpha (α) Cygni is also called Deneb

Flamsteed numbers increase with right ascension (from right to left)

capital letter identifying variable star

DISTANCE

Astronomers measure distances to stars in the same way that a surveyor would: by taking bearings from two different places – in this case, from opposite sides of the Earth's orbit, six months apart. Even then, the shift in position, or parallax, is only tiny. If the shift is too small to detect, astronomers estimate how far away a star is by calculating how much light it emits and comparing this with how bright it appears in the sky.

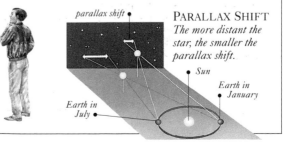

PATTERNS IN THREE DIMENSIONS

The stars in the constellation patterns usually lie at various distances from the Earth and have no real connection with each other. For example, the stars in the Great Square of Pegasus range from 97 to 330 light years away.

parallax shift

PARALLAX SHIFT
The more distant the star, the smaller the parallax shift.

Sun

Earth in July

Earth in January

OBSERVING THE STARS

IDENTIFYING objects in the night sky for the first time can be a daunting experience. A good way to start is by learning to gauge distance and finding a few bright stars and key constellations.

Once these reference points have been identified, imaginary lines can be drawn outwards from them to find other stars and patterns, which in turn act as useful stepping-stones to the rest of the sky.

SCALE IN THE SKY

It can be difficult to judge how large a feature will appear in the sky by looking at a map. Fortunately, a hand held at arm's length acts as a convenient measuring scale. For example, an index finger easily covers the Moon or Sun, both of which are only half a degree across. The back of a hand is about 10 degrees across, the width of the bowl of the Plough (Big Dipper). To cover the Great Square of Pegasus (16 degrees across), the fingers must be splayed.

▽ USING HANDSPANS
A hand held at arm's length can be used as a measuring device by both adults and children.

• *full Moon*

the Plough in Ursa Major •

the Great Square of Pegasus •

ONE FINGER   **CLOSED HAND**   **OPEN HAND**

NORTHERN SKIES

The Plough, or Big Dipper, which is high in northern-hemisphere skies in spring, is a key pattern in the northern sky. Two stars in the bowl of the Plough, Alpha and Beta Ursae Majoris, point to the north pole star, Polaris. On the other side of the celestial pole is the W-shaped constellation Cassiopeia. The Plough's bowl can also be used to locate the bright star Vega, which is prominent in northern skies in summer. A line extended from the curving handle of the Plough leads first to Arcturus, a beacon of spring skies, and then to Spica, the brightest star in Virgo. Also to the south of the bowl of the Plough are Leo and the stars Castor and Pollux in Gemini.

NORTHERN SIGNPOSTS

Vega • LYRA

CASSIOPEIA

URSA MINOR   *North celestial pole*
• Polaris

Alpha

BOÖTES   *Plough*   Beta

Arcturus   URSA MAJOR

Castor
Pollux

LEO   GEMINI

VIRGO   Regulus

• Spica

SCALE

MID-LATITUDE SKIES

Orion is a prominent constellation in the evening skies of northern winter and southern summer. The line of three stars that forms Orion's Belt points to the brightest star in the sky, Sirius (in Canis Major). Sirius marks one corner of a huge triangle (known in the northern hemisphere as the Winter Triangle). The other corners are marked by the bright stars Betelgeuse (in Orion) and Procyon (in Canis Minor). Another prominent star in Orion is Rigel. A line from Rigel through Betelgeuse points to Castor and Pollux in the neighbouring constellation of Gemini. On the other side of Orion is Aldebaran, the brightest star in Taurus; beyond Aldebaran, in the same direction, is the Pleiades open cluster. Almost directly to the north of Orion lies Capella, the brightest star in Auriga, which is overhead on January evenings from mid-northern latitudes.

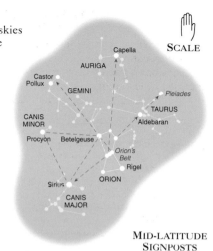

SCALE

MID-LATITUDE
SIGNPOSTS

SOUTHERN SKIES

Two bright stars in Centaurus and the familiar shape of Crux, the Southern Cross – all of which are at their highest on April and May evenings – are the starting points for finding a way around southern skies. A line from Alpha through nearby Beta Centauri points to Crux, the smallest constellation in the sky but also one of the most distinctive. The Southern Cross is not to be confused with the slightly larger False Cross, which is closer to the bright star Canopus. Unlike in the northern hemisphere, there is no bright star near the south celestial pole, but the longer axis of Crux points towards the pole, as does a line at right angles to the one linking Alpha and Beta Centauri (see also p.87). Canopus and Achernar form a large triangle with the south celestial pole.

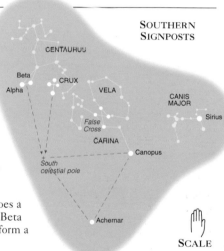

SOUTHERN
SIGNPOSTS

SCALE

SKYWATCHING TIPS

• Always wear warm clothing – even summer evenings can be cold.

• Allow at least 10 minutes for your eyes to adapt to the dark before beginning serious observations.

• If needed, use only a dim red torch, so that your eyes remain adapted to the dark.

PLASTIC-COVERED TORCH

• Observe objects when they are well clear of the horizon wherever possible.

• To see faint objects more easily, look slightly to one side of them; their light will then fall on the more sensitive outer part of your eye. This technique is called averted vision.

• Keep a log of your observations, always noting the date and time.

BINOCULARS AND TELESCOPES

ASTRONOMERS use binoculars and telescopes to make objects appear brighter and larger. These instruments collect more light than the human eye, which means that much fainter objects can be seen than with the eye alone. They also magnify objects, so that small details can be distinguished. Binoculars are usually recommended for beginners; more serious study requires a telescope.

BINOCULARS OR A TELESCOPE?

For simple stargazing, binoculars are ideal, being portable and relatively cheap. They show many more stars than the naked eye, and their wide field of view makes them especially useful for looking at large areas of sky or objects such as comets. They also produce upright images. Telescopes have larger apertures and higher magnifications than binoculars, and show inverted images. The aperture of a telescope is fixed, but the magnification can be altered by changing the eyepiece. When assessing a telescope's performance the aperture is more important than the magnification (see below). Another critical requirement is a steady mounting, to prevent images from shaking. Most amateur astronomers use a telescope of "small" to "moderate" aperture – where small is less than 100 mm (4 in) and moderate is 100–250 mm (4–10 in); anything greater than this is considered large.

finder scope

eyepiece

cradle

equatorial mount

stand

▽ BINOCULARS
Binoculars have apertures up to about 50 mm (2 in) and magnify up to about 10 times. High magnification makes objects look larger, but with magnification greater than 10 times it is not easy to hold binoculars steady enough to see objects clearly.

focusing knob

eyepiece lens

prism

prism

pivot bar

objective lens

◁ REFLECTING TELESCOPE

APERTURE AND MAGNIFICATION

Although magnification makes objects appear larger and closer, there are limits to the magnification that can be used. An image looks fainter as it gets bigger. As a guide, expect a maximum magnification of about twice the telescope aperture in millimetres (50 times the aperture in inches). No matter how large the aperture, as the magnification increases, the unsteadiness of the atmosphere, caused by air currents, becomes more noticeable, which limits the powers that can be used.

MAGNIFICATION
High powers of magnification are useful when viewing the Moon (shown here), planets, or close double stars. Low powers are better for diffuse objects such as comets, nebulae, and galaxies.

 NAKED EYE

 BINOCULARS

 TELESCOPE

REFRACTING TELESCOPES

Refractors have a main lens, called the object glass or objective lens, which collects and focuses light. The image is magnified by an eyepiece at the opposite end of the tube. In some small refractors, a prism is used to bend the light so that the eyepiece is more conveniently positioned for observation, as in the photograph here. Most small refractors have a simple type of mounting known as an altazimuth, which allows the telescope to tilt up and down and swivel from side to side.

REFRACTOR
This small refracting telescope is on an altazimuth mounting.

finder scope (for aiming at objects)

objective lens housing

eyepiece

objective lens

incident light

refracted light

altazimuth mount

tripod

eyepiece

HOW A REFRACTOR WORKS

REFLECTING TELESCOPES

Most reflectors used by amateur observers are of the Newtonian type, in which light is collected by a concave primary mirror and deflected into an eyepiece at the side of the tube by a flat secondary mirror. They often have an equatorial mounting, which allows them to track objects across the sky simply by turning one axis, called the polar axis, which points to the celestial pole; a motor drive can accomplish this automatically. However, a Dobsonian mounting, which is a form of altazimuth mounting, is also now popular.

REFLECTOR
This reflecting telescope of Newtonian design is on a Dobsonian mounting.

eyepiece

lightweight tube

Formica ring

incident light

Teflon pad

eyepiece

reflected light

primary mirror

secondary mirror

HOW A NEWTONIAN REFLECTOR WORKS

CASSEGRAIN TELESCOPES

Another type of reflector, called the Cassegrain, uses a secondary mirror with a convex surface to reflect light back through a hole in the centre of the main mirror, where the eyepiece is inserted. Because the light path is folded back on itself within the tube, this design is more compact than the Newtonian. A modified form, called a Schmidt–Cassegrain, is popular among amateurs. This has a thin lens, known as a corrector plate, across the front of the tube to increase the field of view.

CASSEGRAIN
This Schmidt–Cassegrain telescope is supported on an equatorial fork mounting.

finder scope

reflected light

secondary mirror

primary mirror

eyepiece

motor-driven equatorial mount

incident light

eyepiece

HOW A CASSEGRAIN WORKS

ASTROPHOTOGRAPHY

A SINGLE-LENS REFLEX camera can be used to take attractive pictures of the night sky, from snapshots of bright stars and planets to long, guided exposures that show objects that are far too faint for the naked eye. For close-ups, a telescope can be used to replace the camera lens. More advanced astro-photographers use electronic detectors called CCDs in place of film.

CONVENTIONAL PHOTOGRAPHY

A time exposure with a fixed camera will record star trails like those shown on p.17. Fast film (such as ISO 400) should be used and the camera lens set to its widest aperture. Exposures should be tailored to the sky conditions – in towns, light pollution (p.37) will start to fog the film after only a few minutes. To produce sharp images of stars, the camera must track the stars as the Earth rotates. This can be done by attaching the camera to a motor-driven mounting or to the tube of a telescope that has such a mounting. For detailed views, the camera lens can be removed and the telescope itself used as a telephoto lens. In this case, the telescope must be guided very accurately on the target, particularly during exposures lasting more than a few seconds.

camera attached to tube on mounting bracket

cable shutter-release

eyepiece can be used to align camera

motor-driven mounting to track movement of stars

CAMERA TO EYEPIECE ▷
The lens of the camera is removed and the body attached to the telescope in place of the eyepiece.

adaptor

camera body

cable shutter-release

telescope

△ CAMERA ON TELESOPE
The telescope drive is used to keep the camera pointed at its target, allowing long exposures without star trailing.

CCD CAMERAS

Charge-coupled devices (CCDs) are light-sensitive silicon chips that can be used in place of a conventional camera and film. They are much more sensitive than normal photographic film, so that an exposure of only a few minutes can show as much as an hour-long exposure would on film. CCD images can be stored in a computer and viewed on its screen.

MOUNTING A CCD CAMERA

CCD camera replaces eyepiece

cable connecting CCD camera to computer

CCD MICROCHIP
A CCD chip is much smaller than a frame of 35 mm film, which can be a drawback.

THE SOLAR SYSTEM

HOW THIS SECTION WORKS

THIS SECTION is about the Sun and the bodies in orbit around it. There are entries on the nine planets (including the Earth), each consisting of an illustrated description of the planet, advice on observation, and charts and diagrams that show where it can be located. Other entries cover the Sun itself, the Moon, and smaller bodies such as comets and meteors.

locator strip shows planet's position in relation to Sun and Earth

planet's size compared with that of the Earth

diagram illustrating planet's tilt, rotation, and orbit

observation section contains tips on finding and studying the planet

structure of planet's interior

vertical section through atmosphere

physical properties expressed as ratios to values for the Earth

locator diagram for inner planet (see below)

pie-chart of atmospheric composition

PLANET LOCATORS ▷

The planets are always to be found in one of the 13 constellations of the zodiac (see p.17). The constellation in which the planets Mercury, Venus, Mars, Jupiter, and Saturn can be found at a particular time is shown on a strip diagram.

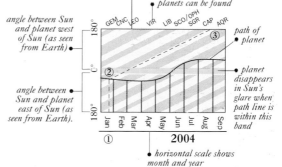

angle between Sun and planet west of Sun (as seen from Earth)

angle between Sun and planet east of Sun (as seen from Earth).

constellations in which planets can be found

path of planet

planet disappears in Sun's glare when path line is within this band

horizontal scale shows month and year

△ THE OUTER PLANETS
Uranus, Neptune, and Pluto seem to move relatively slowly. Their location in the night sky is therefore shown on more conventional charts.

△ HOW TO USE THE STRIP DIAGRAM

1. Find the date on the horizontal scale. For example, to find Venus in January 2004 on the segment above, first locate January at the bottom of the diagram.
2. Read upwards to the curved path line.
3. Read diagonally up along the tinted band to identify the constellation in which the planet appears. In January 2004, Venus is in Aquarius. Use one of the charts in the Monthly Sky Guides to find Aquarius.

THE SUN

THE SUN is our local star. It is a ball of incandescent gas of average size, temperature, and brightness compared with other stars. The Sun dominates the Solar System: it is the source of heat and light for all the planets, and its great mass exerts a gravitational pull that keeps them in orbit around it.

WARNING: Never look directly at the Sun through binoculars or a telescope.

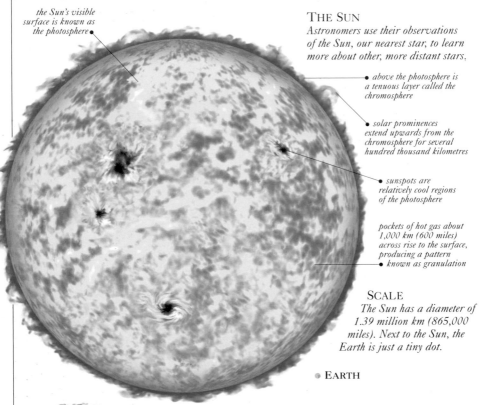

the Sun's visible surface is known as the photosphere

THE SUN
Astronomers use their observations of the Sun, our nearest star, to learn more about other, more distant stars.

above the photosphere is a tenuous layer called the chromosphere

solar prominences extend upwards from the chromosphere for several hundred thousand kilometres

sunspots are relatively cool regions of the photosphere

pockets of hot gas about 1,000 km (600 miles) across rise to the surface, producing a pattern known as granulation

SCALE
The Sun has a diameter of 1.39 million km (865,000 miles). Next to the Sun, the Earth is just a tiny dot.

• EARTH

chromosphere

photosphere

core

radiative zone

convective zone

INTERNAL STRUCTURE

STRUCTURE
The Sun's energy is generated at its core, where temperatures are estimated to reach 15 million°C (27 million°F). Under these extreme conditions, hydrogen is converted to helium by nuclear fusion. Energy from these reactions travels outwards, first by radiation and then by convection, eventually reaching the photosphere. Above the photosphere is a less dense layer of gas, the chromosphere, from which bright clouds called prominences extend into the rarefied outermost region, the corona.

Diameter (Earth = 1) 109	Mass (Earth = 1) 333,000	Volume (Earth = 1) 1,300,000

SUNSPOTS

Sunspots, dark patches on the Sun's surface, are actually areas of cooler gas. They can last from a few days to several months, and range in size from a few hundred kilometres across to complex groups extending for 100,000 km (60,000 miles). Occasional eruptions near sunspots, called flares, shoot out atomic particles that reach the Earth and can cause glows in the atmosphere termed aurorae.

SUNSPOT CYCLES

Sunspot numbers rise and fall in a cycle lasting about 11 years. At the start of the cycle, spots are few in number and appear away from the equator. Approaching solar maximum, the spots become more numerous (with up to 100 visible at one time) and appear closer to the equator.

umbra •   • penumbra   granulation •

△ SUNSPOT GROUP
The centre of a sunspot, known as the umbra, is its darkest, coolest part, at about 4,500°C (8,100°F). The umbra is surrounded by a lighter, warmer area called the penumbra.

first spots of new cycle   *last spots of old cycle*   *spots appear nearer the equator*   *number of spots falls*   *last spots of old cycle*   *first spots of new cycle*

YEAR 1   YEAR 3   YEAR 5   YEAR 7   YEAR 9   YEAR 11
SOLAR MINIMUM   **SOLAR MAXIMUM**   **SOLAR MINIMUM**

OBSERVING SUNSPOTS

Looking at the Sun with binoculars or a telescope can cause blindness. The only safe way to observe the Sun is to project its image on to a white surface, as shown below. The rim of the Sun appears darker than its centre, an effect known as limb darkening. Sunspots appear as small, dark marks that change position daily as the Sun rotates.

sunspot •

1. For safety, place a cap over the finder scope. If you are using a refractor, also cap the main lens.

2. Aim the telescope at the Sun by minimizing the size of the shadow cast by the telescope or the finder.

3. Remove the lens cap (if using a refractor), and focus the Sun's image on to a piece of white card.

| Density (water = 1) 1.41 | Gravity (Earth = 1) 27.94 | Surface temperature 5,500°C (9,900°F) | Magnitude −26.7 |

ECLIPSES OF THE SUN

Occasionally, the Moon passes in front of the Sun, briefly blocking its light to cause a solar eclipse. At least two solar eclipses occur each year, but not everyone will see them. During a solar eclipse, the Moon's shadow falls on the Earth. Anyone within the dark inner part of the shadow (the umbra) will see a total eclipse. From the lighter, outer shadow (the penumbra), a partial eclipse is seen. Because the umbra is quite narrow, total solar eclipses are rare at any one place on the Earth.

When the Sun's disc is entirely covered, its faint outer halo of gas, the corona, becomes visible. Scientists travel the world for the rare glimpses of the corona that an eclipse affords. A total eclipse can last for up to 7½ minutes, but 2 to 3 minutes is more usual; a partial eclipse can last for up to 3 to 4 hours. As with all solar observations, an eclipse is best viewed by projecting the Sun's image, but when the Sun is totally eclipsed the corona can safely be viewed with binoculars.

SEQUENCE OF A TOTAL SOLAR ECLIPSE

1. A partial eclipse – the Moon moves across the face of the Sun.

2. Just before totality, a shape similar to a diamond ring is seen.

3. At totality, the Sun's faint but extensive corona is visible.

4. The Moon moves away again and the eclipse ends.

HOW A SOLAR ECLIPSE OCCURS

outer shadow (penumbra) • • area covered by total eclipse • Earth

Moon •

sunlight

• inner shadow (umbra) • area covered by partial eclipse

ANNULAR ECLIPSE

When the Moon is at its furthest from the Earth, it does not appear quite big enough to cover the Sun completely. This gives rise to an annular eclipse, so named because a ring, or annulus, of light remains visible at mid-eclipse.

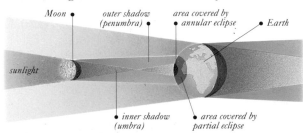

Moon • outer shadow (penumbra) • • area covered by annular eclipse • Earth

sunlight

• inner shadow (umbra) • area covered by partial eclipse

HOW AN ANNULAR ECLIPSE OCCURS

RING OF SUNLIGHT
An annulus of light is seen around the eclipsing Moon. The photosphere (rather than the corona) is visible here.

Diameter (Earth = 1) 109	Mass (Earth = 1) 333,000	Volume (Earth = 1) 1,300,000

MERCURY

MERCURY is the closest planet to the Sun and is difficult to see because it is always low in the sky in the evening or morning twilight. It is a small, rocky planet, less than half the diameter of the Earth, and resembles our own Moon in appearance, being covered with craters. Mercury has no air or water. During the day, its surface is scorched by intense sunlight, while at night its temperature plummets far below freezing.

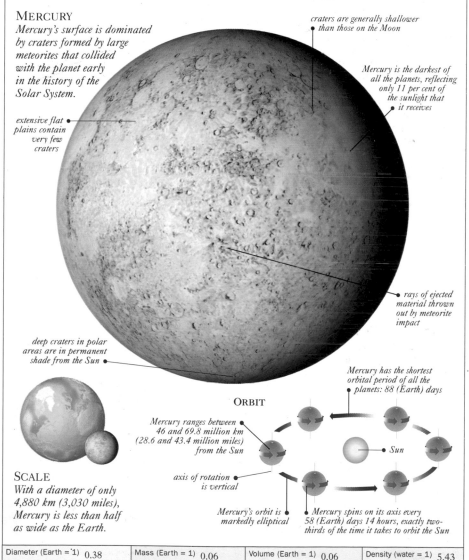

MERCURY
Mercury's surface is dominated by craters formed by large meteorites that collided with the planet early in the history of the Solar System.

craters are generally shallower than those on the Moon

Mercury is the darkest of all the planets, reflecting only 11 per cent of the sunlight that it receives

extensive flat plains contain very few craters

rays of ejected material thrown out by meteorite impact

deep craters in polar areas are in permanent shade from the Sun

SCALE
With a diameter of only 4,880 km (3,030 miles), Mercury is less than half as wide as the Earth.

ORBIT

Mercury ranges between 46 and 69.8 million km (28.6 and 43.4 million miles) from the Sun

Mercury has the shortest orbital period of all the planets: 88 (Earth) days

Sun

axis of rotation is vertical

Mercury's orbit is markedly elliptical

Mercury spins on its axis every 58 (Earth) days 14 hours, exactly two-thirds of the time it takes to orbit the Sun

| Diameter (Earth = 1) 0.38 | Mass (Earth = 1) 0.06 | Volume (Earth = 1) 0.06 | Density (water = 1) 5.43 |

OBSERVATION

Of the five planets visible to the naked eye, Mercury is the most difficult to spot because it is always close to the Sun. Binoculars are usually needed to locate it. The best time to observe Mercury is around greatest elongation (see p.15), when it is furthest from the Sun. At that time, at a magnification of 250 times Mercury will appear as large as the full Moon looks to the naked eye. Like Venus and the Moon, Mercury's disc shows phases, which can be seen through a small telescope. Moderate to large apertures show dark, smudgy surface markings.

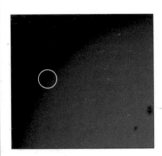

TRANSITS
Occasionally, Mercury can be seen crossing the Sun's disc, an event known as a transit. In this photograph, taken at the transit of 1993, Mercury appears as a small, round dot. Future transits will occur on 8 November 2006, 9 May 2016, and 11 November 2019.

MERCURY IN THE EVENING SKY
At optimal viewing times, Mercury resembles a first-magnitude star. In this picture, it can be seen near the horizon, above and to the right of the large tree.

ATMOSPHERE AND CLIMATE

Mercury is airless and waterless. The barren, rocky surface is blasted by solar radiation, which raises its temperature to above 450°C (840°F) at noon on the equator when the planet is nearest the Sun. However, some shaded areas in craters near the poles are probably permanently below freezing, and it is thought possible that ice exists there. At night the surface temperature plummets to below −180°C (−290°F).

LOCATION OF MERCURY 2001–2012

| Diameter (Earth = 1) 0.38 | Mass (Earth = 1) 0.06 | Volume (Earth = 1) 0.06 | Density (water = 1) 5.43 |

GEOGRAPHY AND GEOLOGY

Mercury looks much like our own Moon, since the rocky surfaces of both bodies have been extensively cratered by impacts from meteorites, and Mercury's diameter is only 40 per cent greater than that of the Moon. One distinct difference is that Mercury has cliffs up to 3 km (2 miles) high running for several hundreds of kilometres, probably caused by shrinking and wrinkling of the planet as it cooled. Mercury is thought to have a large iron core that occupies three-quarters of its diameter.

rocky silicate crust

rocky silicate mantle

iron core

INTERNAL STRUCTURE

CRATERS

As on the Moon, the youngest craters on Mercury are bright and surrounded by rays of material ejected by the force of the meteorite impact. Between Mercury's main craters are older, smoother areas called inter-crater plains, dotted with small craters. Secondary craters, caused by debris from the main impact, lie closer to the main craters than on the Moon because of Mercury's stronger gravity. Mercury has one large lowland plain, the Caloris Basin, which resembles the mare areas of the Moon. There are no known volcanic craters on Mercury.

△ THE CALORIS BASIN
Part of this basin, 1,300 km (800 miles) across, can be seen on the left of this picture. It was formed by a meteorite impact and later flooded with lava.

DEGAS AND BRONTË ▷
These two ray craters (at the centre left in this photograph) are each about 60 km (37 miles) across.

| Gravity (Earth = 1) 0.38 | Number of moons 0 | Average temperature 167°C (333°F) | Maximum magnitude −1.5 |

VENUS

VENUS IS THE PLANET closest in size to the Earth, being only 650 km (400 miles) smaller in diameter. It is the second planet from the Sun and comes within 40 million km (25 million miles) of the Earth, nearer than any other planet. It is the brightest object in the sky after the Sun and Moon, a result of both its closeness to us and the fact that it is entirely covered in bright clouds.

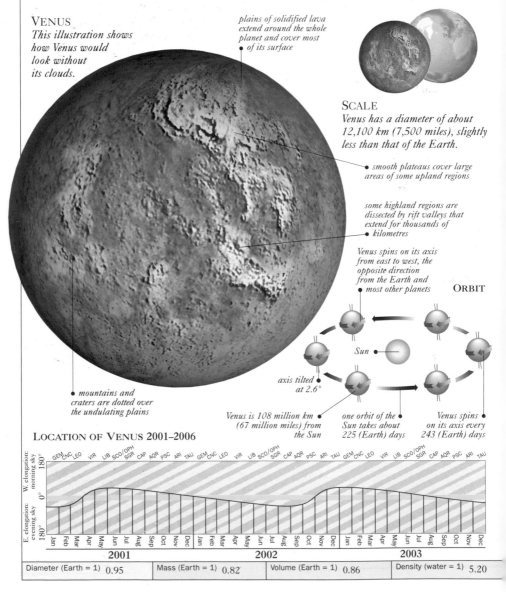

VENUS
This illustration shows how Venus would look without its clouds.

plains of solidified lava extend around the whole planet and cover most of its surface

SCALE
Venus has a diameter of about 12,100 km (7,500 miles), slightly less than that of the Earth.

smooth plateaus cover large areas of some upland regions

some highland regions are dissected by rift valleys that extend for thousands of kilometres

Venus spins on its axis from east to west, the opposite direction from the Earth and most other planets

ORBIT

Sun

axis tilted at 2.6°

mountains and craters are dotted over the undulating plains

Venus is 108 million km (67 million miles) from the Sun

one orbit of the Sun takes about 225 (Earth) days

Venus spins on its axis every 243 (Earth) days

LOCATION OF VENUS 2001–2006

| Diameter (Earth = 1) | 0.95 | Mass (Earth = 1) | 0.82 | Volume (Earth = 1) | 0.86 | Density (water = 1) | 5.20 |

OBSERVATION

Venus can be seen in the morning or evening sky, depending on whether it lies to the west or east of the Sun. It is always dazzling, reaching magnitude –4.7 at its brightest. During each orbit, Venus goes through a cycle of phases (see below). Binoculars will show the crescent phase, which occurs when Venus is closest to the Earth, but a small telescope is needed to see the full series. At half phase, a magnification of 75 times will show Venus the same size as the Moon appears to the naked eye. Due to its covering of clouds, the surface of the planet is invisible to us. Some dusky, V-shaped markings can be seen in the clouds, and the clouds over the poles can look brighter than the rest of the disc.

TELESCOPE VIEW ▷
Two crescent phases of Venus are shown here superimposed on one another.

△ NAKED-EYE VIEW
Venus is always close to the Sun in the sky, usually appearing near the horizon in the twilight. Its brilliance makes it easy to distinguish from adjacent stars.

PHASES

Venus completes a cycle of phases as it orbits the Sun. When on the far side of the Sun, and hence furthest from Earth, it appears as a full disc but is invisible behind the Sun's glare. As it moves closer to us, in the evening sky, it grows in apparent size. When at its greatest eastern elongation (see p.15), it passes through half phase to a crescent. The point when Venus is between the Sun and the Earth is known as inferior conjunction. It then moves into the morning sky, shrinking in apparent size but increasing in phase from a crescent via half to full again.

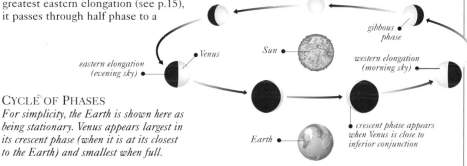

gibbous phase

eastern elongation (evening sky) ●

Venus

Sun ●

western elongation (morning sky) ●

CYCLE OF PHASES
For simplicity, the Earth is shown here as being stationary. Venus appears largest in its crescent phase (when it is at its closest to the Earth) and smallest when full.

Earth ●

● *crescent phase appears when Venus is close to inferior conjunction*

	2004	2005	2006
Gravity (Earth = 1) 0.91	Number of moons 0	Average temperature 464°C (867°F)	Maximum magnitude –4.7

ATMOSPHERE AND CLIMATE

Venus is enveloped in clouds of sulphuric acid, which lie 50–70 km (30–45 miles) above its surface. Below the clouds, the atmosphere consists almost entirely of carbon-dioxide gas. At the surface, the atmospheric pressure is crushing, about 90 times greater than on the Earth. Temperatures soar to 464°C (867°F) due to the greenhouse effect (see below). Surface winds are gentle, only a few kilometres per hour, but above the clouds they reach hundreds of kilometres per hour. As a result, the clouds whip around the planet in four Earth days, far faster than the planet rotates on its axis, which takes 243 days. Like the planet itself, the clouds rotate from east to west.

ATMOSPHERIC STRUCTURE

- upper clouds of sulphuric acid
- thin sulphuric acid haze
- dense clouds producing rain of sulphuric acid
- lower haze of dust and very small sulphuric acid droplets
- lower atmosphere almost entirely carbon dioxide

THERMOSPHERE

TROPOSPHERE

ATMOSPHERIC COMPOSITION

- nitrogen (3.5%) and trace gases
- carbon dioxide (96.5%)

RADIATION BALANCE

km   miles
100 — 60
90 —
80 — 50
70 —
     — 40
60 —
50 — 30
40 —
     — 20
30 —
20 — 10
10 —
0 — 0

- sunlight
- most of the sunlight Venus receives is reflected back by its clouds
- clouds
- less than half of the infra-red radiation from the surface is released back into space
- surface emits infra-red radiation

THE GREENHOUSE EFFECT

Visible light from the Sun streams in through a planet's atmosphere, heating its surface. The surface then releases the heat as invisible infra-red radiation, but certain gases in the atmosphere, notably carbon dioxide, prevent some of the infra-red radiation from escaping directly into space, causing the temperature to increase. This is termed the greenhouse effect. In the case of the Earth, where carbon dioxide makes up only a small fraction of the atmosphere, the greenhouse effect raises the temperature by about 35°C (63°F). On Venus, where the atmosphere is almost entirely carbon dioxide, the increase in temperature due to the greenhouse effect is a massive 500°C (900°F), resulting in an average temperature of 464°C (867°F). Unlike on the Earth, the temperature on Venus differs by only a few degrees between the equator and the poles.

LOCATION OF VENUS 2007–2012

| Diameter (Earth = 1) 0.95 | Mass (Earth = 1) 0.82 | Volume (Earth = 1) 0.86 | Density (water = 1) 5.20 |

GEOGRAPHY AND GEOLOGY

Most of the surface of Venus is covered by undulating plains, which are dotted with mountains and craters formed by volcanic action and meteorite impacts. There are also two main upland regions, similar to continents on the Earth: Aphrodite Terra near the equator, which is over half the area of Africa; and Ishtar Terra in the far north, about the size of Australia. Ishtar contains the highest point on Venus, the Maxwell Montes mountain range, 11 km (7 miles) high – taller than Mount Everest on the Earth. There are signs of recent lava flows, indicating that Venus may still be volcanically active today. Since Venus is so hot, all its water has evaporated.

• silicate crust

• rocky mantle

• iron and nickel core

INTERNAL STRUCTURE

CRATERS

The surface of Venus is dotted with craters caused by meteorite impacts. Most are quite large, up to 300 km (185 miles) in diameter, because large meteorites can penetrate the atmosphere whereas smaller ones burn up. Like the craters on the Moon, many on Venus have central peaks and are surrounded by ejected material. In addition, there are numerous craters formed by volcanic action.

volcanic peak •   flat, rocky plain •   impact crater •   • lava flow

MAAT MONS

This volcanic mountain in Aphrodite Terra is the second-highest peak on Venus.

summit is 8.5 km
• (5.2 miles) high

PLAINS, MOUNTAINS, AND CRATERS

Although its clouds prevent us from seeing its surface with a telescope, Venus has been mapped by radar. This image (and the two below) are based on data from the Magellan space probe.

SAPAS MONS

This volcano has two central peaks surrounded by an expanse of solidified lava.

2010	2011	2012

| Gravity (Earth = 1) 0.91 | Number of moons 0 | Average temperature 464°C (867°F) | Maximum magnitude −4.7 |

THE EARTH

THE EARTH, our home world, is the third planet from the Sun and the largest of the four rocky inner planets. Among the planets of the Solar System, the Earth is unique in having abundant surface water and an atmosphere rich in nitrogen and oxygen. It is also the only planet known with certainty to harbour life, supporting a complex population of plants and animals.

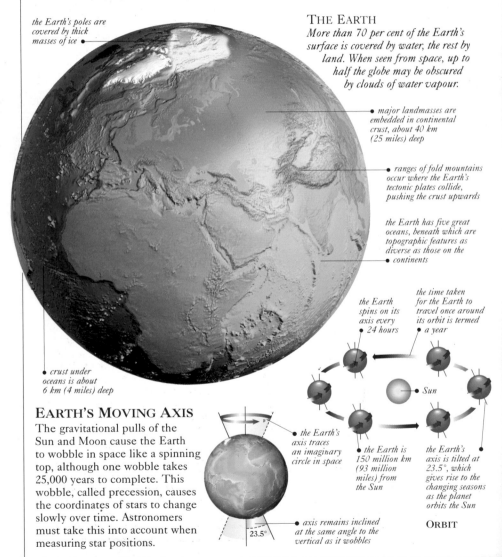

the Earth's poles are covered by thick masses of ice

THE EARTH
More than 70 per cent of the Earth's surface is covered by water, the rest by land. When seen from space, up to half the globe may be obscured by clouds of water vapour.

major landmasses are embedded in continental crust, about 40 km (25 miles) deep

ranges of fold mountains occur where the Earth's tectonic plates collide, pushing the crust upwards

the Earth has five great oceans, beneath which are topographic features as diverse as those on the continents

the Earth spins on its axis every 24 hours

the time taken for the Earth to travel once around its orbit is termed a year

crust under oceans is about 6 km (4 miles) deep

Sun

EARTH'S MOVING AXIS
The gravitational pulls of the Sun and Moon cause the Earth to wobble in space like a spinning top, although one wobble takes 25,000 years to complete. This wobble, called precession, causes the coordinates of stars to change slowly over time. Astronomers must take this into account when measuring star positions.

the Earth's axis traces an imaginary circle in space

the Earth is 150 million km (93 million miles) from the Sun

the Earth's axis is tilted at 23.5°, which gives rise to the changing seasons as the planet orbits the Sun

23.5°

axis remains inclined at the same angle to the vertical as it wobbles

ORBIT

Diameter 12,756 km (7,926 miles)	Mass 5.98 x 10^{21} tonnes	Volume 1.08 x 10^{12} km³ (2.6 x 10^{11} mile³)

ATMOSPHERE AND CLIMATE

The layer of gases that surrounds the Earth plays an important part in protecting and sustaining life. Not only does it shield the surface from excessive solar radiation and meteorite impacts, but its density, combined with Earth's favourable distance from the Sun, provides the right temperature for water to exist as a liquid. Water and carbon dioxide are used as food by plants, which in turn release the oxygen that is essential for animal life. Circulation in the atmosphere is also an important mechanism by which heat energy is redistributed polewards from the equator.

ATMOSPHERIC STRUCTURE

water vapour (1%) and trace gases

meteoroids burn up in the upper atmosphere

nitrogen (78.1%)

oxygen (20.9%)

ATMOSPHERIC COMPOSITION

THERMOSPHERE

MESOSPHERE

STRATOSPHERE

TROPOSPHERE

ozone layer absorbs ultra-violet radiation

clouds of water vapour

GEOGRAPHY AND GEOLOGY

The Earth's crust is made up of sections, called plates, that float on the surface of the viscous mantle and slowly move apart or slip beneath one another. Mountain ranges, volcanoes, and earthquakes occur along the margins of the plates. The Earth has a core of iron and nickel, the outer part of which is liquid. Motions in the liquid outer core give rise to the Earth's magnetic field, which extends into space, creating a magnetic cocoon around our planet termed the magnetosphere.

thin, brittle crust

dense, partially molten mantle

molten metal outer core

solid metal inner core

INTERNAL STRUCTURE

LIGHT POLLUTION

Light pollution is caused by artificial lights shining into the sky. The problem is greatest in urban areas and is so extensive that in some developed countries there are now few places with truly dark skies. As well as being a waste of energy, light pollution is a growing nuisance to astronomers, as relatively faint celestial objects become lost in the glare from surface lighting.

THE EARTH AT NIGHT

At the top left of this picture are the lights of industrialized Europe, and at the top right is Japan. The yellow areas, such as those around the Middle East, represent gas burned off in oil fields, while the red specks in equatorial Africa are due to agricultural burning. The line of light in North Africa is the Nile Valley.

| Density (water = 1) 5.52 | Gravity 1 | Number of moons 1 | Average temperature 15°C (59°F) |

THE MOON

THE MOON is the Earth's only natural satellite. It is so close to the Earth – at an average distance of only 384,400 km (238,900 miles) – that even binoculars will reveal features on its surface in fascinating detail. The Moon has no air or liquid water, and hence no weather; it is also lifeless and without geological activity. Its main landforms have all resulted from meteorite impact.

THE NEAR SIDE OF THE MOON

The Moon's distinctive lowland plains, the maria, are labelled here; other features are cross-referred to the panel on the facing page.

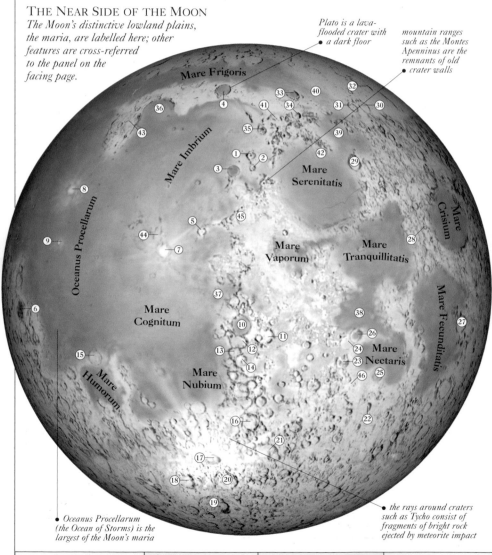

Plato is a lava-flooded crater with a dark floor

mountain ranges such as the Montes Apenninus are the remnants of old crater walls

Mare Frigoris

Mare Imbrium

Oceanus Procellarum

Mare Serenitatis

Mare Crisium

Mare Vaporum

Mare Tranquillitatis

Mare Fecunditatis

Mare Cognitum

Mare Nectaris

Mare Humorum

Mare Nubium

• Oceanus Procellarum (the Ocean of Storms) is the largest of the Moon's maria

• the rays around craters such as Tycho consist of fragments of bright rock ejected by meteorite impact

| Diameter (Earth = 1) 0.27 | Mass (Earth = 1) 0.01 | Volume (Earth = 1) 0.02 | Density (water = 1) 3.34 |

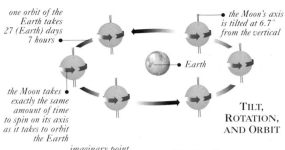

one orbit of the Earth takes 27 (Earth) days 7 hours

the Moon's axis is tilted at 6.7° from the vertical

Earth

SCALE
The Moon's diameter is 3,476 km (2,160 miles), just over a quarter of that of the Earth.

the Moon takes exactly the same amount of time to spin on its axis as it takes to orbit the Earth

TILT, ROTATION, AND ORBIT

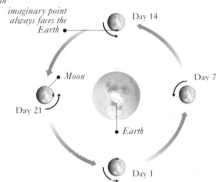

imaginary point always faces the Earth

Moon

Earth

Day 14

Day 7

Day 21

Day 1

OBSERVING THE MOON

Since the Moon spins on its axis exactly once in the time it takes to orbit the Earth, the same hemisphere, termed the near side, is always turned towards Earth. Hence, we only ever see about half of the lunar surface. The main features can be seen with the naked eye. Dark lowland plains, known as maria, contrast with the bright highlands. Binoculars or a small telescope reveal innumerable craters and mountain ranges. Surface relief is most conspicuous near the border between lit and unlit areas, called the terminator, where shadows are longest. When the surface is illuminated at high angles near full Moon, it appears washed out, and even large craters can vanish. However, some features need high contrast to be seen and are at their most prominent near full Moon; these include the dark maria and the bright rays around some craters.

△ CAPTURED ROTATION
The Earth's gravitational influence has slowed the Moon's rotation so that it is exactly synchronized with its orbit.

◁ THE FAR SIDE
The Moon's far side, invisible from the Earth, has been photographed from space.

KEY TO LUNAR FEATURES

CRATERS			LOWLAND FEATURES
1. Aristillus	13. Alpetragius	25. Fracastorius	36. Sinus Iridum
2. Autolycus	14. Arzachel	26. Theophilus	37. Sinus Medii
3. Archimedes	15. Gassendi	27. Langrenus	38. Sinus Asperitatis
4. Plato	16. Walter	28. Proclus	39. Lacus Somniorum
5. Eratosthenes	17. Tycho	29. Posidonius	40. Lacus Mortis
6. Grimaldi	18. Longomontanus	30. Atlas	UPLAND FEATURES
7. Copernicus	19. Clavius	31. Hercules	41. Montes Alpes
8. Aristarchus	20. Maginus	32. Endymion	42. Montes Caucasus
9. Marius	21. Stöfler	33. Aristoteles	43. Montes Jura
10. Ptolemaeus	22. Piccolomini	34. Eudoxus	44. Montes Carpatus
11. Albategnius	23. Catharina	35. Cassini	45. Montes Apenninus
12. Alphonsus	24. Cyrillus		46. Rupes Altai

Gravity (Earth = 1) 0.17	Average temperature −18°C (0°F)	Maximum magnitude −12.7

PHASES OF THE MOON

The Moon's phases arise because we see differing amounts of its sunlit side as it orbits the Earth. At new Moon, the near side of the Moon is in complete shadow. As it orbits the Earth, the visible area grows, or waxes, from a crescent via a gibbous phase to full, when the disc is fully illuminated. The phases then occur in reverse, as the visible area shrinks, or wanes. When the Moon is a thin crescent, the unlit part can be seen faintly illuminated by light reflected from the Earth, an effect known as earthshine.

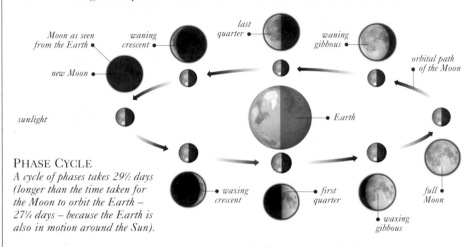

Moon as seen from the Earth

waning crescent

last quarter

waning gibbous

orbital path of the Moon

new Moon

sunlight

Earth

PHASE CYCLE
A cycle of phases takes 29½ days (longer than the time taken for the Moon to orbit the Earth – 27¼ days – because the Earth is also in motion around the Sun).

waxing crescent

first quarter

full Moon

waxing gibbous

ECLIPSES OF THE MOON

Occasionally, the full Moon moves into the Earth's shadow and is eclipsed. From the Moon's first entry into the shadow until it has completely re-emerged can take up to four hours, and the period during which the eclipse is total can be well over an hour. Up to three lunar eclipses may occur in a year, although in some years there are none. Lunar eclipses are widely visible on the Earth's surface, from wherever the Moon is above the horizon.

SEQUENCE OF A LUNAR ECLIPSE
Sunlight bent into the Earth's shadow by its own atmosphere often prevents the eclipsed Moon disappearing completely and makes it appear red.

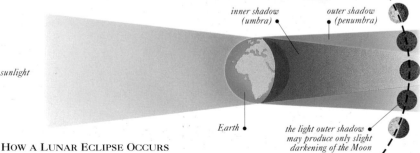

inner shadow (umbra)

outer shadow (penumbra)

sunlight

Earth

the light outer shadow may produce only slight darkening of the Moon

HOW A LUNAR ECLIPSE OCCURS

Diameter (Earth = 1) 0.27	Mass (Earth = 1) 0.01	Volume (Earth = 1) 0.02	Density (water = 1) 3.34

HISTORY AND GEOLOGY

The Moon is thought to have formed about 4.5 billion years ago when a body the size of Mars struck the Earth, which itself was still less than 100 million years old. Debris from the collision was thrown into orbit and coalesced to form the Moon. The young Moon was bombarded by meteorites until about 3.9 billion years ago, when the storm of impacts subsided. Molten lava then oozed out from the interior, creating the maria, a process that continued for more than 2 billion years. Maria are scarce on the far side because the crust is thicker there, and so less lava reached the surface.

crust of granite-like rock

rocky mantle

partly molten outer core

small inner core

INTERNAL STRUCTURE

rim formed from material that falls back to the surface following impact

rays, consisting of fragments of bright rock

concentric steps on crater walls

central peak

METEORITE IMPACT CRATER
Large craters often have a flat floor with one or more mountains at their centre. Since there is no erosion on the Moon, craters are well preserved from the time of impact.

LANDFORMS

The Moon's lowland maria bear few large craters. In contrast, the highlands, which are older, are saturated with craters of all sizes, from tiny pits to huge walled plains over 200 km (125 miles) across. With the exception of a few small volcanic craters, they were all formed by meteorite impacts. Large craters often have central peaks, caused by rebounding of the crater floor during impact, and stepped walls caused by subsequent slumping. Young craters are bright and surrounded by rays of pulverized rock thrown out by the impact. The Moon also has valleys, termed rilles, of which there are two main types: those caused by faulting, which can be straight or curved; and sinuous rilles, which look like rivers but are actually lava channels.

◁ CRATERS AND RILLES
Aristarchus (on the left) is a young ray crater. A long rille leads away from the adjacent crater Herodotus.

▽ OVERLAPPING CRATERS
The crater Theophilus (on the right) has a central peak and terraced wall.

Gravity (Earth = 1)	0.17	Average temperature	–18°C (0°F)	Maximum magnitude	–12.7

MARS

MARS IS A small, rocky planet that in some ways is similar to the Earth. It has a 24-hour day, a pattern of seasons that resembles our own, and polar ice-caps. However, there are important differences: temperatures on Mars rarely rise above freezing, and the atmosphere is thin and contains almost no oxygen. Mars is often called the Red Planet because it is covered by red deserts.

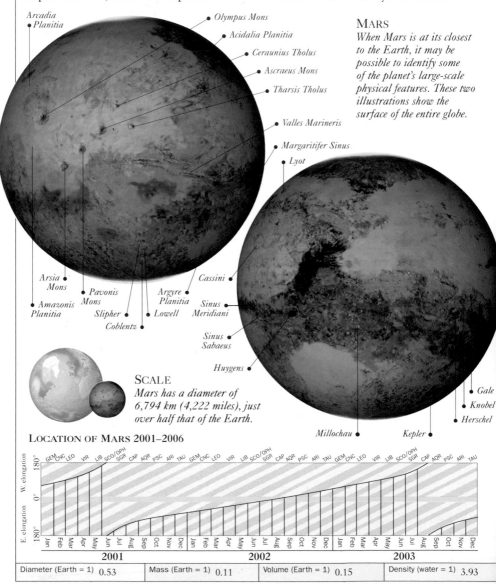

Arcadia Planitia

Olympus Mons

Acidalia Planitia

Ceraunius Tholus

Ascraeus Mons

Tharsis Tholus

Valles Marineris

Margaritifer Sinus

Lyot

MARS
When Mars is at its closest to the Earth, it may be possible to identify some of the planet's large-scale physical features. These two illustrations show the surface of the entire globe.

Arsia Mons

Pavonis Mons

Amazonis Planitia

Slipher

Coblentz

Argyre Planitia

Lowell

Cassini

Sinus Meridiani

Sinus Sabaeus

Huygens

Millochau

Kepler

Gale

Knobel

Herschel

SCALE
Mars has a diameter of 6,794 km (4,222 miles), just over half that of the Earth.

LOCATION OF MARS 2001–2006

| Diameter (Earth = 1) | 0.53 | Mass (Earth = 1) | 0.11 | Volume (Earth = 1) | 0.15 | Density (water = 1) | 3.93 |

OBSERVATION

Mars is easy to spot with the naked eye at or near times of opposition (see below), when it resembles a bright and distinctly orange-coloured star. Binoculars show only a tiny disc, but with a small telescope the planet's polar caps and the largest of its dark surface markings may be seen. For serious observing, a telescope with an aperture of 200 mm (8 in) or more is recommended. At its average opposition distance, a magnification of about 100 times makes Mars appear as large as the full Moon does to the naked eye.

◁ NAKED EYE
Mars is the orange dot above the right-hand side of the spire.

ORBIT

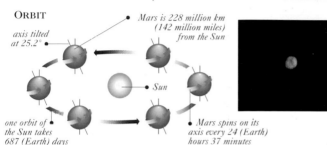

axis tilted at 25.2°

Mars is 228 million km (142 million miles) from the Sun

Sun

one orbit of the Sun takes 687 (Earth) days

Mars spins on its axis every 24 (Earth) hours 37 minutes

△ BINOCULARS
Mars is the disc below centre in this picture.

◁ TELESCOPE
Large-scale surface features appear as light and dark markings.

OPPOSITIONS

Mars comes to opposition (see p.15) roughly every two years and two months, but its highly elliptical orbit means that its distance from us at opposition varies appreciably. At close oppositions – every 15 or 17 years – it appears largest and brightest in the sky.

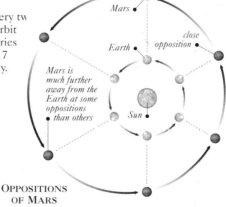

Mars

close opposition

Earth

Mars is much further away from the Earth at some oppositions than others

Sun

OPPOSITIONS OF MARS

DATES OF OPPOSITIONS

DATE	WHERE MARS APPEARS	MAGNITUDE	DISTANCE from Earth (million km)
24 December 2007	Gemini–Taurus	–1.6	89
29 January 2010	Cancer	–1.2	99
3 March 2012	Leo	–1.2	101
8 April 2014	Virgo	–1.5	93
22 May 2016	Scorpius	–2.1	76
27 July 2018	Capricornus	–2.8	58

| Gravity (Earth = 1) 0.38 | Number of moons 2 | Average temperature –63°C (–81°F) | Maximum magnitude –2.8 |

ATMOSPHERE AND CLIMATE

Mars has an atmosphere that consists mostly of carbon dioxide. It is so thin that the pressure at the surface is less than 1 per cent of that on Earth, and the temperature is usually well below freezing. In winter, the atmosphere freezes at the poles, adding a layer of carbon-dioxide frost to the permanent polar caps of frozen water. Morning mists and high-altitude clouds, particularly in polar areas, can be seen from the Earth. Localized dust storms occur throughout the Martian year. However, when Mars is at its closest to the Sun – and temperature and wind speed are at their maximum – storms can cover the whole planet, enveloping it in dust.

ATMOSPHERIC STRUCTURE

thin clouds of frozen carbon dioxide

isolated clouds and fog of icy water vapour

iron-rich red dust

THERMOSPHERE

STRATOSPHERE

TROPOSPHERE

ATMOSPHERIC COMPOSITION

oxygen and carbon monoxide (0.2%), and trace gases

argon (1.6%)

nitrogen (2.7%)

carbon dioxide (95.3%)

MOONS

Mars has two small moons called Phobos and Deimos, with average diameters of about 22 km (14 miles) and 12 km (7 miles). Both moons are irregularly shaped and are thought to be asteroids that have been pulled into orbit around Mars by the planet's gravity. Phobos orbits Mars more quickly than Mars rotates on its axis, so from the planet's surface it appears to rise in the west and set in the east. Phobos and Deimos are too faint to be seen without a large telescope. Close-up photographs from space probes have shown that both are heavily cratered.

Stickney

PHOBOS
The largest crater on Phobos, called Stickney, is about 10 km (6 miles) in diameter.

DEIMOS
The smaller of the two moons, Deimos has no large craters.

Phobos

Deimos

MOON ORBITS
Phobos and Deimos are shown here orbiting Mars (not to scale).

1 2 3 4 5 6 7 8 *Scale in radiuses of Mars*

LOCATION OF MARS 2007–2012

Diameter (Earth = 1)	Mass (Earth = 1)	Volume (Earth = 1)	Density (water = 1)
0.53	0.11	0.15	3.93

GEOGRAPHY AND GEOLOGY

Mars is a planet of two halves: the southern hemisphere is mainly upland, heavily cratered by meteorites; the northern hemisphere is smoother and on average a few kilometres lower in altitude. There are several huge volcanoes, the most impressive being Olympus Mons, a mountain 600 km (400 miles) wide and 27 km (17 miles) high, and often covered by white clouds that can be seen with a telescope on Earth. Another spectacular feature is a system of canyons, Valles Marineris, more than 4,000 km (2,500 miles) long, one-fifth of the planet's circumference and visible through a telescope as a dark streak. The surface of Mars resembles a rock-strewn desert, coloured a rusty red by iron oxide and frozen to a depth of several kilometres. There are signs that water has flowed over the surface in the past, when the climate was warmer.

rock crust

mantle
of silicate
rock

small,
probably
solid core

INTERNAL
STRUCTURE

◁ SYRTIS MAJOR
*Once thought to be an area of
vegetation, this elongated dark
marking actually consists of
darker rock and dust.*

THE THARSIS BULGE ▷
*There are three volcanoes in this
upland region, forming a chain
2,000 km (1,250 miles) long.
The edge of the Valles Marineris
is at the right of the picture.*

CHIMP ROCK ▷
*This boulder seems
to have been scoured
by wind-blown dust.
Winds on Mars can
reach 200 km
(125 miles) an hour.*

PATHFINDER ON MARS ▷
*In 1997, the Pathfinder lander sent back
pictures of a frozen, rocky desert.*

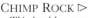

| 2010 | 2011 | 2012 |

| Gravity (Earth = 1) 0.38 | Number of moons 2 | Average temperature −63°C (−81°F) | Maximum magnitude −2.9 |

JUPITER

JUPITER IS THE largest planet in the Solar System, weighing more than twice as much as all the other planets put together. It spins on its axis faster than any other planet – one rotation takes less than 10 hours. The visible surface of Jupiter consists of swirling, distinctively banded clouds. Beneath them, the planet is composed mostly of liquid hydrogen and helium.

JUPITER
Jupiter's constantly changing clouds form bands parallel to its equator.

dark bands, called belts, consist of descending, relatively warm gas

bright bands, known as zones, are higher than the belts and consist of ascending, relatively cool gas

SCALE
At 143,000 km (88,850 miles) in diameter, Jupiter is 11 times wider than Earth.

• *North Equatorial Belt*

• *Equatorial Zone*

• *South Equatorial Belt*

Jupiter spins on its axis in about 9 hours 50 minutes

one orbit of the Sun takes 11.9 (Earth) years •

• *Sun*

the Great Red Spot • is a cloud system three times wider than the Earth

Jupiter is 778 million km • (483 million miles) from the Sun

axis tilted at 3.1° •

ORBIT

LOCATION OF JUPITER 2001–2006

| Diameter (Earth = 1) 11.21 | Mass (Earth = 1) 318 | Volume (Earth = 1) 1,321 | Density (water = 1) 1.33 |

OBSERVATION

Jupiter is one of the most interesting planets for the amateur observer. It is usually the brightest planet after Venus (although at times Mars can become slightly brighter), and it is so large that even binoculars show it as a rounded disc. A small telescope reveals the most prominent cloud bands, which are usually the dark North and South Equatorial Belts, either side of the bright Equatorial Zone. An aperture of 75 mm (3 in) reveals some of the larger features within the clouds.

Over a period of about 10 minutes, these features can be seen to be moving. A small telescope also shows Jupiter's disc to be elliptical – the planet's equatorial diameter is over 9,000 km (5,600 miles) greater than its polar diameter, due to its rapid rotation. Jupiter looks biggest and brightest when it is at opposition (see p.15), which occurs every 13 months. At that time, at a magnification of only 40 times it will appear as large as the full Moon looks to the naked eye.

OBSERVING JUPITER
Through binoculars, Jupiter can be distinguished from stars because it appears as a disc rather than a point of light. Telescopes and CCD cameras show the surface of the disc in greater detail.

BINOCULARS   TELESCOPE   CCD

OBSERVING THE GALILEAN MOONS

Jupiter's four largest moons – Io, Europa, Ganymede, and Callisto – were first seen in 1610 by the Italian scientist Galileo Galilei, and are now known as the Galilean moons. Through a small telescope or binoculars, they appear like faint stars lined up on either side of the planet's equator, and change position as they orbit the planet. Sometimes one or more may be missing, either passing in front of or behind Jupiter, or lost in its shadow.

DAY 1

I G   E   G

DAY 2

E   I   G   C

DAY 3

TRACKING THE MOONS
The moons' positions are shown here over four nights. The moons are shown as coloured discs but appear through binoculars or a telescope as small points of light.

KEY
🔵 Callisto (C)
🔵 Europa (E)
🔵 Ganymede (G)
🔵 Io (I)

E   I   G   C

DAY 4

G   E   C

| Gravity (Earth = 1) | 2.36 | Number of moons | 60+ | Average temperature | −144°C (−227°F) | Maximum magnitude | −2.9 |

STRUCTURE AND ATMOSPHERE

Jupiter is enveloped in a cloudy atmosphere about 1,000 km (600 miles) deep. Clouds of different composition form at various levels depending on the temperature and pressure, which both increase with depth. Beneath the clouds there is no solid surface. Instead, hydrogen and helium are compressed into liquids by Jupiter's great gravitational pull. Deep in the interior, where liquid hydrogen acts like molten metal, convection produces a strong magnetic field that extends for millions of kilometres into space. At Jupiter's centre there is thought to be a rocky core.

ATMOSPHERIC STRUCTURE

- white clouds of ammonia crystals
- dark orange clouds of ammonium hydrosulphide
- bluish clouds of water ice and water droplets

STRATOSPHERE

TROPOSPHERE

- atmosphere
- liquid hydrogen and helium
- liquid metallic hydrogen
- rocky core about twice the size and ten times the mass of Earth

INTERNAL STRUCTURE

ATMOSPHERIC COMPOSITION

- helium (10.2%) and trace gases
- hydrogen (89.8%)

CLOUD BELTS AND STORMS

Jupiter's rapid rotation draws its clouds into light and dark bands. In the lighter areas, termed zones, gas rises from the warm interior and condenses to form high-altitude clouds. The darker clouds, called belts, occur at lower altitudes, where gas descends. The colours of the belts range from red and brown to blue, depending on the compounds that they contain. Individual cloud features seldom last more than a few weeks, but some white oval clouds have lasted for over half a century. The most prominent feature is the Great Red Spot, on the southern edge of the South Equatorial Belt. This swirling, high-altitude storm cloud rotates anti-clockwise once a week or so. It has been tracked since 1831 although a similar feature was seen in the 17th century.

THE GREAT RED SPOT

This image was taken from the Galileo space probe. The colouring of the spot is thought to be due to red phosphorus, or perhaps carbon compounds.

LOCATION OF JUPITER 2007–2012

| Diameter (Earth = 1) 11.21 | Mass (Earth = 1) 318 | Volume (Earth = 1) 1,321 | Density (water = 1) 1.33 |

RINGS AND MOONS

Jupiter has over 60 known satellites, which fall into three groups: the inner eight, including the four Galilean moons, which have circular orbits in the planet's equatorial plane; the middle five, with elliptical orbits inclined at about 25 and 46 degrees to Jupiter's equator; and the remainder, which have elliptical and retrograde (east-to-west) orbits. The last two groups are probably captured asteroids. Apart from the Galilean moons, the satellites are small and faint – a large telescope is needed to see them. Jupiter has a faint ring of dust, over 100,000 km (60,000 miles) wide.

RINGS AND INNERMOST MOONS

Io *Thebe* *Amalthea* *Metis* *Adrastea* *Jupiter*

Main ring *Halo ring*

6   5   4   3   2   1

Scale in radiuses of Jupiter

JUPITER'S LARGEST OUTER MOONS

340 330 320 310 300 290   170 160 150   30 20 10

Sinope | *Pasiphae* | *Carme* | *Ananke*   *Elara* / *Leda*   *Callisto*   *Io*
Lysithea | *Himalia*   *Ganymede* | *Jupiter*
Europa

THE GALILEAN MOONS

Io, the innermost Galilean satellite, is similar in size to our Moon, having a diameter of 3,640 km (2,260 miles). It is covered with yellow-orange sulphur, erupted by volcanoes that are still active. Its interior is kept molten by Jupiter's gravitational forces. Europa, 3,120 km (1,940 miles) in diameter, is the smallest of the four. Its smooth, icy surface resembles a cracked eggshell. Ganymede – diameter 5,260 km (3,270 miles) – is the largest moon in the Solar System, bigger than Mercury. Its complex, partly cratered surface has dark patches and lighter grooves. Outermost of the four moons is Callisto – diameter 4,820 km (2,995 miles) – the dark surface of which is covered with impact craters.

IO

EUROPA

GANYMEDE

CALLISTO

| Gravity (Earth = 1) 2.36 | Number of moons 60+ | Average temperature −144°C (−227°F) | Maximum magnitude −2.9 |

SATURN

SATURN, THE MOST DISTANT planet known to ancient astronomers, is the second largest in the Solar System, and the easiest one to recognize through a telescope because of the broad, bright rings that encircle its equator. Like Jupiter, it has a cloudy atmosphere overlying an interior of liquid hydrogen and helium. Saturn has more than 30 moons, some orbiting among the rings.

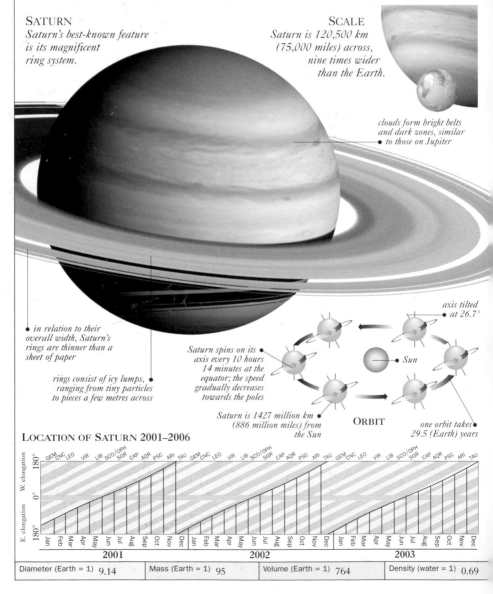

SATURN
Saturn's best-known feature is its magnificent ring system.

SCALE
Saturn is 120,500 km (75,000 miles) across, nine times wider than the Earth.

clouds form bright belts and dark zones, similar to those on Jupiter

axis tilted at 26.7°

in relation to their overall width, Saturn's rings are thinner than a sheet of paper

rings consist of icy lumps, ranging from tiny particles to pieces a few metres across

Saturn spins on its axis every 10 hours 14 minutes at the equator; the speed gradually decreases towards the poles

Sun

Saturn is 1427 million km (886 million miles) from the Sun

ORBIT

one orbit takes 29.5 (Earth) years

LOCATION OF SATURN 2001–2006

| Diameter (Earth = 1) 9.14 | Mass (Earth = 1) 95 | Volume (Earth = 1) 764 | Density (water = 1) 0.69 |

OBSERVATION

To the naked eye, Saturn looks like a bright, yellowish star. Binoculars just reveal a small disc, with a hint of elongation caused by its rings. With a small telescope, the rings, which are over twice as wide as the planet itself, can be seen clearly. Of the five planets visible to the naked eye, Saturn is the slowest-moving, its oppositions (see p.15) occurring a year and two weeks apart. When Saturn is viewed at a magnification of 100 times at opposition, its globe looks the same size as the full Moon seen with the naked eye. Saturn's disc is crossed by cloud belts, but these are not as prominent as those of Jupiter, nor is there an equivalent of the Great Red Spot. However, white spots appear in the equatorial zone about every 30 years, during summer in the planet's northern hemisphere.

NAKED-EYE VIEW △
Saturn is the bright, star-like object at the centre of this picture.

CCD VIEW
With a CCD camera, it is possible to see the major divisions of the rings.

◁ TELESCOPE VIEW
A small telescope shows the outline of Saturn's rings.

VIEWING SATURN'S RINGS

As Saturn orbits the Sun, we see its rings from various angles because of the combined effect of Saturn's axial tilt and the inclination of its orbit to our own. At most, the rings are tipped towards us at about 27 degrees. Twice in each orbit of Saturn around the Sun the rings appear to us edge-on, when they disappear from view because they are so thin. The next time this will happen will be in September 2009.

THE EARTH AND SATURN IN SPACE

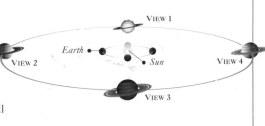

VIEW 1
VIEW 2
Earth
Sun
VIEW 4
VIEW 3

APPEARANCE OF RINGS AS VIEWED FROM THE EARTH

VIEW 1   VIEW 2   VIEW 3   VIEW 4

2004   2005   2006

| Gravity (Earth = 1) 0.92 | Number of moons 30+ | Average temperature −176°C (−285°F) | Maximum magnitude −0.3 |

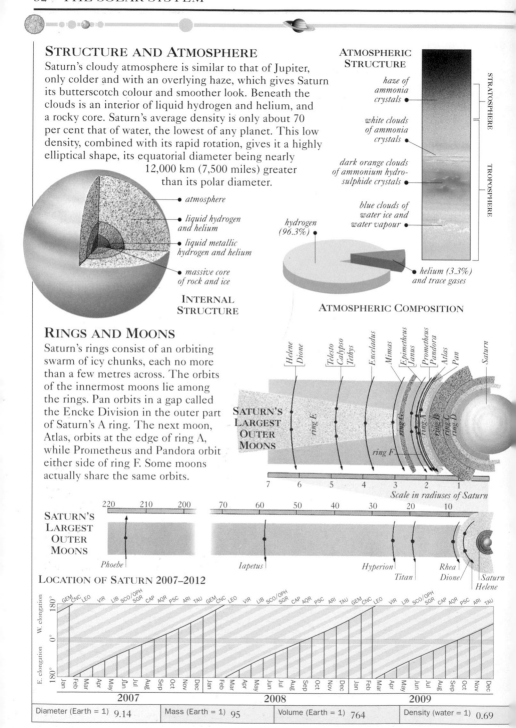

STRUCTURE AND ATMOSPHERE

Saturn's cloudy atmosphere is similar to that of Jupiter, only colder and with an overlying haze, which gives Saturn its butterscotch colour and smoother look. Beneath the clouds is an interior of liquid hydrogen and helium, and a rocky core. Saturn's average density is only about 70 per cent that of water, the lowest of any planet. This low density, combined with its rapid rotation, gives it a highly elliptical shape, its equatorial diameter being nearly 12,000 km (7,500 miles) greater than its polar diameter.

• atmosphere

• liquid hydrogen and helium

• liquid metallic hydrogen and helium

• massive core of rock and ice

INTERNAL STRUCTURE

ATMOSPHERIC STRUCTURE

haze of ammonia crystals •

white clouds of ammonia crystals •

dark orange clouds of ammonium hydro-sulphide crystals •

blue clouds of water ice and water vapour •

STRATOSPHERE

TROPOSPHERE

ATMOSPHERIC COMPOSITION

hydrogen (96.3%)

helium (3.3%) and trace gases

RINGS AND MOONS

Saturn's rings consist of an orbiting swarm of icy chunks, each no more than a few metres across. The orbits of the innermost moons lie among the rings. Pan orbits in a gap called the Encke Division in the outer part of Saturn's A ring. The next moon, Atlas, orbits at the edge of ring A, while Prometheus and Pandora orbit either side of ring F. Some moons actually share the same orbits.

SATURN'S LARGEST OUTER MOONS

Helene | Dione — Telesto Calypso Tethys — Enceladus — Mimas — Epimetheus Janus — Prometheus Pandora — Atlas — Pan — Saturn

ring E   ring F

ring G   ring A   ring B   ring C   ring D

7   6   5   4   3   2   1
Scale in radiuses of Saturn

SATURN'S LARGEST OUTER MOONS

220   210   200   70   60   50   40   30   20   10

Phoebe | Iapetus | Hyperion | Rhea | Saturn
Titan   Dione | Helene

LOCATION OF SATURN 2007–2012

W. elongation   180°

E. elongation   0°   180°

GEM CNC LEO   VIR   LIB SCO/OPH SGR   CAP   AQR   PSC   ARI   TAU   GEM CNC LEO   VIR   LIB SCO/OPH SGR   CAP   AQR   PSC   ARI   TAU   GEM CNC LEO   VIR   LIB SCO/OPH SGR   CAP   AQR   PSC   ARI   TAU

Jan Feb Mar Apr May Jun Jul Aug Sep Oct Nov Dec | Jan Feb Mar Apr May Jun Jul Aug Sep Oct Nov Dec | Jan Feb Mar Apr May Jun Jul Aug Sep Oct Nov Dec

2007   2008   2009

Diameter (Earth = 1)	Mass (Earth = 1)	Volume (Earth = 1)	Density (water = 1)
9.14	95	764	0.69

INNER RINGS

The outermost part of Saturn's ring system visible from the Earth is ring A, which is nearly 275,000 km (170,000 miles) across. This is separated from the brightest and widest part, ring B, by the Cassini Division, a gap of about 4,500 km (2,800 miles), visible with a 75 mm (3 in) telescope. Next is the partly transparent ring C (or crepe ring). Fainter rings, called D and F, lie inside and outside the visible rings. Two other very faint rings, known as G and E, lie beyond ring F but are not shown here.

Saturn's cloud top

ring D

ring C (*crepe ring*)

ring B

Cassini Division

ring F

INNER RINGS AND DIVISIONS

Encke Division   *ring A*

VOYAGER'S VIEW OF SATURN'S RINGS

This enhanced image of ring C and part of ring B (taken by the probe Voyager 2 in 1981) shows that each of the main rings consists of thousands of tiny ringlets. Saturn's rings are 420,000 km (260,000 miles) wide, but have a thickness of just a few hundred metres.

MOONS

Saturn has over 30 known moons. The largest is Titan, 5,150 km (3,200 miles) in diameter. It is the second-largest moon in the Solar System (after Jupiter's Ganymede) and the only one with a substantial atmosphere. At magnitude 8, it can be seen with a small telescope as it orbits the planet every 16 days. An aperture of 150 mm (6 in) should show several other moons – notably Rhea, Tethys, Dione, Iapetus, Enceladus, and perhaps Mimas. Iapetus is unusual in being over four times fainter when on one side of Saturn than on the other, because it has one bright and one dark hemisphere.

TITAN

Titan's surface is obscured by orange hazes suspended in its nitrogen-rich atmosphere.

Gravity (Earth = 1)	0.92	Number of moons	30+	Average temperature	-176°C (-285°F)	Maximum magnitude	-0.3

URANUS

A COLD GAS GIANT, Uranus is the third-largest planet in the Solar System. Its most unusual characteristic is that its axis of rotation lies almost in the plane of its orbit, and so it seems to orbit the Sun on its side. Although it can be seen with the naked eye when at its brightest, Uranus was not discovered until 1781, when it was found by a British astronomer, William Herschel.

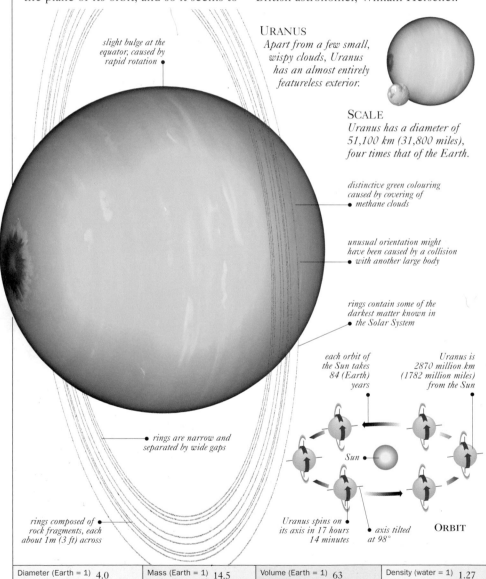

slight bulge at the equator, caused by rapid rotation

URANUS
Apart from a few small, wispy clouds, Uranus has an almost entirely featureless exterior.

SCALE
Uranus has a diameter of 51,100 km (31,800 miles), four times that of the Earth.

distinctive green colouring caused by covering of methane clouds

unusual orientation might have been caused by a collision with another large body

rings contain some of the darkest matter known in the Solar System

each orbit of the Sun takes 84 (Earth) years

Uranus is 2870 million km (1782 million miles) from the Sun

rings are narrow and separated by wide gaps

Sun

rings composed of rock fragments, each about 1m (3 ft) across

Uranus spins on its axis in 17 hours 14 minutes

axis tilted at 98°

ORBIT

Diameter (Earth = 1) 4.0	Mass (Earth = 1) 14.5	Volume (Earth = 1) 63	Density (water = 1) 1.27

ATMOSPHERE AND CLIMATE

Uranus is covered in methane clouds that absorb red light, giving the planet a greenish appearance. Its disc is nearly featureless, but some bright clouds were seen by the Voyager 2 space probe in 1986 and later by the Hubble Space Telescope. The planet's extreme axial tilt means that in the course of each orbit the Sun appears overhead at the equator and both poles; each pole experiences 42 years of daylight followed by 42 years of darkness. The interior is probably significantly different from those of Jupiter and Saturn, consisting mostly of water, methane, ammonia, and rock, rather than liquid hydrogen.

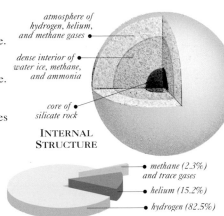

atmosphere of hydrogen, helium, and methane gases

dense interior of water ice, methane, and ammonia

core of silicate rock

INTERNAL STRUCTURE

methane (2.3%) and trace gases

helium (15.2%)

hydrogen (82.5%)

ATMOSPHERIC COMPOSITION

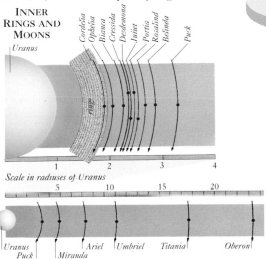

INNER RINGS AND MOONS

Uranus

Cordelia
Ophelia
Bianca
Cressida
Desdemona
Juliet
Portia
Rosalind
Belinda
Puck

rings

Scale in radiuses of Uranus

1   2   3   4
5   10   15   20

Uranus
Puck
Miranda
Ariel
Umbriel
Titania
Oberon

OUTER MOONS

RINGS AND MOONS

Uranus has 11 thin rings and over 20 known moons (several of them only recently identified and whose orbits are not yet accurately known). The rings are too faint to be seen with the size of telescope used by amateur observers. The outermost ring, called the Epsilon ring, is 100 km (60 miles) wide and has "shepherd" moons, Cordelia and Ophelia, one on each side. The moons, too, are faint; even the biggest and brightest, Titania, is of only 14th magnitude and hence cannot be seen without a large telescope.

OBSERVATION

Under good conditions, and when its position is known, Uranus can be located with the naked eye, resembling a star of 6th magnitude. It is easy to find with binoculars, even from urban areas. Its identity can be confirmed by watching its movements from night to night. At oppositions, which occur a year and four days apart, a magnification of 500 times will show Uranus about the same size as the full Moon.

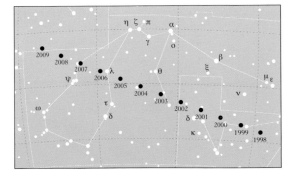

LOCATION OF URANUS 1998–2009

| Gravity (Earth = 1) | 0.89 | Number of moons | 20+ | Average temperature | −215°C (−355°F) | Maximum magnitude | 5.5 |

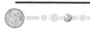

NEPTUNE

NEPTUNE IS THE outermost of the gas giants. Like Uranus, it has an atmosphere rich in hydrogen, helium, and methane, and a faint ring system. Neptune was discovered in 1846, after its position had been predicted based on disturbances to the motion of Uranus caused by its gravitational pull. The planet remained poorly known until the space probe Voyager 2 flew past in 1989.

NEPTUNE
A distant gas giant with some bright cloud features.

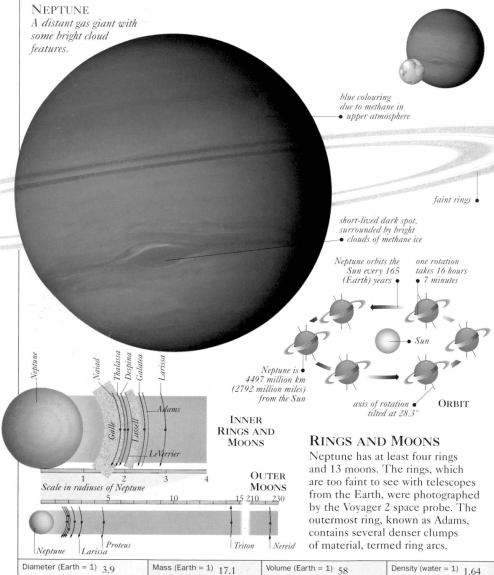

blue colouring due to methane in upper atmosphere

faint rings

short-lived dark spot, surrounded by bright clouds of methane ice

Neptune orbits the Sun every 165 (Earth) years

one rotation takes 16 hours 7 minutes

Sun

Neptune is 4497 million km (2792 million miles) from the Sun

axis of rotation tilted at 28.3°

ORBIT

Neptune

Naiad

Thalassa

Despina

Galatea

Larissa

Galle

Lassell

Adams

LeVerrier

1 2 3 4
Scale in radiuses of Neptune
5 10 15 210 230

INNER RINGS AND MOONS

OUTER MOONS

Neptune

Larissa

Proteus

Triton

Nereid

RINGS AND MOONS

Neptune has at least four rings and 13 moons. The rings, which are too faint to see with telescopes from the Earth, were photographed by the Voyager 2 space probe. The outermost ring, known as Adams, contains several denser clumps of material, termed ring arcs.

Diameter (Earth = 1)	Mass (Earth = 1)	Volume (Earth = 1)	Density (water = 1)
3.9	17.1	58	1.64

ATMOSPHERE AND CLIMATE

The atmospheres of Neptune and Uranus are similar, although Neptune's is stormier and appears blue (rather than blue-green) because there is more methane in its upper levels. In 1989 Voyager 2 photographed a large dark spot, reminiscent of Jupiter's Great Red Spot, in the southern hemisphere. Five years later, when the Hubble Space Telescope observed Neptune, the spot had vanished but another dark spot, this time in the northern hemisphere, appeared late in 1994. Bright streaks of methane cirrus clouds were recorded by both Voyager and Hubble. The composition of the main cloud deck is not known with certainty, but hydrogen sulphide and ammonia are probably present. Neptune's interior is thought to resemble that of Uranus, consisting of water, ammonia, and methane above a rocky core.

INTERNAL STRUCTURE

atmosphere of hydrogen, helium, and methane gases

mantle of icy water, methane, and ammonia

core of silicate rock

hydrogen (80%)

methane (about 1%) and trace gases

helium (19%)

ATMOSPHERIC COMPOSITION

MOONS

Of Neptune's eight known moons, Triton is the only one of any significance. It is also the largest, having a diameter of 2,700 km (1,680 miles). The surface is covered with nitrogen and methane frost and, at −235°C (−391°F), is the coldest known place in the Solar System. Liquid nitrogen bursts through the surface to create geysers that leave dark streaks. Triton has a retrograde orbit (it moves in the opposite direction to Neptune), and is thought to have been a separate body, like Pluto, that was captured by Neptune's gravity. Triton is actually larger than Pluto, and the two may be physically similar.

TRITON'S SOUTH POLE
The nitrogen and methane ice at Triton's poles has a slight but distinctive pink colouring.

AQUARIUS

2009
2007
2008 2005
2006 2003
2004 2001
2002
2000
1999
1998

LOCATION OF NEPTUNE 1998–2009

OBSERVATION

Neptune never becomes brighter than 8th magnitude and so is invisible to the naked eye, but it can be located with binoculars, through which it resembles a faint star. Sightings of Neptune can be confirmed by observing its gradual movement against the background of stars over several nights. Through a telescope, the planet appears as a featureless bluish disc about two-thirds the apparent size of Uranus. Neptune comes to opposition (see p.15) only two-and-a-half days later each year.

Gravity (Earth = 1)	Number of moons	Average temperature	Maximum magnitude
1.12	13	−215°C (−355°F)	7.6

PLUTO

A TINY WORLD of rock and ice, Pluto is the smallest of all the planets, only two-thirds the size of our Moon. It is usually the outermost planet, but it has a highly elliptical orbit that for short periods takes it closer to the Sun than Neptune. Pluto was discovered in 1930 by Clyde Tombaugh, an American astronomer, who used photographs to search for a planet beyond Neptune.

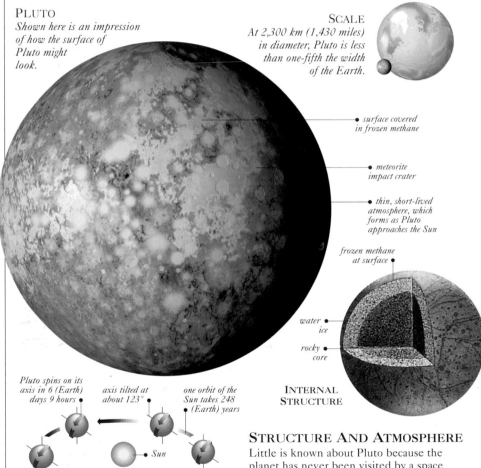

PLUTO
Shown here is an impression of how the surface of Pluto might look.

SCALE
At 2,300 km (1,430 miles) in diameter, Pluto is less than one-fifth the width of the Earth.

surface covered in frozen methane

meteorite impact crater

thin, short-lived atmosphere, which forms as Pluto approaches the Sun

frozen methane at surface

water ice

rocky core

INTERNAL STRUCTURE

Pluto spins on its axis in 6 (Earth) days 9 hours

axis tilted at about 123°

one orbit of the Sun takes 248 (Earth) years

Sun

ORBIT

Pluto's axis is so steeply tilted that its north pole lies below the plane of its orbit

Pluto ranges between 4,400 and 7,300 million km (2,700 and 4,500 million miles) from the Sun

STRUCTURE AND ATMOSPHERE

Little is known about Pluto because the planet has never been visited by a space probe. Its surface is thought to be covered with methane ice, some of which evaporates to form a thin temporary atmosphere for a few decades when Pluto is at its closest to the Sun. Below the methane ice is thought to be a layer of frozen water and a large rocky core.

| Diameter (Earth = 1) 0.18 | Mass (Earth = 1) 0.002 | Volume (Earth = 1) 0.006 | Density (water = 1) 2.0 |

CHARON

Pluto's only moon, Charon, was discovered in 1978. It has more than half the diameter and about one-fifth the mass of Pluto, making it the largest moon in relation to its parent in the Solar System. In effect, the two bodies form a double planet. Charon orbits about 18,400 km (11,400 miles) above Pluto's surface every 6.4 days. Pluto and Charon each spin on their axes in 6.4 days as well, so each body always presents the same face to the other.

CHARON'S SURFACE
Charon is thought to be covered in frozen water (as shown here), unlike Pluto, which is coated with methane ice.

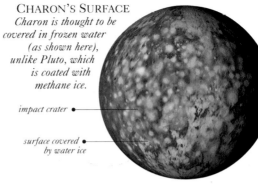

impact crater •——

surface covered •——
by water ice

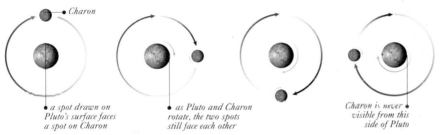

• *Charon*

• *a spot drawn on Pluto's surface faces a spot on Charon*

• *as Pluto and Charon rotate, the two spots still face each other*

Charon is never •
visible from this side of Pluto

△ SYNCHRONIZED ORBITS
From one hemisphere of Pluto, Charon is always visible and remains motionless in the sky. It can never be seen from the other hemisphere.

PLUTO AND CHARON ▷
It is very difficult to separate Pluto and Charon using a telescope on Earth. This image, taken by the Hubble Space Telescope, is the best picture that has so far been taken of Pluto and its moon.

LOCATION OF PLUTO 1998–2009

OBSERVATION

Pluto is of only 14th magnitude. This means that a telescope with an aperture of 200 mm (8 in) is needed just to see it. Even through a large telescope, Pluto appears as a mere star-like point of light. No detail can be detected on its surface. The easiest way to identify Pluto is to study its motion against the stars on a series of photographs – this is similar to the technique used by Clyde Tombaugh in his search for the planet. Pluto's orbit is tilted at 17 degrees to that of the Earth, and so it strays further from the ecliptic (see p.15) than any other planet.

| Gravity (Earth = 1) 0.07 | Number of moons 1 | Average temperature −223°C (−369°F) | Maximum magnitude 14 |

COMETS AND METEORS

COMETS, consisting of frozen gas and dust, exist in a swarm at the edge of the Solar System. Sometimes they approach the Sun on highly elongated orbits, warming up and releasing gas and dust, before receding back into the darkness. Dust particles from comets can enter the Earth's atmosphere, where they burn up to create bright streaks in the sky called meteors or shooting stars.

COMETS

Comets are icy remnants from the formation of the outer planets. They usually orbit unseen in the so-called Oort Cloud, which extends to one light year or more from the Sun. Sometimes the gravity of a passing star nudges a comet from the cloud into the inner Solar System, so that it becomes visible from Earth. Over 1,000 comets are known, but the Oort Cloud and its inner region, called the Kuiper Belt, are thought to contain billions of them.

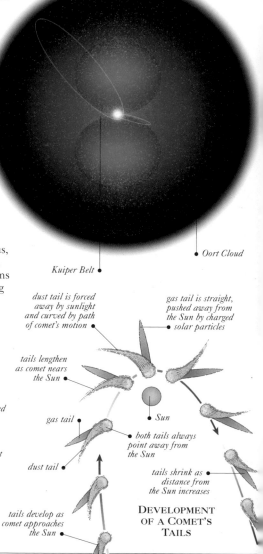

THE SOURCES OF COMETS
Comets of long orbital period are thought to come from the Oort Cloud (at the edge of this picture); those of shorter period come from a flattened inner region, the Kuiper Belt.

NUCLEI AND TAILS

The only solid part of a comet is its nucleus, which is typically about a kilometre across. As it approaches the Sun, the nucleus warms up, emitting gas and dust to form a glowing head, termed the coma, up to 100,000 km (60,000 miles) across. In some comets, gas and dust from the coma form tails.

Oort Cloud

Kuiper Belt

escaping gas and dust form tails

nucleus covered in a crust of dark dust

large, bright coma

fountains of gas and dust

dust tail is forced away by sunlight and curved by path of comet's motion

tails lengthen as comet nears the Sun

gas tail is straight, pushed away from the Sun by charged solar particles

gas tail

Sun

dust tail

both tails always point away from the Sun

tails shrink as distance from the Sun increases

tails develop as comet approaches the Sun

FEATURES OF A COMET

DEVELOPMENT OF A COMET'S TAILS

COMET OBSERVATION

About two dozen comets can be seen each year with a large telescope, but only rarely is one bright enough to be visible to the naked eye. There are two main classes: periodic comets orbit the Sun in under 200 years, while long-period comets may take hundreds of thousands of years to return. Large, bright comets develop tails, of which there are two types: one consists of gas and looks bluish; the other consists of dust and appears yellowish. Gas tails are usually narrow and straight, while dust tails are often broad and curved. Both are visible through binoculars.

COMET HALE–BOPP
This bright comet was easily visible to the naked eye in 1997. It will not return for 2,400 years.

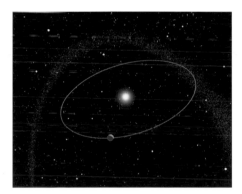

THE ORIGIN OF A METEOR SHOWER
Individual meteor showers occur at the same time each year as the Earth's orbit passes through the trail of dust left along a comet's orbit.

METEORS

On any clear night bright streaks can be seen in the sky from time to time. They appear suddenly and last for less than a second. These are meteors, or shooting stars, caused by specks of dust from comets burning up in the atmosphere at a height of about 100 km (60 miles). A handful of so-called sporadic (random) meteors can usually be seen in an hour, but several times each year the Earth passes through a trail of dust left by a comet, resulting in a meteor shower. Meteors in a shower appear to diverge from a single point called the radiant, and the shower is named after the constellation in which the radiant is found – hence, the Leonids appear to come from Leo. Meteors are easy to see with the naked eye, and useful data have been derived from the records kept by amateur observers.

SHOWER	DATE	CONSTELLATION	HOURLY RATE
Quadrantids	3–4 January	Boötes	100
Lyrids	21 April	Lyra	10
Eta Aquarids	5 May	Aquarius	35
Delta Aquarids (S)	29 July	Aquarius	25
Delta Aquarids (N)	6 August	Aquarius	10
Perseids	12 August	Perseus	80
Orionids	20–22 October	Orion	25
Taurids	5 November	Taurus	10
Leonids	17 November	Leo	10
Geminids	13 December	Gemini	100
Ursids	23 December	Ursa Minor	10

BRIGHT METEOR SHOWERS
This table shows the main meteor showers that the Earth encounters each year. The hourly rate is the maximum number visible under ideal conditions. The date given indicates the time of maximum activity – smaller numbers of meteors can usually be seen for some days either side of this date.

ASTEROIDS AND METEORITES

ASTEROIDS – or minor planets – are small bodies of iron and rock left over from the formation of the Solar System. Most asteroids orbit the Sun in a belt between Mars and Jupiter, but some stray from this group to cross the paths of the inner planets. Meteorites are small fragments, usually from asteroids, that have entered the Earth's atmosphere and fallen to the surface.

ASTEROIDS

Over a million asteroids are thought to exist, although only about 20,000 have so far been discovered. Most asteroids orbit in the belt between Mars and Jupiter, but there is a group, known as the Trojan asteroids, that moves along Jupiter's orbit. Members of another group, named the Apollo asteroids, cross the Earth's orbit and may therefore collide with our planet. The largest asteroid, known as Ceres, is 940 km (580 miles) in diameter. The brightest is Vesta, 580 km (360 miles) across, which can be as bright as 5th magnitude, making it easily visible with binoculars.

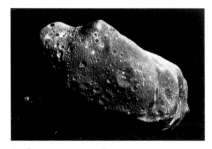

△ IDA
This asteroid, 55 km (34 miles) in length, is orbited by a small satellite known as Dactyl.

• Trojan asteroids

• asteroid belt

• orbit of an Apollo asteroid

Venus

Sun   Earth

Mercury   Mars

Jupiter

Trojan asteroids •

△ ASTEROID ORBITS
The asteroid belt lies between about 320 and 490 million km (200 and 305 million miles) from the Sun. The Trojans orbit either side of Jupiter.

METEORITES

Every day about 10 meteorites fall to Earth, although most land in remote areas or the oceans and go unnoticed. Over 20,000 meteorites have been found, many long after their fall. Meteorites are composed of rock, or iron, or a mixture of both. Large meteorites are usually moving fast enough to dig a crater when they hit the Earth, but smaller ones are slowed by the atmosphere and drop harmlessly to the surface.

METEOR CRATER ▷
This crater, 1.2 km (0.75 miles) wide, was formed in the desert of Arizona, USA, by the impact of an iron meteorite about 50,000 years ago.

STONY-IRON METEORITE

THE CONSTELLATIONS

HOW THIS SECTION WORKS

THIS SECTION contains entries on the 88 constellations, arranged alphabetically by their internationally accepted names. The charts are the most detailed in the book, showing all stars above the approximate threshold of naked-eye visibility. The text covers the origin of the constellations and a selection of the stars and deep-sky objects that they contain.

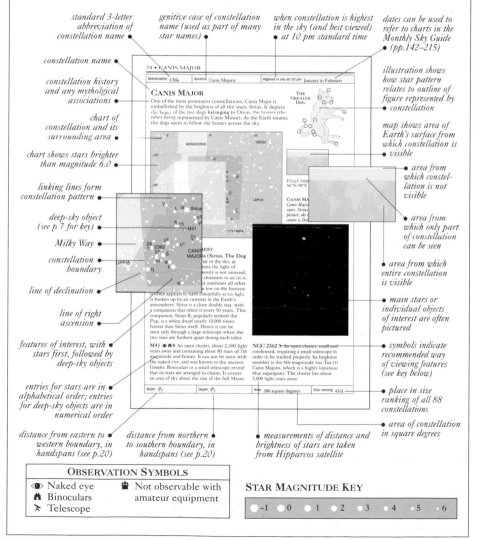

standard 3-letter abbreviation of constellation name

genitive case of constellation name (used as part of many star names)

when constellation is highest in the sky (and best viewed) at 10 pm standard time

dates can be used to refer to charts in the Monthly Sky Guide (pp.142–215)

constellation name

constellation history and any mytholgical associations

chart of constellation and its surrounding area

chart shows stars brighter than magnitude 6.0

linking lines form constellation pattern

deep-sky object (see p.7 for key)

Milky Way

constellation boundary

line of declination

line of right ascension

features of interest, with stars first, followed by deep-sky objects

entries for stars are in alphabetical order; entries for deep-sky objects are in numerical order

distance from eastern to western boundary, in handspans (see p.20)

distance from northern to southern boundary, in handspans (see p.20)

measurements of distance and brightness of stars are taken from Hipparcos satellite

illustration shows how star pattern relates to outline of figure represented by constellation

map shows area of Earth's surface from which constellation is visible

area from which constellation is not visible

area from which only part of constellation can be seen

area from which entire constellation is visible

main stars or individual objects of interest are often pictured

symbols indicate recommended way of viewing features (see key below)

place in size ranking of all 88 constellations

area of constellation in square degrees

Chart detail

74 • CANIS MAJOR

| Abbreviation CMa | Genitive Canis Majoris | Highest in sky at 10 pm January to February |

CANIS MAJOR

THE GREATER DOG

One of the most prominent constellations, Canis Major is embellished by the brightest of all the stars, Sirius. It depicts the larger of the two dogs belonging to Orion, the hunter (the other being represented by Canis Minor). As the Earth rotates, the dogs seem to follow the hunter across the sky.

MONOCEROS

ORION

FULLY VISIBLE 56°N–90°S

CANIS MAJOR
Canis Major's stars, Sirius picture, she li centre is Del

CANIS MAJORIS (Sirius, The Dog star in the sky, at mits the light of nosity is not unusual, closeness to us (it is us outshines all other n low on the horizon it often appears to flash colourfully as its light is broken up by air currents in the Earth's atmosphere. Sirius is a close double star, with a companion that orbits it every 50 years. This companion, Sirius B, popularly termed the Pup, is a white dwarf nearly 10,000 times fainter than Sirius itself. Hence it can be seen only through a large telescope when the two stars are furthest apart during each orbit.

M41 An open cluster, about 2,300 light years away and containing about 80 stars of 7th magnitude and fainter. It can just be seen with the naked eye, and was known to the ancient Greeks. Binoculars or a small telescope reveal that its stars are arranged in chains. It covers an area of sky about the size of the full Moon.

NGC 2362 An open cluster, small and condensed, requiring a small telescope in order to be studied properly. Its brightest member is the 4th-magnitude star Tau (τ) Canis Majoris, which is a highly luminous blue supergiant. The cluster lies about 5,000 light years away.

| Width | Depth | Area 380 square degrees | Size ranking 43rd |

OBSERVATION SYMBOLS

◉ Naked eye	♨ Not observable with
♣ Binoculars	amateur equipment
✦ Telescope	

STAR MAGNITUDE KEY

−1 0 1 2 3 4 5 6

Abbreviation And	Genitive Andromedae	Highest in sky at 10 pm October to November

ANDROMEDA

One of the most famous constellations, Andromeda depicts the princess in Greek myth who was chained to a rock as a sacrifice to a sea monster but was saved by the hero Perseus. The constellation contains the nearest major galaxy to us, M31, the Andromeda Galaxy, which is the most distant object visible to the naked eye.

ANDROMEDA

FULLY
VISIBLE
90°N–37°S

M31 (THE ANDROMEDA GALAXY)
This spiral galaxy looks elliptical because it is tilted at an angle to us.

AROUND M31
M31 is at the top of this picture. The bright star at the bottom left is Beta (β) Andromedae.

FEATURES OF INTEREST

Gamma (γ) Andromedae ⚹ One of the most attractive double stars in the sky. It appears to the naked eye as single star of magnitude 2.1, but even a small telescope will reveal an orange-coloured primary, which is a giant star, and a blue companion of 5th magnitude.

M31 (The Andromeda Galaxy) 👁 ♠ ⚹
A spiral galaxy, similar to the Milky Way but larger. On a clear, dark night, it can be seen by the naked eye as an elongated smudge. With binoculars or a small telescope, it looks much

larger, extending for several Moon diameters. Even so, this is only the central part of the galaxy, and a larger telescope is needed to see any trace of its spiral arms. Lying about 2.4 million light years away, M31 is the largest galaxy in the Local Group. It has two small elliptical companion galaxies (the equivalent of our Magellanic Clouds), M32 and NGC 205 (or M110), which can be seen with a telescope with an aperture of 100 mm (4 in) or more.

NGC 752 ♠ An open cluster, visible through binoculars, consisting of faint stars spread over an area of sky wider than the full Moon. It lies about 1,300 light years away.

NGC 7662 ⚹ A planetary nebula, about 4,000 light years away. It looks small but prominent through a telescope, like a blue-green star of 9th magnitude; high magnification reveals a rounded outline, like an out-of-focus star.

Width 🖐🖐	Depth 🖐🖐	Area 722 square degrees	Size ranking 19th

Abbreviation Ant	Genitive Antliae	Highest in sky at 10 pm March to April

ANTLIA

Antlia is a faint constellation, considerably overshadowed by its glorious southern neighbours Centaurus and Vela. Antlia was invented in the 18th century by the French astronomer Nicolas Louis de Lacaille and represents a mechanical air pump. Its brightest star is Alpha (α) Antliae, magnitude 4.3.

THE
AIR PUMP

FULLY VISIBLE
49°N–90°S

FEATURES OF INTEREST

Zeta (ζ) Antliae 🖐🔭 A multiple star that appears as a wide 6th-magnitude double when viewed through binoculars. When a small telescope is turned on it, the brighter star of the pair is seen also to be double. All three stars lie 370 light years away.

Width 🖐	Depth 🖐	Area 239 square degrees	Size ranking 62nd

Abbreviation Aps	Genitive Apodis	Highest in sky at 10 pm May to July

APUS

Apus lies near the south celestial pole, to the south of Centaurus. It is not easy to identify and contains few objects of note. It is one of the constellations invented at the end of the 16th century by the Dutch navigators Pieter Dirkszoon Keyser and Frederick de Houtman, and represents a bird of paradise of New Guinea. Its brightest star is Alpha (α) Apodis, magnitude 3.8.

THE BIRD
OF PARADISE

FULLY VISIBLE
7°N–90°S

FEATURES OF INTEREST

Delta (δ) Apodis 🖐🔭 A wide double star, easily divided with binoculars. The two stars are of magnitudes 4.7 and 5.3. They are both red giants but are estimated to lie at different distances from us, 760 and 660 light years respectively, so they probably form an optical double rather than a genuine binary.

Width 🖐	Depth 🖐	Area 206 square degrees	Size ranking 67th

Abbreviation Aqr	Genitive Aquarii	Highest in sky at 10 pm August to October

AQUARIUS

This well-known constellation represents a youth pouring water from a jar. The "Water-jar" is represented by a Y-shaped group of four stars, Gamma (γ), Zeta (ζ), Eta (η), and Pi (π) Aquarii. The stream of water flows into the mouth of a large fish, represented by the constellation of Piscis Austrinus to the south. Aquarius is a constellation of the zodiac, the Sun passing through it from 16 February to 11 March.

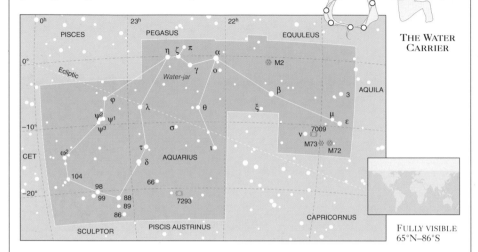

THE WATER CARRIER

FULLY VISIBLE
65°N–86°S

FEATURES OF INTEREST

Zeta (ζ) Aquarii ⊁ A close binary, consisting of two white, 4th-magnitude stars that orbit each other every 760 years. Using high magnification, a telescope with an aperture of 75 mm (3 in) or more should separate them.

M2 ♁⊁ A globular cluster, just too faint to be seen with the naked eye in all but the best conditions, but easy to see with binoculars or a small telescope. It resembles a fuzzy star.

NGC 7009 (The Saturn Nebula) ⊁
A planetary nebula. When seen through a telescope with an aperture of 200 mm (8 in) or more, it appears to have appendages that resemble the rings of Saturn, hence its popular name. A smaller telescope will show it as an 8th-magnitude disc of similar apparent size to the globe of Saturn.

NGC 7293 (The Helix Nebula) ♁⊁
Possibly the closest planetary nebula to Earth (only about 300 light years away), and one of the largest in apparent size, at over a third

the diameter of the full Moon. Being so large, its light is spread over a wide area, making it difficult to spot. Under clear, dark skies, it can be seen through binoculars or a wide-field telescope as a pale grey patch.

NGC 7293 (THE HELIX NEBULA)
On colour photographs, the Helix Nebula resembles an exotic flower. The shell of gas has been discarded from the faint star at the centre of the nebula.

Width 🖐🖐✋	Depth 🖐✋	Area 980 square degrees	Size ranking 10th

Abbreviation Aql	Genitive Aquilae	Highest in sky at 10 pm July to August

AQUILA

Aquila lies on the celestial equator and represents the eagle that carried the thunderbolts of the Greek god Zeus. The Milky Way passes through the constellation, and there are dense star fields towards the border with Scutum; the brightest part is an area known as the Scutum Star Cloud.

THE
EAGLE

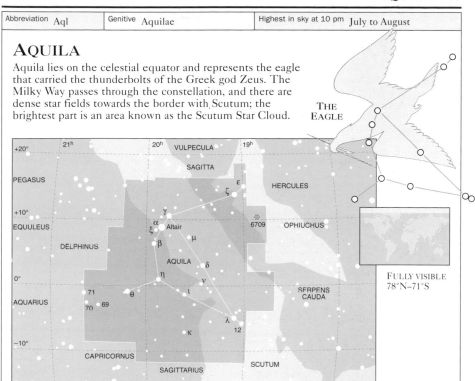

FULLY VISIBLE
78°N–71°S

FEATURES OF INTEREST

Alpha (α) Aquilae (Altair) 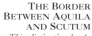 Among the 20 brightest stars in the sky, at magnitude 0.8, and also one of the closest first-magnitude stars to us, only 17 light years away. It marks the neck of the eagle and forms one corner of the Summer Triangle, completed by Deneb (in Cygnus) and Vega (in Lyra). Altair is flanked by two stars, the 4th-magnitude Beta (β) Aquilae (also known as Alshain) and 3rd-magnitude Gamma (γ) Aquilae (or Tarazed).

Eta (η) Aquilae A Cepheid variable star, one of the brightest in this important class. Its magnitude varies from 3.6 to 4.5 in a cycle lasting 7 days 4 hours, and the changes can be followed with the naked eye or through binoculars. It is a supergiant star, estimated to lie about 1,200 light years away.

THE BORDER
BETWEEN AQUILA
AND SCUTUM
This distinctive hook-shaped group of stars is in the southern part of Aquila. The brightest star in the group (centre left) is Lambda (λ) Aquilae, magnitude 3.4.

THE MAIN STARS IN AQUILA
Altair is the bright star at the top left of this picture, flanked on its left and right by Beta (β) and Gamma (γ) Aquilae, also known as Alshain and Tarazed.

Width	Depth	Area 652 square degrees	Size ranking 22nd

Abbreviation Ara	Genitive Arae	Highest in sky at 10 pm June to July

ARA

Ara lies in the Milky Way, south of Scorpius. It is well to the south of the celestial equator but was known to the ancient Greeks, who visualized it as the altar on which their gods swore an oath of allegiance before challenging the Titans for control of the Universe. It is also depicted as the altar on which Centaurus is about to sacrifice Lupus, the wolf.

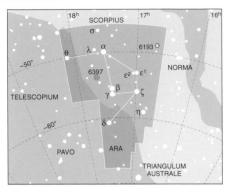

THE ALTAR

FULLY VISIBLE 22°N–90°S

FEATURES OF INTEREST

NGC 6193 **♙** An open cluster, consisting of a handful of stars scattered over an area half the apparent size of the full Moon. Its brightest star is of 6th magnitude, and the whole cluster is best seen with binoculars.

NGC 6397 **♙ ☄** A large globular cluster, about two-thirds the apparent size of the full Moon and one of the closest to us, at slightly over 7,000 light years away. It is just visible to the naked eye and easy to find with binoculars. The stars, less densely packed than in many globulars, form chains in the outer regions that can be seen with a moderate-sized telescope.

Width ♙	Depth ♙	Area 237 square degrees	Size ranking 63rd

Abbreviation Ari	Genitive Arietis	Highest in sky at 10 pm November to December

ARIES

THE RAM

Aries depicts the ram with the golden fleece, famous from Greek mythology. Its only noticeable feature is a line of three stars: Alpha (α), Beta (β), and Gamma (γ) Arietis. It is a constellation of the zodiac, the Sun passing through it from 18 April to 14 May. Aries lies between Pisces and Taurus.

THE CENTRAL PART OF ARIES
Alpha (α), Beta (β), and Gamma (γ) Arietis are to the right in this picture.

FEATURES OF INTEREST

Gamma (γ) Arietis ☄ A wide double star, easily divided with a small telescope. The two stars are nearly identical, both being blue-white and of magnitude 4.6. Found by the English scientist Robert Hooke in 1664, when telescopes were still quite crude, this was one of the first double stars to be discovered.

FULLY VISIBLE 90°N–58°S

Width ♙	Depth ♙	Area 441 square degrees	Size ranking 39th

Abbreviation Aur	Genitive Aurigae	Highest in sky at 10 pm December to February

AURIGA

THE CHARIOTEER

Auriga represents the driver of a horse-drawn chariot. According to one myth, he is Erichthonius, a legendary king of Athens. However, there is no explanation in mythology for his depiction in the sky with a goat and its kids on his left arm. The goat is marked by the constellation's brightest star, Capella (a Latin name, meaning "she-goat"), while the kids (also known as the Haedi, another Latin name) are depicted by Zeta (ζ) and Eta (η) Aurigae. In Greek and Roman times, the figure's right foot was represented by a star now assigned to Taurus, Beta (β) Tauri.

FULLY VISIBLE
90°N–34°S

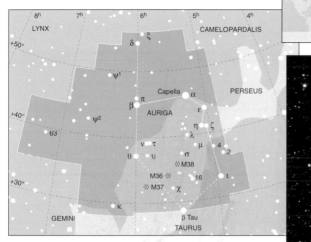

FEATURES OF INTEREST

Alpha (α) Aurigae (Capella) ◉ The sixth-brightest star in the sky, at magnitude 0.1. To the naked eye, it appears yellowish. It is, in fact, a spectroscopic binary, consisting of two yellow-coloured giants that orbit each other every 104 days. It lies 42 light years away.

Epsilon (ε) Aurigae ◉ One of the most extraordinary variable stars in the sky. It is an eclipsing binary, consisting of a brilliant white supergiant orbited by an odd dark companion that passes in front of it every 27 years, the longest known period between eclipses of any variable star. The star's brightness is more than halved by the eclipse, from magnitude 2.9 to 3.8, and it remains dimmed for over a year. After observing the last eclipse, which ended in 1984, astronomers think that the mystery partner might be a close binary, surrounded by an elongated cloud of dark dust and gas. The next eclipse is due to start at the end of 2009.

THE MAIN STARS IN AURIGA
Capella is at the top of this picture. M36, M37, and M38 are just visible.

Zeta (ζ) Aurigae ◉ An eclipsing binary, comprising an orange giant orbited every 2.7 years by a smaller blue star. During an eclipse, which lasts 40 days, the star's brightness drops from magnitude 3.7 to 4.0.

M36, M37, and M38 ♠ ⚹ Just visible with the naked eye and easy to see with binoculars, these three open clusters lie 4,000–4,500 light years away. In a binocular field of 6 degrees or more, all three can be seen as misty patches. The smallest of the trio, M36, is the easiest to spot, a small telescope resolving its brightest stars. M37, the largest of the clusters at about two-thirds the width of the full Moon, contains more stars but they are fainter. M38 is the most scattered cluster; a small telescope reveals that many of its stars form chains.

Width 🖐🖐	Depth 🖐🖐	Area 657 square degrees	Size ranking 21st

Abbreviation Boo	Genitive Boötis	Highest in sky at 10 pm May to June

BOÖTES

THE HERDSMAN

Boötes is an elongated constellation depicting a man herding a bear, represented by Ursa Major. The name of its brightest star, Arcturus, is Greek for "bear guard". The northern part of Boötes contains the faint stars that formed the now-defunct constellation of Quadrans Muralis, the mural (or wall) quadrant, which gave its name to the Quadrantid meteor shower that radiates from this area every January.

FULLY VISIBLE 90°N–35°S

THE MAIN STARS IN BOÖTES
The bright star at the bottom of this picture is Arcturus.

FEATURES OF INTEREST

Alpha (α) Boötis (Arcturus) 👁 The brightest star north of the celestial equator, and, at magnitude –0.1, the fourth brightest overall. It is a red giant, 100 times more luminous than the Sun but with a cooler (and hence redder) surface. To the naked eye, it has a noticeably warm tint, which becomes stronger when it is viewed with binoculars.

Epsilon (ε) Boötis ✱ A beautiful double star but a difficult one to divide. To the naked eye, it appears of magnitude 2.4. A telescope of aperture 75 mm (3 in) or more shows a red-giant primary and a close, blue-green partner of 5th magnitude. High magnification and a steady night are needed to separate the stars.

Kappa (κ) Boötis ✱ A double star, easily divided with a small telescope into a pair of white stars of 5th and 7th magnitudes.

Mu (μ) Boötis ♠✱ A multiple star. Binoculars show a wide double, with stars of magnitudes 4.3 and 6.5. The fainter star is itself double, with 7th- and 8th-magnitude components that orbit each other every 260 years. They should be divisible in moderate apertures, but are just too close to be split with a small telescope.

Xi (ξ) Boötis ✱ A double star, divisible with a small telescope. The stars, of magnitudes 4.7 and 7.0, are both yellow-orange, one slightly deeper in tone than the other. They form a true binary with an orbital period of 152 years.

Width 🖐✌🤚	Depth 🖐🖐🤚	Area 907 square degrees	Size ranking 13th

Abbreviation Cae	Genitive Caeli	Highest in sky at 10 pm December to January

CAELUM
THE CHISEL

Caelum is a small, faint constellation in an inconspicuous area of the southern-hemisphere sky. It represents a stone-mason's chisel and was introduced into the sky in the 18th century by the French astronomer Nicolas Louis de Lacaille. Its brightest star, Alpha (α) Caeli, is of magnitude 4.4.

FULLY VISIBLE
41°N–90°S

FEATURES OF INTEREST

Gamma (γ) Caeli ☌ A double star, although a moderate-sized telescope is needed to show it as such. It is of magnitude 4.6, with a close companion of 8th magnitude.

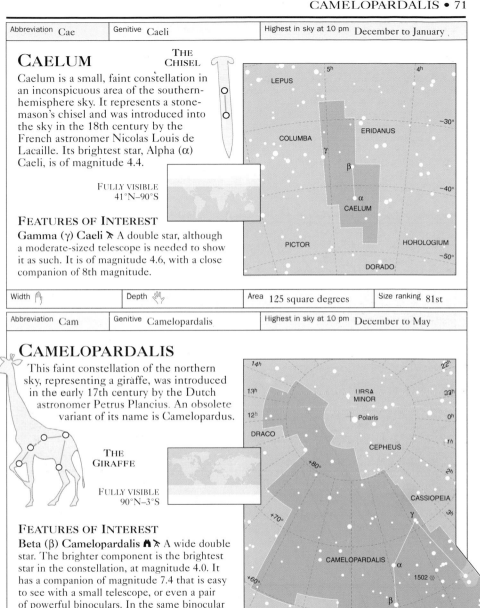

Width	Depth	Area 125 square degrees	Size ranking 81st

Abbreviation Cam	Genitive Camelopardalis	Highest in sky at 10 pm December to May

CAMELOPARDALIS

This faint constellation of the northern sky, representing a giraffe, was introduced in the early 17th century by the Dutch astronomer Petrus Plancius. An obsolete variant of its name is Camelopardus.

THE GIRAFFE

FULLY VISIBLE
90°N–3°S

FEATURES OF INTEREST

Beta (β) Camelopardalis ♠☌ A wide double star. The brighter component is the brightest star in the constellation, at magnitude 4.0. It has a companion of magnitude 7.4 that is easy to see with a small telescope, or even a pair of powerful binoculars. In the same binocular field, an even wider pairing can be seen; the two stars, 11 and 12 Camelopardalis, are of magnitudes 5.2 and 6.1.

NGC 1502 ♠☌ An open cluster, visible with binoculars or a small telescope. Although small, its stars are moderately bright, and include a noticeable 7th-magnitude double.

Width	Depth	Area 757 square degrees	Size ranking 18th

Abbreviation Cnc	Genitive Cancri	Highest in sky at 10 pm February to March

CANCER

Cancer represents the crab that, in Greek mythology, was crushed underfoot by Hercules during his battle with the multi-headed Hydra. It lies between Gemini and Leo and is the faintest constellation of the zodiac; its brightest star, Beta (β) Cancri, is of magnitude 3.5. The Sun is within Cancer's boundaries from 20 July until 10 August.

THE CRAB

FULLY VISIBLE
90°N–57°S

M44 (PRAESEPE)
M44 is too large to fit in the field of view of most telescopes. This picture shows the cluster as it looks through binoculars. The two stars known as the aselli that are useful in locating the cluster are just out of view.

FEATURES OF INTEREST

Zeta (ζ) Cancri ✻ A multiple star. Through a small telescope, it is seen to consist of two stars, of magnitudes 5.1 and 6.2. A telescope with an aperture larger than about 150 mm (6 in) will show that the brighter component has a much closer companion, of magnitude 6.1, which orbits it every 60 years.

Iota (ι) Cancri ✻ A wide double star, with components of magnitudes 4.2 and 6.6 that are easy to divide with a small telescope.

M44 (Praesepe) ♙ An open cluster, also known as the Beehive Cluster or the Manger. (Praesepe is Latin, meaning both "manger" and "hive".) It appears as a cloudy patch at the limit of naked-eye visibility – its brightest stars are of 6th magnitude, and it was known to the ancient Greeks – but binoculars show it as a field of stars more than three times the apparent width of the full Moon. It lies about 520 light years away. To the north and south of the cluster are the stars Gamma (γ) Cancri

(magnitude 4.7) and Delta (δ) Cancri (magnitude 3.9). In ancient times, these were visualized as donkeys feeding at the manger, hence they are known as the aselli, or asses.

M67 ♙✻ An open cluster. It contains more stars than M44 (Praesepe), but it is further away from us (about 2,600 light years) and so appears fainter and smaller.

Width 〰	Depth 〰	Area 506 square degrees	Size ranking 31st

Abbreviation CVn	Genitive Canum Venaticorum	Highest in sky at 10 pm April to May

CANES VENATICI

Canes Venatici represents two hunting dogs, held on a leash by the herdsman Boötes. The constellation was formed in 1687 by Johannes Hevelius from stars that had formerly been part of Ursa Major.

THE
HUNTING DOGS

FULLY VISIBLE
90°N–37°S

M51 (THE WHIRLPOOL GALAXY)
This spiral galaxy is interacting with a smaller companion galaxy, NGC 5195. M51 appears to us face-on, with NGC 5195 at the end of one of its spiral arms.

FEATURES OF INTEREST

Alpha (α) Canum Venaticorum (Cor Caroli) ⚹ A double star. A small telescope will easily separate the two components, of magnitudes 2.9 and 5.6. Although both should appear white, some observers have reported delicate colour tints. This is possibly because the brighter star has an unusual composition, as revealed by spectroscopic studies. The name Cor Caroli means "Charles's heart", and commemorates King Charles I of England.

M3 � ⚹ A globular cluster on the verge of naked-eye visibility. It is easy to find with binoculars or a small telescope, in which it appears about half the size of the full Moon. A telescope with an aperture of about 100 mm (4 in) or more is needed to see the cluster's individual stars.

M51 (The Whirlpool Galaxy) ♚ ⚹ A spiral galaxy, seen almost face-on. This is one of the most famous galaxies in the sky, and one of the easiest in which to see spiral structure. The galaxy can be located using binoculars. A small telescope reveals its bright nucleus,

as well as the nucleus of a smaller, irregularly shaped galaxy, NGC 5195, which is passing close by. Using a telescope of moderate to large aperture – 200 mm (8 in) or more – it should be possible to trace the outline of M51's arms. M51 and NGC 5195 are both about 25 million light years away.

Width	Depth	Area 465 square degrees	Size ranking 38th

Abbreviation CMa	Genitive Canis Majoris	Highest in sky at 10 pm January to February

CANIS MAJOR

One of the most prominent constellations, Canis Major is embellished by the brightest of all the stars, Sirius. It depicts the larger of the two dogs belonging to Orion, the hunter (the other being represented by Canis Minor). As the Earth rotates, the dogs seem to follow the hunter across the sky.

THE GREATER DOG

FULLY VISIBLE
56°N–90°S

CANIS MAJOR
Canis Major contains several bright stars. Sirius is near the top of this picture; the bright star nearest the centre is Delta (δ) Canis Majoris.

FEATURES OF INTEREST

Alpha (α) Canis Majoris (Sirius, The Dog Star) ◉ The brightest star in the sky, at magnitude –1.44. Sirius emits the light of about 20 Suns. This luminosity is not unusual, but because of its relative closeness to us (it is 8.6 light years away), Sirius outshines all other stars. It is white, but when low on the horizon it often appears to flash colourfully as its light is broken up by air currents in the Earth's atmosphere. Sirius is a close double star, with a companion that orbits it every 50 years. This companion, Sirius B, popularly termed the Pup, is a white dwarf nearly 10,000 times fainter than Sirius itself. Hence it can be seen only through a large telescope when the two stars are furthest apart during each orbit.

M41 ◉♉✶ An open cluster, about 2,300 light years away and containing about 80 stars of 7th magnitude and fainter. It can just be seen with the naked eye, and was known to the ancient Greeks. Binoculars or a small telescope reveal that its stars are arranged in chains. It covers an area of sky about the size of the full Moon.

NGC 2362 ✶ An open cluster, small and condensed, requiring a small telescope in order to be studied properly. Its brightest member is the 4th-magnitude star Tau (τ) Canis Majoris, which is a highly luminous blue supergiant. The cluster lies about 5,000 light years away.

Width 🖐	Depth 🖐	Area 380 square degrees	Size ranking 43rd

Abbreviation CMi	Genitive Canis Minoris	Highest in sky at 10 pm February

CANIS MINOR

Canis Minor represents the smaller of the two dogs of Orion, the hunter. Both Orion and Canis Major, which depicts the larger dog, lie nearby. Apart from its two brightest stars, Canis Minor contains little of note.

THE
LESSER DOG

FULLY VISIBLE
89°N–77°S

FEATURES OF INTEREST
Alpha (α) Canis Minoris (Procyon)
The 8th-brightest star in the sky, at magnitude 0.4. The name Procyon is of Greek origin, meaning "before the dog", from the fact that it rises before the other dog star, Sirius. It is a white star, slightly less luminous than Sirius, and slightly further away, at 11.4 light years. It shares with Sirius the peculiarity of having a white-dwarf partner, Procyon B, which is over 10,000 times fainter than Procyon and orbits it every 41 years. The two appear so close that only large telescopes, of the type used by professional astronomers, can separate them.

Width	Depth	Area 183 square degrees	Size ranking 71st

Abbreviation Cap	Genitive Capricorni	Highest in sky at 10 pm August to September

CAPRICORNUS

The smallest constellation of the zodiac, lying between Sagittarius and Aquarius, Capricornus depicts a fish-tailed goat. The constellation originated among the Babylonian and Sumerian peoples of the Middle East, but in Greek myth it is linked with the goat-like god Pan, who turned his lower half into a fish to escape the sea monster Typhon. Capricornus is not prominent: its brightest star, Delta (δ) Capricorni (Deneb Algedi), is of magnitude 2.9. The Sun passes through it from 19 January to 16 February.

THE
SEA GOAT

FULLY VISIBLE
62°N–90°S

FEATURES OF INTEREST
Alpha (α) Capricorni (Algedi, Giedi)
A wide double star. Ordinary binoculars, or good eyesight, reveal two stars, of magnitudes 3.6 and 4.3. Both are yellowish in colour, but they are unrelated. The brighter star is a giant, 110 light years away, while the fainter one is a supergiant, over six times more distant.

Beta (β) Capricorni A wide double star. The primary is a yellow giant, magnitude 3.1, visible to the naked eye. Binoculars or a small telescope show the second star, of magnitude 6.0. Both stars lie about 300 light years away.

Width	Depth	Area 414 square degrees	Size ranking 40th

Abbreviation Car	Genitive Carinae	Highest in sky at 10 pm January to April

CARINA

Carina is an impressive constellation, containing the second-brightest star of all, Canopus, and lying in a rich part of the Milky Way. In Greek times, it formed part of a much larger constellation, Argo Navis, representing the ship of the Argonauts, but was made separate in the 18th century by the Frenchman Nicolas Louis de Lacaille. It represents the ship's keel, with Canopus marking the rudder. The other parts of the ship – Vela (the sails) and Puppis (the stern) – lie to the north of Carina.

THE KEEL

FULLY VISIBLE
14°N–90°S

STAR CLUSTERS AND NEBULAE IN CARINA
This picture shows the whole of this magnificent southern constellation, with the bright star Canopus at the top right. The Eta Carinae Nebula (NGC 3372) lies on the far left, with the open cluster IC 2602 (also known as the Southern Pleiades) below and to its right. NGC 2516, another prominent cluster, is to the right of centre.

Width	Depth	Area 494 square degrees	Size ranking 34th

FEATURES OF INTEREST

Alpha (α) Carinae (Canopus) ◉
The second-brightest star in the sky, at
magnitude –0.6. It is a white supergiant,
14,000 times more luminous than the Sun,
lying 310 light years away.

Eta (η) Carinae ♠ ☀ A remarkable variable
star. Currently it is of 5th magnitude, but it
has been much brighter in the past, most
noticeably in the 19th century, when it flared
up to nearly –1. Eta Carinae is thought to
be either a supergiant with a mass of 100
Suns, one of the most massive stars known,
or possibly a massive binary. Through a
telescope, it appears as a hazy orange ellipse,
because of matter thrown off in its last
outburst. Its distance is estimated at over
8,000 light years, and it lies within the
extensive nebula NGC 3372 (see below).

NGC 2516 ◉ ♠ An open cluster, visible to
the naked eye. Using binoculars, it is possible
to pick out its individual stars, the brightest
being a 5th-magnitude red giant, scattered
over an area of sky the size of the full Moon.
It is about 1,300 light years away.

NGC 3114 ◉ ♠ An open cluster, visible to
the naked eye and appearing about the same

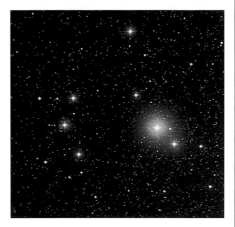

IC 2602 (THE SOUTHERN PLEIADES)
*This large, bright open cluster contains several stars
visible to the naked eye. The bright star at the right
of the picture is Theta (θ) Carinae.*

size as the disc of the full Moon. Its individual
stars can be seen through binoculars. It lies
nearly 3,000 light years away.

NGC 3372 (The Eta Carinae Nebula)
◉ ♠ ☀ A large, bright diffuse nebula, four
times the apparent width of the full Moon,
surrounding the star Eta (η) Carinae (see
above). The nebula is visible to the naked
eye against the Milky Way and is best seen
with binoculars. A V-shaped lane of dark
dust runs through it. Near Eta Carinae itself,
telescopes show a dark and bulbous cloud
of dust called the Keyhole Nebula.

NGC 3532 ◉ ♠ A bright and dense open
cluster, elliptical in shape. It is visible to
the naked eye and is a glorious sight through
binoculars, being nearly twice the apparent
diameter of the full Moon at its widest. It is
1,300 light years away.

IC 2602 (The Southern Pleiades) ◉ ♠
A large and prominent open cluster, containing
eight stars brighter than magnitude 6. The
brightest member is Theta (θ) Carinae, a
blue-white star of magnitude 2.7. The cluster
appears twice the size of the full Moon and
lies about 500 light years away.

NGC 3372 (THE ETA CARINAE NEBULA)
*This magnificent nebula surrounds the peculiar
variable star Eta (η) Carinae. It is dissected by dark
lanes of dust. Eta Carinae itself is in the brightest part
of the nebula, just above centre in this photograph.*

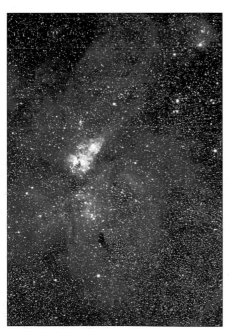

Abbreviation Cas	Genitive Cassiopeiae	Highest in sky at 10 pm October to December

CASSIOPEIA

This attractive constellation represents the mythical Queen Cassiopeia. Her husband and daughter are represented by the adjacent constellations Cepheus and Andromeda. Cassiopeia was notoriously vain, and is depicted sitting on a throne, fussing with her hair. Cassiopeia's brightest stars form a distinctive W-shape. Epsilon (ε) Cassiopeiae, at one end of the W, marks the queen's ankle while Beta (β), at the other end, lies in her shoulder.

CASSIOPEIA

FULLY VISIBLE
90°N–12°S

THE MAIN STARS IN CASSIOPEIA
The distinctive W-shape formed by Cassiopeia's brightest stars makes the constellation easy to recognize.

FEATURES OF INTEREST

Gamma (γ) Cassiopeiae ◉ A variable star, currently about magnitude 2.2. Its rapid spin causes rings of gas to be thrown off its equator, changing its brightness temporarily.

Eta (η) Cassiopeiae ⋇ A double star. It consists of a yellow star of magnitude 3.5 and an orange companion of magnitude 7.2 that can be seen with a small telescope. The two stars lie 19 light years away, forming a genuine binary pair with an orbital period of 480 years.

Rho (ρ) Cassiopeiae ◉ ♟ A highly luminous yellow supergiant. As a result of pulsations in its size, it varies between about 4th and 5th magnitudes in a cycle that lasts just under a year.

M52 ♟ ⋇ An open cluster. It is visible with binoculars, covering an area about one-third

the apparent size of the full Moon, although a telescope is needed to show its individual stars. It lies 5,200 light years away. A 5th-magnitude star that appears to be a member of the cluster actually lies much closer to us.

NGC 457 ♟ ⋇ An elongated open cluster, about one-third the apparent size of the full Moon and visible through binoculars or a small telescope. The cluster's appearance has been compared to an owl, with its two brightest stars marking the owl's eyes. The brightest star is the 5th-magnitude Phi (φ) Cassiopeiae, a luminous supergiant.

Width 🖐🖐	Depth 🖐🖐	Area 598 square degrees	Size ranking 25th

Abbreviation Cen	Genitive Centauri	Highest in sky at 10 pm April to June

CENTAURUS

This large constellation in the southern Milky Way depicts a centaur, the mythical beast with the legs of a horse and the upper body of a man. In Greek mythology, this centaur is identified as Chiron, tutor to the offspring of the gods. Its brightest star, Alpha (α) Centauri, is the third brightest in the sky. A line drawn between Alpha (α) and Beta (β) Centauri points to the Southern Cross, Crux.

THE CENTAUR

FULLY VISIBLE 25°N–90°S

NGC 5139 (OMEGA CENTAURI)
When seen through a telescope, this bright globular cluster often appears elliptical rather than circular.

FEATURES OF INTEREST

Alpha (α) Centauri (Rigil Kentaurus) ◉ ♙

A nearby multiple star. To the naked eye, it appears of magnitude –0.3, the third-brightest star in the sky. A small telescope shows it to be a glorious binary, consisting of two yellow and orange stars of magnitudes 0.0 and 1.4. They orbit each other every 80 years, so one complete orbit can just be followed in a human lifetime. Lying 2 degrees away from this pair is a much fainter third star, an 11th-magnitude red dwarf called Proxima Centauri. This is the closest star to the Sun, 4.2 light years away, about 0.2 light years closer to us than the two brighter members of the Alpha Centauri system.

Beta (β) Centauri ◉

A blue-white giant star, magnitude 0.6 and 11th brightest in the sky, about 525 light years away.

NGC 5139 (Omega (ω) Centauri) ◉ ♙ ⊁

The largest and brightest globular cluster in the sky, about 17,000 light years away. Seen with the naked eye or binoculars, it appears as a hazy 4th-magnitude patch larger than the full Moon. A small telescope shows its main stars.

NGC 3918 (The Blue Planetary) ⊁

A planetary nebula, visible through a small telescope as a rounded blue disc.

NGC 5128 (Centaurus A) ⊁

An unusual galaxy. With a small telescope, it looks like an elliptical galaxy, but larger apertures and long-exposure photographs show that it is bisected by a dark dust lane, evidently due to a merger with another galaxy. It is a strong radio source, referred to as Centaurus A.

Width 🖐🖐🖐🤚	Depth 🖐🤚🖐	Area 1,060 square degrees	Size ranking 9th

Abbreviation Cep	Genitive Cephei	Highest in sky at 10 pm September to October

CEPHEUS

This far-northern constellation, adjoining Cassiopeia and extending almost to the north celestial pole, represents the mythical King Cepheus, the husband of the vain Queen Cassiopeia and father of Andromeda. Its brightest star is Alpha (α) Cephei, of magnitude 2.5.

CEPHEUS

FULLY VISIBLE
90°N–1°S

DELTA AND MU CEPHEI
The following stars are useful for gauging the magnitude of Delta (δ) and Mu (μ) Cephei: Zeta (ζ), magnitude 3.4, Epsilon (ε), magnitude 4.2, and Lambda (λ), magnitude 5.1.

KEY

FEATURES OF INTEREST

Beta (β) Cephei ⚹ A double and variable star. The brighter component is a blue giant of magnitude 3.2, about 600 light years away. It is a pulsating variable star (the prototype of a group called Beta Cephei stars), although its variations are so small that they are barely perceptible to the eye. A small telescope shows a companion of magnitude 7.9.

Delta (δ) Cephei ◉ 🔭⚹ A double star and a famous variable. The brighter star, a yellow supergiant, is the prototype of the so-called Cepheid variables, which astronomers use for finding distances in space. Such stars change in brightness as they pulsate in size. Delta Cephei itself varies between magnitudes 3.5 and 4.4 every 5 days 9 hours. It lies about 1,000 light years away. A small telescope shows a wide companion of magnitude 6.3.

Mu (μ) Cephei (The Garnet Star) ◉ 🔭⚹
A variable star with a strong red colour, hence its popular name, which is noticeable through binoculars or a small telescope. It is a red supergiant that pulsates in size, varying from magnitude 3.4 to 5.1 about every 2 years.

Width 〰	Depth 〰〰	Area 588 square degrees	Size ranking 27th

Abbreviation Cet	Genitive Ceti	Highest in sky at 10 pm October to December

CETUS

Cetus, which straddles the celestial equator south of Pisces and Aries, is a large constellation representing the mythical sea monster from whose jaws Andromeda was rescued by the hero Perseus. The brightest star in the constellation is Beta (β) Ceti, magnitude 2.0.

THE SEA MONSTER OR WHALE

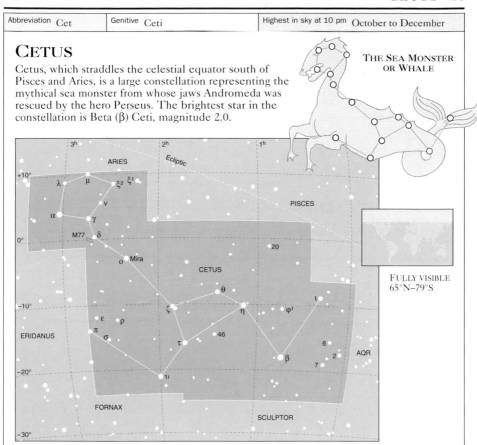

FULLY VISIBLE
65°N–79°S

FEATURES OF INTEREST

Omicron (o) Ceti (Mira) ⊙ ♟ A famous variable star. Mira is a red giant star, about 300 times larger than the Sun, that varies widely in brightness as it swells and contracts in size in a cycle that lasts approximately 11 months.

OMICRON (o) CETI (MIRA) *The variable star Mira (below centre in picture) is seen here at its maximum brightness.*

At its brightest, it can reach 3rd or even 2nd magnitude, but it drops to 10th magnitude at its minimum. Mira, which was first identified as being variable in 1596, is the prototype of a class of long-period variables; referred to as Mira stars, they form the largest group of variable stars. Mira is Latin for "wonderful".

Tau (τ) Ceti ⊙ A nearby, Sun-like star. It is similar to the Sun in temperature and luminosity, and at a distance of 11.9 light years it is among the 20 closest stars to Earth. It appears of magnitude 3.5.

M77 ⤧ A spiral galaxy, seen face-on from Earth. A telescope shows it as a small, round patch. It is the brightest of a class of galaxies known as Seyfert galaxies, which have particularly bright centres.

Width	Depth	Area 1,231 square degrees	Size ranking 4th

Abbreviation Cha	Genitive Chamaeleontis	Highest in sky at 10 pm February to May

CHAMAELEON

Chamaeleon is a small, faint constellation near the south celestial pole. Introduced at the end of the 16th century by the Dutch navigators Pieter Dirkszoon Keyser and Frederick de Houtman, it depicts a chameleon, the lizard that changes its skin colour to camouflage itself. Its brightest stars are of 4th magnitude.

THE
CHAMELEON

FULLY VISIBLE
7°N–90°S

FEATURES OF INTEREST

Delta (δ) Chamaeleontis �釘 A wide double star. With binoculars, it is easy to see the two components, of magnitudes 4.4 and 5.5. Both stars lie about 360 light years away.

NGC 3195 ⟡ A faint planetary nebula, of similar apparent size to the disc of Jupiter, visible with a moderate-sized telescope.

Width	Depth	Area 132 square degrees	Size ranking 79th

Abbreviation Cir	Genitive Circini	Highest in sky at 10 pm May to June

CIRCINUS

This small constellation next to Centaurus was introduced in the 18th century by the French astronomer Nicolas Louis de Lacaille. It represents a pair of dividing compasses, of the type used by surveyors and chart makers, and is suitably placed in the sky next to Norma, the level. Despite its insignificance, Circinus is easy to find, since it lies next to Alpha (α) Centauri in Centaurus. Although it is in the Milky Way, it contains no notable star clusters.

THE
COMPASSES

FULLY VISIBLE
19°N–90°S

FEATURES OF INTEREST

Alpha (α) Circini ⟡ A double star. The primary, of magnitude 3.2, is the brightest star in the constellation. It lies 53 light years away. Its companion, of magnitude 8.6, is visible through a small telescope.

Width	Depth	Area 93 square degrees	Size ranking 85th

Abbreviation Col	Genitive Columbae	Highest in sky at 10 pm January

COLUMBA

THE DOVE

Columba was introduced in the late 16th century by the Dutch astronomer Petrus Plancius, who created it from stars near Canis Major. It represents Noah's dove.

FEATURES OF INTEREST

Alpha (α) Columbae ◉
A blue-white star, 270 light years away, of magnitude 2.6.

Mu (μ) Columbae ◉ ♓
A so-called runaway star, moving through our Galaxy at unusually high speed, about 100 km (60 miles) per second. At least two fainter stars, 53 Arietis and AE Aurigae (not shown on the chart), seem to be diverging from the same point, south of Orion's belt. They might all have been part of a pair of multiple-star systems that were disrupted by a close encounter 2–3 million years ago.

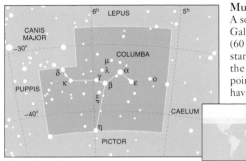

FULLY VISIBLE 46°N–90°S

Width 🖐	Depth 🖐	Area 270 square degrees	Size ranking 54th

Abbreviation Com	Genitive Comae Berenices	Highest in sky at 10 pm April to May

COMA BERENICES

This constellation represents the hair of Queen Berenice of Egypt. According to legend, she cut off her locks to thank the gods for the safe return of her husband, King Ptolemy, from battle. It was formed in the 16th century by Gerardus Mercator, the Dutch cartographer, from a group of faint stars that the Greeks regarded as the tail of Leo. The galaxies in its southern region belong to the Virgo Cluster.

BERENICE'S HAIR

NGC 4565
A telescope of moderate size reveals the shape of this spiral galaxy, seen edge-on. A lane of dark dust runs across it.

FULLY VISIBLE
90°N–55°S

FEATURES OF INTEREST

M64 (The Black Eye Galaxy) ⚹ A spiral galaxy, visible through a small telescope as an elliptical haze. Larger apertures show a dark cloud of dust silhouetted against the galaxy's centre, which gives rise to its popular name.

The Coma Star Cluster (Melotte 111) ◉ ♓
An open cluster, consisting of a scattered group of stars stretching southwards in a fan shape from Gamma (γ) Comae Berenices, magnitude 4.4, which is not a true member but a fore-ground star. The cluster is 260 light years away.

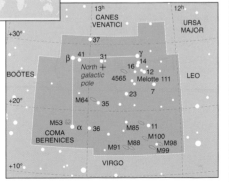

Width 🖐	Depth 🖐	Area 386 square degrees	Size ranking 42nd

Abbreviation CrA	Genitive Coronae Australis	Highest in sky at 10 pm July to August

CORONA AUSTRALIS

The ancient Greeks visualized this small but pretty constellation as a wreath lying at the forefeet of Sagittarius. Its main feature is an arc of stars, distinctive even though the brightest is of only 4th magnitude.

THE
SOUTHERN
CROWN

FEATURES OF INTEREST

Gamma (γ) Coronae Australis ☆ A close binary, divisible through a telescope with a moderate-sized aperture. The stars, both of 5th magnitude, orbit each other every 122 years. They lie 58 light years away.

Kappa (κ) Coronae Australis ☆ A double star, with components of magnitudes 5.7 and 6.3, easily divided with a small telescope.

NGC 6541 🔭☆ A globular cluster, visible with a small telescope, or even binoculars. It covers an area about one-third the apparent size of the full Moon.

FULLY VISIBLE 44°N–90°S

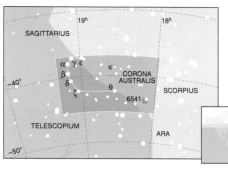

Width 🖐	Depth 🖐	Area 128 square degrees	Size ranking 80th

Abbreviation CrB	Genitive Coronae Borealis	Highest in sky at 10 pm June

CORONA BOREALIS

Corona Borealis is a semi-circular pattern lying between Boötes and Hercules. It depicts the crown worn by the mythical Princess Ariadne of Crete when she married the god Dionysius, who threw it into the sky, where its jewels turned into stars. Appropriately, its brightest star, Alpha (α) Coronae Borealis, magnitude 2.2, is named Gemma, Latin for "jewel".

THE
NORTHERN
CROWN

ARC OF CORONA
BOREALIS
*Seven stars form the
Northern Crown.*

FEATURES OF INTEREST

Zeta (ζ) Coronae Borealis ☆ A double star, with components of magnitudes 5.0 and 6.0, divisible with a small telescope.

Nu (ν) Coronae Borealis 🔭 A double star. Binoculars show the two stars, both red giants, of magnitudes 5.2 and 5.4; they lie about 550 light years away but do not orbit each other.

R Coronae Borealis 🔭☆ An unusual variable star, usually of around 6th magnitude. It is a highly luminous yellow supergiant about 7,000 light years away. Occasionally and unpredictably, it can fade within a few weeks to as faint as 15th magnitude, remaining there for some months before increasing in brightness again.

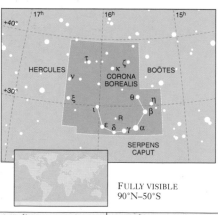

FULLY VISIBLE
90°N–50°S

Width 🖐	Depth 🖐	Area 179 square degrees	Size ranking 73rd

Abbreviation Crv	Genitive Corvi	Highest in sky at 10 pm April to May

CORVUS

This small constellation south of Virgo represents a crow perched on the coils of Hydra, the water-snake. In Greek mythology, the crow was sent by Apollo to fetch water in a cup (represented by the adjoining constellation of Crater), but greedily stopped to eat figs instead. On its return, the crow blamed the water-snake for delaying it. But Apollo, who was not fooled by the lie, condemned the crow to a life of thirst, just out of reach of the cup in the heavens. Its brightest star, Gamma (γ) Corvi, is of magnitude 2.6.

THE CROW

FULLY VISIBLE
65°N–90°S

THE MAIN STARS IN CORVUS
Four bright stars in Corvus form a distinctive shape called a keystone. Beta (β) Corvi is at the bottom left.

FEATURES OF INTEREST

Delta (δ) Corvi ⊁ A double star, with components of widely differing brightness. The brighter star, of magnitude 3.0, has a 9th-magnitude partner, which is visible through a small telescope.

NGC 4038 and 4039 (The Antennae) ⊁ A famous pair of interacting galaxies. They are small and of 11th magnitude, so a telescope of moderate to large aperture is needed to see them. Long-exposure photographs show two streamers of stars and gas that extend from the colliding galaxies like the feelers of an insect, giving rise to the popular name.

Width	Depth	Area 184 square degrees	Size ranking 70th

Abbreviation Crt	Genitive Crateris	Highest in sky at 10 pm April

CRATER

This undistinguished constellation represents a cup or chalice. In Greek myth, it is linked with its neighbouring constellations, Corvus, the crow, and Hydra, the water-snake. Crater's brightest star is Delta (δ) Crateris, magnitude 3.6, but it contains no objects of interest for observers using small telescopes.

THE CUP

FULLY VISIBLE
65°N–90°S

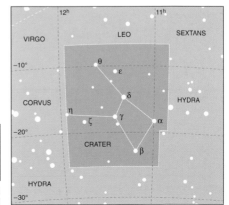

Width	Depth	Area 282 square degrees	Size ranking 53rd

Abbreviation Cru	Genitive Crucis	Highest in sky at 10 pm April to May

CRUX

The smallest constellation in the sky, Crux covers a mere
5 per cent of the area of the largest constellation, Hydra.
Nevertheless, it is one of the most famous and easily recognized
star patterns of all. To the ancient Greeks, its stars formed part
of the hind legs of Centaurus, the centaur. Crux became a
recognized constellation in its own right in the late 16th century
as Europeans explored the southern oceans, although no one is
credited with its invention. It lies in a brilliant region of the
Milky Way. Its longer axis points to the south celestial pole.

THE
SOUTHERN CROSS

FULLY VISIBLE
25°N–90°S

FEATURES OF INTEREST

Alpha (α) Crucis (Acrux) 👁 🏃 🔭 A double
star, appearing to the naked eye as a single
object of magnitude 0.8, the 13th-brightest
star in the sky. A small telescope divides it
into a glittering blue-white pair, of magnitudes
1.3 and 1.7. Both stars are 320 light years away
and probably form a true binary, although the
orbital period is unknown. There is a much
wider 5th-magnitude star, visible through
binoculars, which is not related.

Beta (β) Crucis 👁 A blue-white giant, lying
350 light years away. At magnitude 1.3, it
is among the 20 brightest stars in the sky.
It pulsates in size five times a day, varying
by under a tenth of a magnitude as it does so,
not enough to be noticeable to the naked eye.

THE SOUTHERN CROSS
*The four brightest stars of Crux form a distinctive
shape known as the Southern Cross. A fifth bright star,
Epsilon (ε) Crucis, lies close to the centre of the cross.*

Width 🖐	Depth 🖐	Area 68 square degrees	Size ranking 88th

THE COALSACK
This dark cloud of dust, seen below and to the left of the cross-shape of Crux, is easy to see with the naked eye. The stars that are visible in this area lie between us and the nebula.

NGC 4755 (THE JEWEL BOX)
This sparkling open cluster was given its name in the 19th century by the English astronomer John Herschel, who described it as resembling a "casket of variously coloured precious stones".

Gamma (γ) Crucis ◉ ♄ A wide optical double star. The brighter star is a red giant of magnitude 1.6, 88 light years away. Binoculars show an unrelated 6th-magnitude companion, which is over three times more distant.

Iota (ι) Crucis ♄ A wide double star, with components of magnitudes 4.7 and 9.5 that can be separated with a small telescope.

Mu (μ) Crucis ◉ ♄ A wide optical double. A small telescope, or powerful binoculars, shows the two stars, of magnitudes 4.0 and 5.1. The fainter component is a rapidly rotating star that throws off rings of gas, causing occasional small variations in its brightness.

NGC 4755 (The Jewel Box, The Kappa (κ) Crucis cluster) ◉ ♄♄ A magnificent open cluster, visible to the naked eye as a bright knot in the Milky Way between Beta (β) Crucis and the Coalsack. It is, in fact, far more distant than either of them, lying 7,600 light years away. Binoculars or a small telescope show its individual stars, of 6th magnitude and fainter, covering an area of sky about one-third the apparent size of the full Moon. Most of its stars are blue-white super-giants, although near its centre there is a prominent red supergiant of 8th magnitude. The star near the centre of the cluster that is

actually designated Kappa (κ) Crucis is a blue-white supergiant of magnitude 5.9.

The Coalsack ◉ ♄ A prominent dark nebula, a wedge-shaped cloud of dust and gas about 600 light years away that blots out the light from the stars in the Milky Way behind it. The Coalsack is large enough for 13 full Moons to be lined up across it. It has no NGC or other catalogue number. Although the Coalsack lies mainly in Crux, it spills over the borders of Crux into Centaurus and Musca.

USING CRUX TO LOCATE THE
SOUTH CELESTIAL POLE
The south celestial pole lies roughly at the intersection of two imaginary lines. One is formed by extending the line between Alpha (α) and Gamma (γ) Crucis (top of picture); the other lies at right angles to a line joining Alpha (α) and Beta (β) Centauri (bottom).

Abbreviation Cyg	Genitive Cygni	Highest in sky at 10 pm August to September

CYGNUS

This large constellation depicts the swan into which, according to Greek myth, the god Zeus transformed himself for one of his illicit love trysts. One story says that the object of his desire was Queen Leda of Sparta, and that their union produced either one or two eggs, from which hatched the twins Castor and Pollux, as well as Helen of Troy. The swan's beak is marked by Beta (β) Cygni and its tail by Alpha (α) Cygni, named Deneb (from an Arabic word meaning "tail"). Deneb forms one corner of the Summer Triangle, with Vega (in Lyra) and Altair (in Aquila) marking the other two. Since it is also identifiable by its cross-shape, Cygnus is sometimes called the Northern Cross. It lies in a rich part of the Milky Way.

THE SWAN

FULLY VISIBLE
90°N–28°S

FEATURES OF INTEREST

Alpha (α) Cygni (Deneb) ◉ The brightest star in Cygnus, at magnitude 1.3. It is a luminous blue-white supergiant lying more than 3,000 light years away, which makes it the most distant of all first-magnitude stars.

Beta (β) Cygni (Albireo) ♠ ➤ A beautiful double star. The two stars, magnitudes 3.1 and 5.1, can be divided with powerful binoculars. They are easy to separate with a telescope, through which they present a striking contrast of orange and blue-green. Both stars lie about 380 light years away, but it is not known whether they form a true binary.

CYGNUS (INSET: ALBIREO)
Cygnus, the swan, forms a large cross-shape in the northern Milky Way. The star marking the head of the swan (or the foot of the cross) is Albireo, a beautiful double star, divisible with a small telescope.

Width	Depth	Area 804 square degrees	Size ranking 16th

NGC 7000 (THE NORTH AMERICA NEBULA)
This large nebula can be found between Deneb and Xi (ξ) Cygni. Its resemblance to the outline of the North American continent is evident in this photograph; a dark inlet similar in shape to the Gulf of Mexico can be made out at the bottom of the picture. The nebula is a bright cloud of gas, which is thought to be lit up by a partially obscured star within it.

Omicron-1 (o¹) Cygni (31 Cygni) ♉ ✯ An orange-coloured giant, magnitude 3.8, which has a wide 5th-magnitude, bluish companion (30 Cygni), ideal for binocular observation. A closer bluish star of 7th magnitude is also visible with binoculars or a small telescope.

Chi (χ) Cygni ◉ ♉ A pulsating red giant, one of the Mira class of variable stars, that ranges in brightness between 3rd and 14th magnitudes every 13 months or so.

61 Cygni ✯ An attractive double star. The two components, of magnitudes 5.2 and 6.1, can be seen separately through a small telescope or even powerful binoculars. Both are orange dwarfs, smaller and fainter than the Sun, and are easily visible only because they are relatively close to us, 11.4 light years away. They orbit each other every 650 years.

NGC 6992 (THE VEIL NEBULA)
The Veil Nebula, in the southern part of Cygnus, is the wispy remnant of an exploded star.

M39 ♉ ✯ An open cluster, just visible to the naked eye under good conditions. Binoculars or a small telescope show its brightest stars. It covers the same area of sky as the full Moon, and lies nearly 900 light years away.

NGC 6826 (The Blinking Planetary) ✯ A planetary nebula visible with a small telescope as a bluish disc of similar size to the disc of Jupiter. Looking alternately at it and to one side gives the impression that it is blinking on and off, which explains its popular name.

NGC 6992 (The Veil Nebula) ♉ ✯ Part of a large, complex nebula called the Cygnus Loop which is the remains of a star that exploded as a supernova perhaps 5,000 years ago. In clear skies, the Veil Nebula section can be seen with binoculars or a small telescope, but the whole nebula is best seen on photographs.

NGC 7000 (The North America Nebula) ♉ ✯ A large nebula, visible under dark skies with binoculars or a wide-field telescope, extending for up to four Moon diameters. It is best seen on long-exposure photographs, where it takes the shape of the continent of North America, hence its popular name.

Cygnus A ⌗ A peculiar galaxy, thought to be two distant galaxies in collision. A large telescope is needed to see it, as it is of 15th magnitude. It is also a strong radio source.

Cygnus X-1 ⌗ A possible black hole, and one of the strongest X-ray sources in the sky. It appears optically as a 9th-magnitude blue supergiant, about 8,000 light years away. The X-rays come from an invisible companion, which orbits the supergiant every 5.6 days. This companion is the supposed black hole.

Abbreviation Del	Genitive Delphini	Highest in sky at 10 pm August to September

DELPHINUS

This small but distinctive constellation is tucked in between Aquila and Pegasus. Delphinus is associated with two different Greek myths. According to one account, it represents the dolphin sent by Poseidon, the sea god, to fetch Amphitrite, a sea nymph, to be his bride. It has also been identified as the dolphin that saved Arion, a poet and musician, when he was attacked on board a ship by a gang of robbers. The constellation's two brightest stars are Alpha (α) and Beta (β) Delphini, magnitudes 3.8 and 3.6 respectively. These stars bear the unusual names Sualocin and Rotanev. When written backwards, the names spell Nicolaus Venator. This is the Latinized version of Niccolò Cacciatore, an astronomer at Palermo Observatory, Italy, who named the stars after himself in the early 19th century.

THE
DOLPHIN

THE MAIN STARS IN
DELPHINUS
The attractive shape of Delphinus represents a leaping dolphin. Four stars, at the top left of this picture, form the shape called Job's Coffin.

FULLY VISIBLE
90°N–69°S

FEATURES OF INTEREST

Job's Coffin ◉ ♄ A name given to the box shape formed by the four stars Alpha (α), Beta (β), Gamma (γ), and Delta (δ) Delphini, all of which are of 4th magnitude.

Gamma (γ) Delphini ⋋ A double star. A small telescope will separate the two components, which appear yellow and white, of magnitudes 4.3 and 5.2. Both stars lie approximately 100 light years away. A fainter and closer pair of 8th-magnitude stars, known as Struve 2725 (about 125 light years away), should be visible in the same field of view.

NOVA DELPHINI
This nova is now very faint but in 1967, when this photograph was taken, it flared to naked-eye visibility.

Width ✋	Depth ✋	Area 189 square degrees	Size ranking 69th

Abbreviation Dor	Genitive Doradus	Highest in sky at 10 pm December to January

DORADO

Dorado, one of several southern constellations representing exotic creatures, was introduced in the late 16th century by the Dutch navigators Pieter Dirkszoon Keyser and Frederick de Houtman. It represents not the goldfish found in ornamental ponds but the dolphinfish of tropical seas, a member of the family Coryphaenidae. It has also been depicted as a swordfish. For astronomers, Dorado is significant because it contains the bulk of the Large Magellanic Cloud, our nearest neighbouring galaxy. Its brightest star is Alpha (α) Doradus, magnitude 3.3.

THE "GOLDFISH" OR SWORDFISH

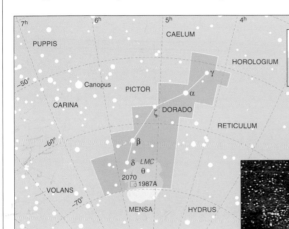

FULLY VISIBLE 20°N–90°S

NGC 2070 (THE TARANTULA NEBULA)
Loops of glowing gas extending from the Tarantula Nebula give it the appearance of a large spider.

FEATURES OF INTEREST

Beta (β) Doradus ◆ A bright Cepheid variable, ranging between magnitudes 3.5 and 4.1 every 9.8 days. It is a yellow-white super-giant and lies about 1,000 light years away.

NGC 2070 (The Tarantula Nebula)
◆ ♠ ☆ A bright nebula in the Large Magellanic Cloud (see below), visible to the naked eye. It appears about the the same size as the full Moon, but its true diameter is about 800 light years, making it far larger than the Orion Nebula. The nebula is a star-forming region, and binoculars or a small telescope reveal a star cluster, 30 Doradus, at its centre.

Supernova 1987A ♣ The brightest super-nova visible from Earth since 1604. In 1987 it flared up in the Large Magellanic Cloud, near the Tarantula Nebula, reaching magnitude 2.8 at its brightest. It remained visible to the naked eye for 10 months.

The Large Magellanic Cloud (LMC)
◆ ♠ ☆ A small galaxy, a satellite of our own, lying 170,000 light years away. It resembles a detached part of the Milky Way, somewhat elongated in shape. It has about one-tenth the mass of our Galaxy and a true diameter of 20,000 light years. It is usually classified as an irregular galaxy, but there are traces of a barred spiral structure. Scanning across it with binoculars or a small telescope brings numerous star clusters and glowing nebulae into view. The largest and brightest nebula is NGC 2070, also known as the Tarantula Nebula (see above).

Width 🖐	Depth 🖐	Area 179 square degrees	Size ranking 72nd

Abbreviation Dra	Genitive Draconis	Highest in sky at 10 pm March to September

DRACO

This extensive constellation of the far-northern sky winds around Ursa Minor. It represents the dragon that in Greek mythology guarded the golden apples of the Hesperides, the daughters of Atlas, and which was slain by Hercules as one of his labours. In the sky, Hercules is represented with one foot on the dragon's head. Despite its considerable size, Draco contains no really prominent stars, the brightest being Gamma (γ) Draconis, magnitude 2.2, a red giant about 150 light years away. With the stars Beta (β), Nu (ν), and Xi (ξ) Draconis, it forms a lozenge shape that marks the head of the dragon. The constellation is noted chiefly for its double stars.

THE DRAGON

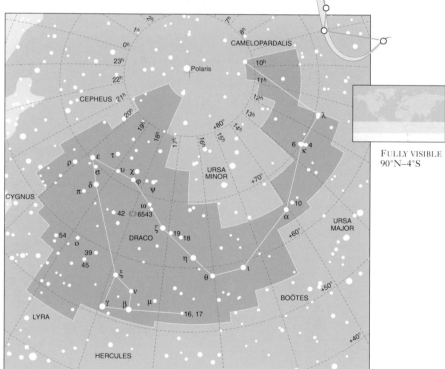

FULLY VISIBLE
90°N–4°S

FEATURES OF INTEREST

Mu (μ) Draconis ✹ A double star, with components that are too close be separated with a small telescope. An aperture of at least 75 mm (3 in), with high magnification, will usually be needed to see the two 6th-magnitude stars. They are 88 light years away and orbit each other every 670 years.

Nu (ν) Draconis ✹✹ A wide double star with twin white 5th-magnitude components that are virtually identical in colour and brightness. The pair form an excellent sight through binoculars and are easy to see with the smallest telescopes. Both stars lie 100 light years away.

Width	Depth	Area 1,083 square degrees	Size ranking 8th

Psi (ψ) Draconis �A double star, easy to divide through a small telescope. The two components, of magnitudes 4.6 and 5.8, may even be divided with powerful binoculars.

16 and 17 Draconis ♏ A multiple star. Binoculars show a wide double with 5th- and 6th-magnitude components. A telescope with high magnification reveals that the brighter star, 17 Draconis, is itself a close double.

39 Draconis ♏ A multiple star. Through a small telescope, or even binoculars, it appears as a wide pair of 5th- and 8th-magnitude stars. Examination of the brighter star under high magnification will show a much closer star, also of 8th magnitude.

NGC 6543 ⚹ A planetary nebula, visible with a small telescope. It appears as a bluish disc of similar size to the globe of Saturn.

THE HEAD OF DRACO
A group of four stars represents the head of Draco. The brightest of them, at the lower left in this photograph, is Gamma (γ) Draconis.

Abbreviation Equ	Genitive Equulei	Highest in sky at 10 pm September

EQUULEUS

The second-smallest constellation in the sky, Equuleus represents a small horse that lies next to Pegasus, the well-known flying horse. It first appeared among the 48 constellations described by the Greek astronomer Ptolemy, but there appear to be no legends about it. Its brightest star is Alpha (α) Equulei, magnitude 3.9.

THE LITTLE HORSE OR FOAL

FULLY VISIBLE
90°N–77°S

FEATURES OF INTEREST

Gamma (γ) Equulei ♏ An optical double star, divisible with binoculars. It consists of a star of magnitude 4.7 with a very wide companion, 6 Equulei, of magnitude 6.1.

Epsilon (ε) Equulei ⚹ A multiple star. A small telescope shows it as a double, with components of magnitudes 5.2 and 7.4. The brighter star is, in fact, a binary with an orbital period of 100 years, but the stars are too close together to be separated with a small aperture.

Width	Depth	Area 72 square degrees	Size ranking 87th

Abbreviation Eri	Genitive Eridani	Highest in sky at 10 pm November to January

ERIDANUS

This long, straggling constellation represents a river in Greek mythology. The River Eridanus features in the story of Phaethon, who fell into it after a disastrous attempt to drive the chariot of his father, the sun-god Helios. The constellation extends for nearly 60 degrees from north to south, the greatest range in declination of any constellation.

THE RIVER

FULLY VISIBLE
32°N–89°S

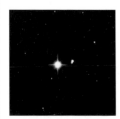

OMICRON-2 (o²) ERIDANI

All three components of this multiple star are visible in this telescopic view. The primary is in the centre with the two dwarf stars, overlapping each other, to its right.

FEATURES OF INTEREST

Alpha (α) Eridani (Achernar) ◉ A blue-white star of magnitude 0.5, the brightest star in Eridanus and the ninth brightest in the sky. It lies 140 light years away. Its name, Achernar, is of Arabic origin, meaning "river's end", and the star marks the constellation's southernmost tip. Nearby is p Eridani, a wide pair of 6th-magnitude stars visible with a small telescope.

Width 🖐️🖐️	Depth 🖐️🖐️✊	Area 1,138 square degrees	Size ranking 6th

Epsilon (ε) Eridani One of the closest naked-eye stars to the Sun. It is 10.5 light years distant and appears of magnitude 3.7. Although somewhat cooler and fainter than the Sun, it is otherwise similar.

Theta (θ) Eridani An attractive double star. The two components, twin white stars of magnitudes 3.2 and 4.3, can be separated with a small telescope.

Omicron-2 (o²) Eridani (40 Eridani) A multiple star with three components, including a red dwarf and a white dwarf together. The brightest of the trio, magnitude 4.4, is similar to the Sun. A small telescope shows that this star has a 10th-magnitude companion, which is the white dwarf; this is the easiest white dwarf to see with small instruments. It forms a binary with an 11th-magnitude red dwarf, although a larger aperture may be needed to spot this. The remarkable trio lies 16.5 light years away.

32 Eridani A double star, with components of contrasting colours. A small telescope reveals a red giant of magnitude 4.8 and a blue-white companion of magnitude 6.1.

THE SOUTHERN TIP OF ERIDANUS
A small part of this large constellation can be seen here. Achernar is just above the horizon, while Chi (χ) and Phi (φ) Eridani are below and just to the left of centre.

Abbreviation For	Genitive Fornacis	Highest in sky at 10 pm November to December

FORNAX

Fornax is an undistinguished constellation in an unremarkable area of sky. It lies on the shores of the celestial river Eridanus and the southern border of Cetus. Invented in the 18th century by the French astronomer Nicolas Louis de Lacaille, it represents a chemical furnace.

THE
FURNACE

FULLY VISIBLE
50°N–90°S

FEATURES OF INTEREST

Alpha (α) Fornacis The brightest star in the constellation, appearing to the naked eye as a single star of magnitude 3.8. A small telescope shows that it has a 7th-magnitude companion. The two stars form a true binary, orbiting each other every 300 years or so. They lie 46 light years away from the Earth.

The Fornax Cluster A cluster of galaxies about 75 million light years away, the brightest of which, notably NGC 1316 and NGC 1365, can be seen with a small telescope. NGC 1316 is a peculiar spiral, also known as radio source Fornax A. NGC 1365 is a barred spiral.

Width	Depth	Area 398 square degrees	Size ranking 41st

Abbreviation Gem	Genitive Geminorum	Highest in sky at 10 pm January to February

GEMINI

A constellation of the zodiac, Gemini depicts the mythological twins Castor and Pollux, after whom its two brightest stars are named. The twins sailed with the Argonauts in search of the golden fleece, and they were later regarded by the ancient Greeks as patron saints of seafarers. The two stars themselves are not related, though, lying at different distances from us. Gemini sits between Taurus and Cancer, and the Sun passes through it from 21 June to 20 July.

THE TWINS

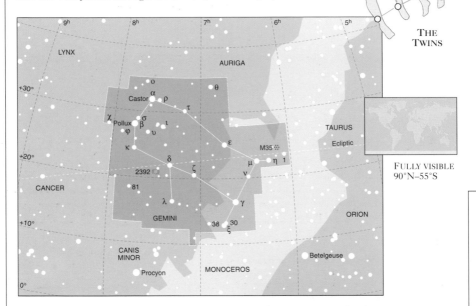

FULLY VISIBLE
90°N–55°S

FEATURES OF INTEREST

Alpha (α) Geminorum (Castor) 👁 🔭

A remarkable multiple star. To the naked eye, it appears as a single star, of magnitude 1.6. A small telescope divides it into a blue-white pair of stars, of magnitudes 1.9 and 2.9. These form a genuine binary with an orbital period of about 470 years. Both of these stars are spectroscopic binaries. A wider companion, of 9th magnitude, can also be seen with a small telescope. This is, in fact, a close pair of red dwarfs, forming an eclipsing binary. The whole six-star family is just over 50 light years away.

CASTOR AND POLLUX
The two brightest stars in Gemini are Castor (top right) and Pollux (bottom left). Although it has been assigned the letter Beta (β), Pollux is actually the brighter star.

Width 🤚👐	Depth 🤚👐	Area 514 square degrees	Size ranking 30th

Beta (β) Geminorum (Pollux) ◉ ♏ The brightest star in the constellation and among the 20 brightest in the sky, at magnitude 1.2. It is an orange-coloured giant, 34 light years away. The coloration is more noticeable when the star is viewed through binoculars.

Zeta (ζ) Geminorum ◉ ♏ A Cepheid variable star, ranging between magnitudes 3.6 and 4.2 in a cycle lasting just over 10 days. It is a yellow supergiant, about 1,200 light years away. Binoculars show a wide 8th-magnitude companion, which is unrelated.

Eta (η) Geminorum ◉ ♏ A variable red giant, about 350 light years away. It pulsates in size in a cycle lasting about 8 months, varying between magnitudes 3.2 and 3.9 as it does so.

M35 ♏ ✶ A rich open cluster, just visible to the naked eye and easy to see with binoculars. It appears almost as large as the full Moon. Binoculars or a small telescope resolve its individual stars, of 8th magnitude and fainter. The cluster lies nearly 3,000 light years away.

NGC 2392 (The Clown-Face Nebula, The Eskimo Nebula) ✶ A planetary nebula. Its bluish disc, similar in size to the globe of Saturn, is visible through a small telescope, but large apertures are needed to detect the surrounding features that lend it the appearance of a face and give rise to its popular names.

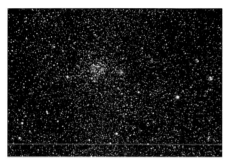

M35
The open cluster M35, discernible at the centre of this photograph with Iota (ι) Geminorum to its lower right, contains about 200 stars. Inspection with a telescope reveals that the stars are arranged in curved lines.

Abbreviation Gru	Genitive Gruis	Highest in sky at 10 pm September to October

GRUS

Grus is one of the dozen southern constellations introduced at the end of the 16th century by the Dutch navigators Pieter Dirkszoon Keyser and Frederick de Houtman. It represents the long-necked wading bird of the family Gruidae. Its brightest star is Alpha (α) Gruis, known as Al Na'ir, magnitude 1.7.

THE CRANE

FULLY VISIBLE
33°N–90°S

FEATURES OF INTEREST

Beta (β) Gruis ◉ A variable red giant, 170 light years away, that fluctuates from magnitude 2.0 to 2.3 with no set period.

Delta (δ) Gruis ◉ A double star, with components that can be separated with the naked eye. Both stars lie about 300 light years away. Delta-1 is a yellow giant of magnitude 4.0; Delta-2 is a red giant of magnitude 4.1.

Mu (μ) Gruis ◉ ♏ A wide naked-eye double. Both stars are yellow giants: Mu-1 (μ¹), 260 light years distant, is of magnitude 4.8; Mu-2 (μ²), 240 light years away, is of magnitude 5.1.

Width 🖐	Depth 🖐	Area 366 square degrees	Size ranking 45th

Abbreviation Her	Genitive Herculis	Highest in sky at 10 pm June to August

HERCULES

A large but not prominent constellation depicting the hero of Greek myth, Hercules lies between the bright stars Arcturus and Vega. The body of Hercules is inverted in the sky, the head being marked by Alpha (α) Herculis, in the south, and the feet by the stars to the north. Hercules was ordered by King Eurystheus of Mycenae to perform 12 labours, one of which was to slay a dragon (marked by adjacent Draco). Hercules is depicted resting on his right knee, with his left foot on the dragon's head. The constellation features the brightest globular cluster in northern skies, M13, and some notable double stars. Its brightest star is Beta (β) Herculis, magnitude 2.8.

HERCULES

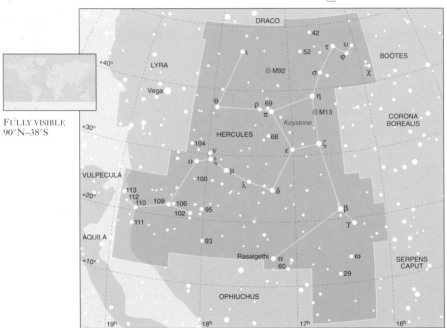

FULLY VISIBLE
90°N–38°S

FEATURES OF INTEREST

Alpha (α) Herculis (Rasalgethi) ◉ ➤

A red giant of variable brightness. It ranges between 3rd and 4th magnitudes, with no set period, as a result of fluctuations in its size. A small telescope shows a companion of magnitude 5.4. Hercules is depicted kneeling, and the name Rasalgethi is derived from an Arabic term meaning "the kneeler's head".

Rho (ρ) Herculis ➤ An optical double star.

The two components, of magnitudes 4.6 and 5.4, can be separated using a small telescope with high magnification.

95 Herculis ➤ A silver and gold pair of stars,

of magnitudes 5.0 and 5.2, divisible through a small telescope.

100 Herculis ➤ A pair of almost identical

white stars, both of magnitude 5.8, that can be separated with a small telescope. The two stars do not form a true binary.

Width 🖐🖐	Depth 🖐🖐🖐	Area 1,225 square degrees	Size ranking 5th

M13 ♙ ⚑ ⚐ The brightest globular cluster in the northern sky. Under dark skies, it appears to the naked eye like a hazy star. Binoculars show it clearly, about half the apparent width of the full Moon, and a small telescope shows its brightest stars. It is 23,500 light years away.

M92 ♙ ⚐ A globular cluster, fainter and smaller than M13 but still worthy of attention. Binoculars are needed to find it, and a telescope of moderate aperture will show its stars.

HERCULES, INCLUDING THE KEYSTONE
Pi (π), Eta (η), Zeta (ζ), and Epsilon (ε) Herculis (at the centre of this picture) form a four-sided figure called the Keystone that marks the pelvis of Hercules.

M13
This spectacular cluster lies on one side of the Keystone, a third of the way between Eta (η) and Zeta (ζ) Herculis. It contains hundreds of thousands of stars.

Abbreviation Hor	Genitive Horologii	Highest in sky at 10 pm November to December

HOROLOGIUM

This unrenowned southern constellation, invented in the 18th century by the French astronomer Nicolas Louis de Lacaille, lies between the bright stars Achernar and Canopus. It represents a pendulum clock, with its brightest star, Alpha (α) Horologii (magnitude 3.9), marking the pendulum weight.

THE PENDULUM CLOCK

FULLY VISIBLE
23°N–90°S

FEATURES OF INTEREST

R Horologii ♙ ⚐ A variable red giant, of the type known as a Mira star. It ranges between 5th and 14th magnitudes every 13 months or so.

TW Horologii ♙ A variable red giant. Over a period of approximately five or six months, it ranges between about 5th and 6th magnitudes.

Width 🖐	Depth 🖐	Area 249 square degrees	Size ranking 58th

Abbreviation Hya	Genitive Hydrae	Highest in sky at 10 pm February to June

HYDRA

Despite being the largest of all the 88 constellations, Hydra is far from prominent. Its head, formed by a loop of six stars of 3rd and 4th magnitudes, lies just north of the celestial equator, under Cancer, while the tip of its tail is 90 degrees away, between Libra and Centaurus. In Greek mythology, Hydra was a multi-headed monster slain by Hercules as one of his 12 labours. During the fight, Hercules was attacked by a crab, represented by the constellation Cancer. Hydra is also linked with a moral tale involving a crow sent to fetch a cup of water; the crow and cup are depicted by the constellations Corvus and Crater, which are represented lying on Hydra's back.

THE WATER-SNAKE

FULLY VISIBLE
54°N–83°S

M83
The bright core and spiral arms of this galaxy, seen face-on from Earth, are visible on photographs and digital images, such as this one taken using a CCD camera.

FEATURES OF INTEREST

Alpha (α) Hydrae (Alphard) ◉ An orange-coloured giant about 175 light years away. The name Alphard comes from an Arabic term that means "the solitary one". It is an apt name because, at magnitude 2.0, Alphard is the only star in Hydra brighter than 3rd magnitude.

Epsilon (ε) Hydrae ⋆ A double star. A telescope of moderate aperture is needed to split the two close components, of magnitudes 3.4 and 6.5, which orbit each other every 1000 years or so. They lie 135 light years away.

R Hydrae ◉ ♁ ⋆ A variable red giant of the Mira type that ranges between 3rd and 11th magnitudes every 13 months or so.

U Hydrae ♁ A variable red giant that fluctuates between 4th and 6th magnitudes

with little regularity as the star changes in size. It lies about 530 light years away.

M48 ♁ ⋆ An open cluster, just visible to the naked eye under good conditions but best seen with binoculars or a wide-field telescope. It is larger in apparent size than the full Moon and lies nearly 2,000 light years away.

M83 ⋆ A spiral galaxy that appears face-on to us, so that its arms are clearly visible through a large-aperture telescope and on photographs. When viewed through a small telescope, it appears as a rounded patch.

NGC 3242 (The Ghost of Jupiter) ⋆ A planetary nebula, visible through a small telescope as a bluish, planet-like disc, hence its popular name.

Width 🖐🖐🖐🖐	Depth 🖐🖐	Area 1,303 square degrees	Size ranking 1st

Abbreviation Hyi	Genitive Hydri	Highest in sky at 10 pm October to December

HYDRUS

This constellation of the far-southern skies was invented in the late 16th century by the Dutch navigators Pieter Dirkszoon Keyser and Frederick de Houtman. Lying between the bright star Achernar and the south celestial pole, it depicts a small water-snake. It should not be confused with the large water-snake, Hydra, known since the time of the ancient Greeks. The constellation's brightest star is Beta (β) Hydri, magnitude 2.8.

FULLY VISIBLE
8°N–90°S

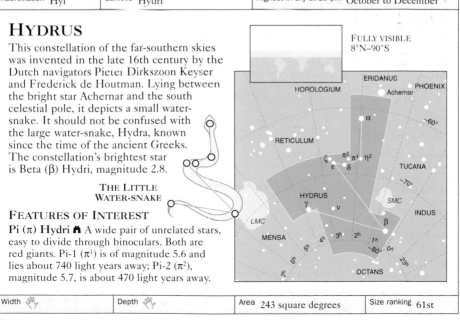

THE LITTLE
WATER-SNAKE

FEATURES OF INTEREST

Pi (π) Hydri � A wide pair of unrelated stars, easy to divide through binoculars. Both are red giants. Pi-1 (π¹) is of magnitude 5.6 and lies about 740 light years away; Pi-2 (π²), magnitude 5.7, is about 470 light years away.

Width 🖐	Depth 🖐	Area 243 square degrees	Size ranking 61st

Abbreviation Ind	Genitive Indi	Highest in sky at 10 pm August to October

INDUS

THE INDIAN

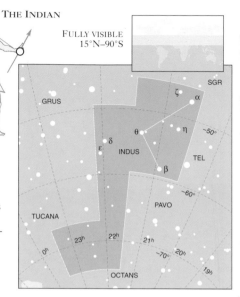

This southern constellation, lying between Pavo and Tucana, was introduced in the late 16th century by the Dutch navigators Pieter Dirkszoon Keyser and Frederick de Houtman. It depicts a native Indian, although from exactly where remains unclear; on old maps, the figure is shown holding arrows and a spear. Indus's brightest star, Alpha (α) Indi, is of magnitude 3.1.

FULLY VISIBLE
15°N–90°S

FEATURES OF INTEREST

Epsilon (ε) Indi 👁 Among the nearest stars to us, Epsilon Indi is only 11.8 light years away and has a magnitude of 4.7. It is a somewhat smaller and cooler star than the Sun.

Theta (θ) Indi ⚹ A double star, consisting of components of magnitudes 4.5 and 6.9 that are visible through a small telescope.

Width	Depth	Area 294 square degrees	Size ranking 49th

Abbreviation Lac	Genitive Lacertae	Highest in sky at 10 pm September to October

LACERTA

Lacerta is a small and insignificant constellation of the northern sky on the edge of the Milky Way, sandwiched between Cygnus and Andromeda. It was introduced in the 17th century by the Polish astronomer Johannes Hevelius. Its brightest star is Alpha (α) Lacertae, magnitude 3.8. Three naked-eye novae have erupted within its boundaries during the 20th century.

THE LIZARD

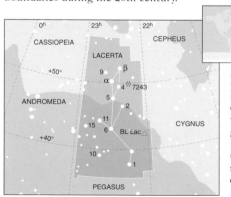

FULLY VISIBLE
90°N–33°S

FEATURES OF INTEREST

BL Lacertae ♟ The nucleus of a distant elliptical galaxy, originally classified as a variable star, hence its designation. It has given its name to a class of similar objects, the BL Lacertae (or BL Lac) objects, which are thought to be galaxies with powerful energy sources, perhaps massive black holes, at their centres. BL Lacertae varies between about 12th and 16th magnitudes.

Width	Depth	Area 201 square degrees	Size ranking 68th

Abbreviation Leo	Genitive Leonis	Highest in sky at 10 pm March to April

LEO

This large, impressive constellation depicts a crouching lion. In Greek myth, this was the lion that Hercules killed as one of his 12 labours. Leo is a constellation of the zodiac, lying between Cancer and Virgo. The Sun passes through it from 10 August to 16 September.

THE LION

FULLY VISIBLE
82°N–57°S

THE MAIN STARS IN LEO
Leo's main stars form a shape that closely resembles the outline of a crouching lion. Regulus and the Sickle are at the right of the picture.

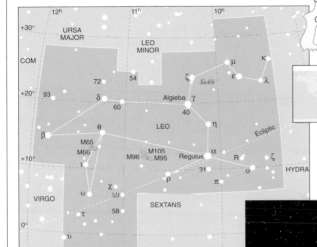

FEATURES OF INTEREST

The Sickle ◉ An easily recognizable pattern of six stars, shaped like a reversed question mark or a hook, which forms the head and chest of the lion. It consists of the stars Epsilon (ε), Mu (μ), Zeta (ζ), Gamma (γ), Eta (η), and Alpha (α) Leonis.

Alpha (α) Leonis (Regulus) ◉ ♯ ⊀ The faintest of the first-magnitude stars, magnitude 1.4. It is a blue-white star about 77 light years away. Binoculars or a small telescope show that it has a wide companion of 8th magnitude.

Gamma (γ) Leonis (Algieba) ⊀ A glorious double star, consisting of two golden orange giants of magnitudes 2.4 and 3.5, which make an excellent sight through a small telescope. They are a genuine binary pair, orbiting each other every 600 years or so. Binoculars (or even sharp eyesight) show a much wider 5th-magnitude star, 40 Leonis, which is unrelated.

Zeta (ζ) Leonis ♯ A wide triple, formed by unrelated stars. Zeta itself is of magnitude 3.4. Binoculars show a 6th-magnitude star, 35 Leonis, to its north. Further south is 39 Leonis, also of 6th magnitude.

R Leonis ♯ ⊀ A red-giant Mira variable, ranging in brightness between about 4th and 11th magnitudes every 10 months or so.

M65 and M66 ⊀ Two 9th-magnitude spiral galaxies, visible with a small telescope. Being tilted at an angle to us, they appear elliptical.

M95 and M96 ⊀ A pair of spiral galaxies, visible through a small telescope as elongated smudges. They lie at similar distances to M65 and M66, namely 20–25 million light years.

Width 🖐🖐	Depth 🖐🖐	Area 947 square degrees	Size ranking 12th

Abbreviation LMi	Genitive Leonis Minoris	Highest in sky at 10 pm March to April

LEO MINOR

**THE
LESSER
LION**

This faint constellation, representing a lion cub, is squeezed between Leo and Ursa Major. It was invented in the 17th century by Johannes Hevelius. Its brightest star is 46 Leonis Minoris, magnitude 3.8, but it contains little to interest owners of small instruments.

FULLY VISIBLE
90°N–48°S

FEATURES OF INTEREST

Beta (β) Leonis Minoris ♊ A close double star. It appears to the naked eye as a single star of magnitude 4.2, and its components can be separated only through a telescope of very large aperture. The two stars, which are 145 light years away, have an orbital period of 37 years. This is the only star in the constellation to have been assigned a Greek letter.

Width 🖐	Depth 🖐	Area 232 square degrees	Size ranking 64th

Abbreviation Lep	Genitive Leporis	Highest in sky at 10 pm January

LEPUS

THE HARE

Lepus lies under the feet of Orion, the hunter, and is pursued across the sky by his dog Canis Major. The constellation was known to the ancient Greeks. Its brightest star is Alpha (α) Leporis, magnitude 2.6, whose name, Arneb, comes from an Arabic term meaning "the hare".

FULLY VISIBLE
62°N–90°S

FEATURES OF INTEREST

Gamma (γ) Leporis ♊ A double star, with components of magnitudes 3.6 and 6.2 that are visible through binoculars. Both stars are at a similar distance from us, about 30 light years.

R Leporis ♊ ⭐ A Mira variable, noted for its deep red colour. It ranges from about 6th to 12th magnitude every 14 months or so.

M79 ⭐ A small globular cluster of 8th magnitude, visible with a small telescope. It lies about 40,000 light years away. In the same field of view is a triple star called h3752 (the h stands for John Herschel, who first catalogued it). This consists of a close pair

of stars, of 5th and 7th magnitudes, with a wider companion of 9th magnitude.

NGC 2017 ⭐ A small star cluster, the main members of which are catalogued as the multiple star h3780. A small telescope reveals a 6th-magnitude star with four companions of 8th to 10th magnitude. A larger aperture will separate two of the components into close doubles, and there is also a fainter 12th-magnitude star that completes the group.

Width 🖐	Depth 🖐	Area 290 square degrees	Size ranking 51st

Abbreviation Lib	Genitive Librae	Highest in sky at 10 pm May to June

LIBRA

A constellation of the zodiac, Libra lies just south of the celestial equator, between Virgo and Scorpius. Originally it was seen to represent the claws of Scorpius, the scorpion, which is why its brightest stars have names that mean the northern and southern claw. Libra was first visualized as a balance by the Romans, over 2,000 years ago, and it is now usually depicted as the scales held by the adjacent figure of Virgo, who is seen as the goddess of justice. The Sun passes through Libra from 31 October to 23 November.

THE SCALES

FULLY VISIBLE
60°N–90°S

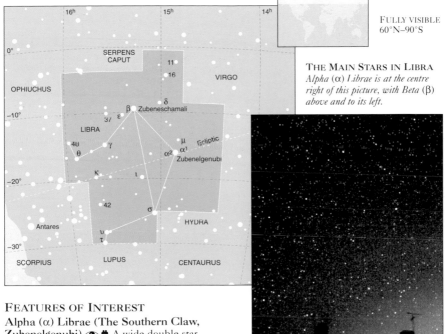

THE MAIN STARS IN LIBRA
Alpha (α) Librae is at the centre right of this picture, with Beta (β) above and to its left.

FEATURES OF INTEREST

Alpha (α) Librae (The Southern Claw, Zubenelgenubi) ◉ ♁ A wide double star. The two components, of magnitudes 2.8 and 5.2, can be separated with binoculars or even good eyesight.

Beta (β) Librae (The Northern Claw, Zubeneschamali) ♁ ➤ The constellation's brightest star, at magnitude 2.6. It is said by some observers to have a greenish tinge, which is highly unusual. Binoculars or a small telescope should reveal its colour.

Delta (δ) Librae ♁ An eclipsing binary of the same type as Algol (in Perseus). Its variations in magnitude, from 4.9 to 5.9 over 2 days 8 hours, are easy to follow through binoculars.

Iota (ι) Librae ♁ ➤ A complex multiple star, appearing to the naked eye as a single star of magnitude 4.5. Binoculars show a wide 6th-magnitude companion, 25 Librae. A telescope with an aperture of 75 mm (3 in) or more shows that the primary has a 9th-magnitude partner. High magnification should reveal that this fainter companion is itself a close pair.

Mu (μ) Librae ➤ A double star, with components of magnitudes 5.7 and 6.7. A telescope with an aperture of about 75 mm (3 in) is needed to separate them.

Width 🖐🤚	Depth 🖐🤚	Area 538 square degrees	Size ranking 29th

Abbreviation Lup	Genitive Lupi	Highest in sky at 10 pm May to June

LUPUS

Lupus lies in the Milky Way to the south of Libra.
It represents a wolf that in Greek and Roman times was
visualized as being held on a pole by a centaur, depicted
by the adjacent Centaurus. It seems, however, that there
are no myths specifically about the wolf. Lupus's brightest
star is Alpha (α) Lupi, magnitude 2.3.

THE
WOLF

FULLY VISIBLE
34°N–90°S

FEATURES OF INTEREST

Kappa (κ) Lupi ☆ A double star. The
components, of magnitudes 3.9 and 5.7, are
easy to divide with a small telescope.

Mu (μ) Lupi ☆ A multiple star. With a small
telescope, it appears as a wide double star with
components of magnitudes 4.3 and 6.9. An
aperture of 100 mm (4 in) or more, with high
magnification, shows that the primary is, in
fact, a close pair of 5th-magnitude stars.

Xi (ξ) Lupi ☆ A double star. Its components,
of magnitudes 5.1 and 5.6, can be separated
with a small telescope.

Pi (π) Lupi ☆ A matching pair of 5th-
magnitude blue-white stars. A telescope with
an aperture of 75 mm (3 in) or more is needed
to see them separately.

NGC 5822 ♙☆ A rich open cluster, of similar
apparent size to the full Moon. Visible with
binoculars or a small telescope, it contains over
100 faint stars and lies 1,800 light years away.

NGC 5822
*This large open cluster is shown here as it would
look through a small telescope.*

Width ♙	Depth ♙♙	Area 334 square degrees	Size ranking 46th

Abbreviation Lyn	Genitive Lyncis	Highest in sky at 10 pm January to March

LYNX

The Polish astronomer Johannes Hevelius, who invented this faint constellation in the 17th century, named it the Lynx because, he said, only the lynx-eyed would be able to spot it. It lies in the northern sky between Ursa Major and Auriga, and is surprisingly large – greater in area than Gemini, for example. Except in good dark-sky conditions, naked-eye observers will see little more than its brightest star, Alpha (α) Lyncis, magnitude 3.1. There are, however, numerous double stars to attract telescope users.

THE LYNX

FULLY VISIBLE
90°N–28°S

FEATURES OF INTEREST

12 Lyncis ⚹ A multiple star. Through a small telescope, it appears double, with components of magnitudes 4.9 and 7.3. An aperture of 75 mm (3 in) or more reveals that the brighter star is a close pair of 5th- and 6th-magnitude stars, which orbit each other every 700 years.

19 Lyncis ⚹ An easily divided multiple star. A small telescope separates it into a double, with components of magnitudes 5.8 and 6.9. Further away, a third star, of 8th magnitude, should also be visible.

38 Lyncis ⚹ A tight double star, requiring a telescope of 75 mm (3 in) aperture to split it into components of magnitudes 3.9 and 6.3.

NGC 2419 ♙ A globular cluster, notable for its remoteness. At 300,000 light years away, it is more distant than the Magellanic Clouds and so appears small and of only 10th magnitude.

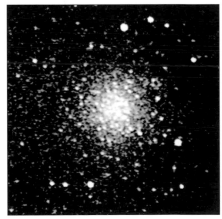

NGC 2419
It is thought likely that this cluster, seen here in a CCD image, lies outside our Galaxy in intergalactic space.

Width 🖐🖐	Depth 🖐🖐	Area 545 square degrees	Size ranking 28th

Abbreviation Lyr	Genitive Lyrae	Highest in sky at 10 pm July to August

LYRA

This prominent constellation of the northern sky lies between Cygnus and Hercules. It represents the lyre played by Orpheus, the great musician of Greek mythology. Arab astronomers, though, visualized the pattern as an eagle, and the name of its brightest star, Vega, comes from their term meaning "swooping eagle". Vega forms one corner of a large triangle of stars known to northern observers as the Summer Triangle, and completed by Deneb (in Cygnus) and Altair (in Aquila).

THE LYRE

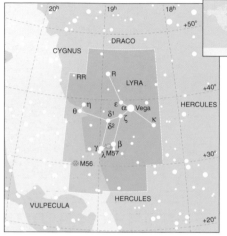

FULLY VISIBLE
90°N–42°S

FEATURES OF INTEREST

Alpha (α) Lyrae (Vega) ◉ The fifth-brightest star in the sky, at magnitude 0.0. It is a blue-white star, 25 light years away.

Beta (β) Lyrae ⊁ A double star, the brighter component of which is variable. Beta Lyrae itself is an eclipsing binary that varies between magnitudes 3.3 and 4.4 in a cycle that lasts 12 days 22 hours. A small telescope shows that it has a wide companion of magnitude 7.2.

Delta (δ) Lyrae ♻ A wide pair of unrelated stars, divisible with binoculars or the naked eye. One is a red giant that varies slightly, between about magnitudes 4.2 and 4.3, and the other is a blue-white star of magnitude 5.6.

Epsilon (ε) Lyrae (The Double Double) ♻ ⊁ A striking quadruple star. When viewed with binoculars, or even sharp eyesight, it appears as a pair of 5th-magnitude stars. A telescope with an aperture of 60–75 mm (2½–3 in), with high magnification, will divide each star into a closer binary. The slightly wider pair, of magnitudes 5.0 and 6.1, has a calculated orbital period of over 1,000 years. The other pair, of magnitudes 5.2 and 5.5, has an orbital period of about 600 years. All four stars lie about 130 light years away.

Zeta (ζ) Lyrae ♻ ⊁ A double star. The two components, magnitudes 4.3 and 5.7, are easy to divide with binoculars or a small telescope.

M57 (The Ring Nebula) ⊁ A planetary nebula, visible through a small telescope as an elliptical disc. Larger apertures show it as a ring, which is how it appears on photographs.

EPSILON (ε) LYRAE
AND VEGA
The famous Double Double, Epsilon (ε) Lyrae, is at the top left in this picture, with the bright star Vega to its right.

M57 (THE RING
NEBULA)
Through a small telescope, this planetary nebula is visible as an elliptical disc.

Width 🖐	Depth 🖐	Area 286 square degrees	Size ranking 52nd

Abbreviation Men	Genitive Mensae	Highest in sky at 10 pm December to February

MENSA

This small and faint constellation near the south celestial pole was introduced in the 18th century by the French astronomer Nicolas Louis de Lacaille. He named it after Table Mountain, near the modern Cape Town in South Africa, from where he charted the southern sky. Mensa's only notable feature is part of the Large Magellanic Cloud, which extends into it from neighbouring Dorado.

THE TABLE
MOUNTAIN

FULLY VISIBLE
5°N–90°S

FEATURES OF INTEREST

Alpha (α) Mensae ☀ A yellow star, 30 light years away and similar in nature to the Sun. At magnitude 5.1, it is the brightest star in the constellation.

Width	Depth	Area 153 square degrees	Size ranking 75th

Abbreviation Mic	Genitive Microscopii	Highest in sky at 10 pm August to September

MICROSCOPIUM

Microscopium is a faint constellation to the south of Capricornus. It was introduced in the 18th century by the French astronomer Nicolas Louis de Lacaille and represents a microscope. The constellation's brightest stars, Gamma (γ) and Epsilon (ε) Microscopii, are both of magnitude 4.7.

THE
MICROSCOPE

FULLY VISIBLE
45°N–90°S

FEATURES OF INTEREST

Alpha (α) Microscopii ✦ An orange giant star of magnitude 4.9. A telescope shows a companion of 10th magnitude.

Width	Depth	Area 210 square degrees	Size ranking 66th

| Abbreviation Mon | Genitive Monocerotis | Highest in sky at 10 pm January to February |

MONOCEROS

THE
UNICORN

Monoceros straddles the celestial equator between Orion and Canis Minor. Introduced in the early 17th century by the Dutchman Petrus Plancius, it represents the mythical unicorn. Its brightest star is Alpha (α) Monocerotis, magnitude 3.9. Monoceros is often overlooked in favour of its glittering neighbouring constellations, but it lies in the Milky Way and contains much of interest for owners of any size of instrument.

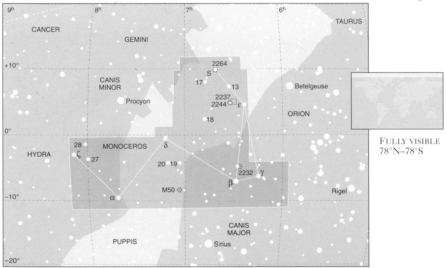

FULLY VISIBLE
78°N–78°S

FEATURES OF INTEREST

Beta (β) Monocerotis ✶ A triple star, divisible with a small telescope. The three stars, magnitudes 4.6, 5.0, and 5.4, form an arc.

Epsilon (ε) Monocerotis (8 Monocerotis) ✶ A double star, with components of magnitudes 4.4 and 6.7 that are easy to divide through a small telescope.

S Monocerotis (15 Monocerotis) ✶ A highly luminous blue-white star, magnitude 4.7 (but slightly variable), in the cluster NGC 2264 (see next page). It has a companion of 8th magnitude, visible with a small telescope.

M50 ♁✶ An open cluster, about half the apparent size of the full Moon and visible with binoculars. A small telescope reveals its individual stars, of 8th magnitude and fainter. It lies 3,000 light years away.

NGC 2244 AND THE ROSETTE NEBULA
The stars of the open cluster NGC 2244 (at the centre of this picture) are enveloped in the Rosette Nebula.

| Width 🖐🖐 | Depth 🖐 | Area 482 square degrees | Size ranking 35th |

NGC 2232 ♄ A scattered open cluster. The
same apparent size as the full Moon, it is just
visible to the naked eye. Its brightest star is
5th-magnitude 10 Monocerotis, and several
other individual member stars are visible with
binoculars. It lies 1,300 light years away.

NGC 2244 ♄ An open cluster at the heart of
the much larger Rosette Nebula. The cluster
is easily visible through binoculars as an
elongated group about two-thirds the apparent
width of the full Moon. However, excellent
skies are needed to trace the outline of the
surrounding Rosette Nebula, which is three
to four times larger and shows up well only
on photographs. The cluster and nebula lie
5,500 light years away.

NGC 2264 ♄ An open cluster. It is visible
with binoculars, and when viewed through a
small telescope it appears triangular in shape.
Its brightest member is S Monocerotis (see
previous page). Long-exposure photographs
show a surrounding area of faint nebulosity,
which includes a dark lane known as the Cone
Nebula. The cluster and associated nebula are
about 2,500 light years away.

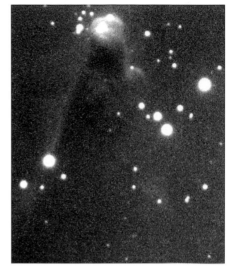

THE CONE NEBULA
*The Cone Nebula is a tapering column of dark dust in
the southern part of the faint area of nebulosity that
surrounds the star cluster NGC 2264.*

Abbreviation Mus	Genitive Muscae	Highest in sky at 10 pm April to May

MUSCA

Musca lies in the Milky Way, to the south of Centaurus
and Crux. It depicts a fly and is one of the dozen southern
constellations invented in the late 16th century by the
Dutch navigators Pieter Dirkszoon Keyser and Frederick
de Houtman. Its brightest star is Alpha
(α) Muscae, magnitude 2.7.

THE
FLY

FULLY VISIBLE
14°N–90°S

FEATURES OF INTEREST

Beta (β) Muscae ✸ A close binary, which
appears through a small telescope as a single
star of magnitude 3.0. An aperture of around
100 mm (4 in) will divide it into two stars of
magnitudes 3.6 and 4.1, which orbit each other
every 400 years or so.

Theta (θ) Muscae ✸ A double star. The two
components, of magnitudes 5.6 and 7.6, are
divisible with a small telescope. The brighter
star is a luminous blue supergiant, while its
companion is an example of a Wolf–Rayet star,
a hot star that has lost its outer layers.

Width	Depth	Area 138 square degrees	Size ranking 77th

Abbreviation Nor	Genitive Normae	Highest in sky at 10 pm June

NORMA

Norma lies in the Milky Way between Ara and Lupus. Introduced in the 18th century by the French astronomer Nicolas Louis de Lacaille, it depicts a draughtsman's level or set square. It adjoins another Lacaille invention, Circinus, the compasses. There are no stars labelled Alpha (α) or Beta (β) Normae due to boundary changes since Lacaille's time.

THE LEVEL

FULLY VISIBLE
29°N–90°S

FEATURES OF INTEREST

Gamma (γ) Normae ◐ A double star, consisting of unrelated components that can be separated with the naked eye. The primary, Gamma-2 (γ²), is the brightest star in the constellation; it is an orange giant star of magnitude 4.0, 130 light years away. Gamma-1 (γ¹), magnitude 5.0, is an immensely luminous yellow supergiant more than 100 times further away.

Epsilon (ε) Normae ⊁ A double star, with components of magnitudes 4.5 and 6.7 that can be separated with a small telescope.

Iota-1 (ι¹) Normae ⊁ A double star. The components, of magnitudes 4.6 and 8.1, can be divided with a small telescope. Iota-2 (ι²) is an unrelated 6th-magnitude star that lies some distance away.

Width	Depth	Area 165 square degrees	Size ranking 74th

Abbreviation Oct	Genitive Octantis	Highest in sky at 10 pm October

OCTANS

Octans contains the south celestial pole. The constellation, which represents a navigator's octant, a predecessor of the sextant, was introduced in the 18th century by the French astronomer Nicolas Louis de Lacaille. Its brightest star is Nu (ν) Octantis, an orange giant of magnitude 3.7. Other than its location at the south celestial pole, there is little notable about Octans.

FULLY VISIBLE
0°–90°S

THE OCTANT

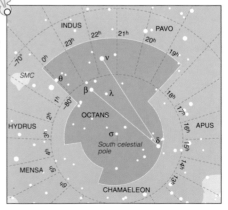

FEATURES OF INTEREST

Sigma (σ) Octantis ◐ This is the nearest naked-eye star to the south celestial pole (lying about 1 degree away), although at magnitude 5.5 it is hardly prominent. It is a yellow-white giant star, 270 light years away.

Lambda (λ) Octantis ⊁ A close double star, divisible with a small telescope. The two components are of magnitudes 5.5 and 7.2.

Width	Depth	Area 291 square degrees	Size ranking 50th

OPHIUCHUS

Abbreviation Oph	Genitive Ophiuchi	Highest in sky at 10 pm June to July

THE SERPENT HOLDER

This large constellation extends from Hercules in the north, across the celestial equator, to Scorpius in the south. It represents the Greek god of medicine, Asclepius, who is depicted holding a serpent (the constellation Serpens), a traditional symbol for healing. The constellation contains several globular clusters. Its brightest star is Alpha (α) Ophiuchi, magnitude 2.1, also known as Rasalhague, derived from an Arabic term meaning "head of the serpent collector".

FULLY VISIBLE
59°N–75°S

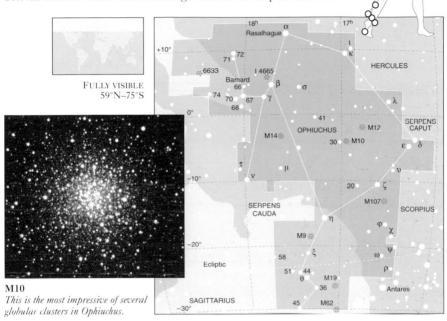

M10
This is the most impressive of several globular clusters in Ophiuchus.

FEATURES OF INTEREST

Rho (ρ) Ophiuchi ♠ ☀ A multiple star. Binoculars show it as a star of magnitude 4.6 with two wide companions, of magnitudes 6.8 and 7.3. A small telescope, with high magnification, reveals that the brightest star has a closer companion of magnitude 5.7.

36 Ophiuchi ☀ A pair of near-identical orange dwarf stars of 5th magnitude, divisible with a small telescope. They lie 20 light years away and orbit each other every 500 years or so.

70 Ophiuchi ☀ A binary star, consisting of yellow and orange dwarfs, magnitudes 4.2 and 6.1, that lie 17 light years away and orbit each other every 88 years. They are slowly moving apart as seen from Earth, and should currently be divisible with all but the smallest apertures.

Barnard's Star ☀ The second-closest star to the Sun, 5.9 light years away. It is a cool and faint red dwarf of magnitude 9.5, and is hence far too faint to be seen with the naked eye.

M10 and M12 ♠ ☀ Two globular clusters about 3 degrees apart. Both are visible through binoculars, appearing about half the size of the full Moon, although a telescope of moderate aperture is needed to resolve individual stars. M10 is the closer cluster at 14,000 light years, compared with 18,000 light years for M12.

NGC 6633 ♠ An open cluster of similar apparent size to the full Moon, visible through binoculars.

IC 4665 ♠ A large and scattered open cluster, visible with binoculars.

Width 🖐🖐	Depth 🖐🖐	Area 948 square degrees	Size ranking 11th

| Abbreviation Ori | Genitive Orionis | Highest in sky at 10 pm December to January |

ORION

Orion is the most magnificent of all the constellations. Being positioned on the celestial equator, it is visible from most places on Earth. It represents a hunter with his dogs (marked by Canis Major and Canis Minor) at his heels. In Greek mythology, Orion was the son of Poseidon, the sea god. He was supposedly killed by the sting of a scorpion, and his position in the sky is such that he sets as the scorpion (the constellation Scorpius) rises. According to another story, Orion became enamoured of a group of nymphs called the Pleiades, depicted by a star cluster in the adjoining constellation of Taurus. As the Earth turns, Orion seems to chase the Pleiades across the sky. The constellation contains several bright stars, but its most celebrated feature is the huge nebula (M42) that lies within the hunter's sword, south of the line of three stars marking his belt.

ORION

FULLY VISIBLE
79°N–67°S

ORION
The magnificent constellation of Orion, with Betelgeuse at the top left, Rigel at the bottom right, and the Orion Nebula and the stars of the belt in the centre.

FEATURES OF INTEREST

Alpha (α) Orionis (Betelgeuse) A red supergiant star of variable brightness, ranging from about magnitude 0 to 1.3 every 6 years or so. It lies 430 light years away. The name Betelgeuse is derived from an Arabic term that incorporates a reference to a hand, although the star actually lies on the hunter's shoulder.

Beta (β) Orionis (Rigel) A blue supergiant star of magnitude 0.2, the brightest star in the constellation and the seventh brightest in the sky. It is 770 light years away. The name Rigel is derived from an Arabic word meaning "foot", which is the part of the hunter's body that the star represents.

| Width | Depth | Area 594 square degrees | Size ranking 26th |

1
2
3
4
5
6
7

DETAIL OF THE M42 (ORION
NEBULA) REGION

M42 (ORION NEBULA) WITH
THE TRAPEZIUM INSET
*M42 is a mass of glowing gas where stars are forming.
At its heart is the multiple star Theta-1 (θ^1) Orionis.*

Theta-1 (θ^1) Orionis (The Trapezium) ✷
A multiple star, located at the heart of the
Orion Nebula (see below). A small telescope
shows it as a quadruple star, with components
of magnitudes 5.1, 6.7, 6.7, and 8.0 arranged in
a trapezium shape. A larger aperture reveals
two other 11th-magnitude stars in the group.

Theta-2 (θ^2) Orionis ♙ A double star. The
two stars, magnitudes 5.0 and 6.4, are divisible
through binoculars. Theta-2 also forms a wide,
bright binocular double with Theta-1 Orionis.

Iota (ι) Orionis ♙ ✷ A double star. The two
components, of magnitudes 2.8 and 7.0, can be
split with a small telescope. Binoculars show
another double nearby: called Struve 747, it
consists of stars of magnitudes 4.8 and 5.7.

Sigma (σ) Orionis ✷ A remarkable multiple
star. The main star, of magnitude 3.8, has two
7th-magnitude companions to one side, and
a 9th-magnitude companion on the other.
A faint triple star, called Struve 761, should
be visible in the same telescopic field of view.

M42 (The Orion Nebula) ◉ ♙ ✷ One
of the most spectacular objects in the sky.
It is a cloud of glowing gas with an apparent
diameter over twice that of the full Moon.
Visible to the naked eye, it becomes larger and
more complex when viewed with binoculars
and telescopes of increasing aperture. It is
1,500 light years away and is lit up by the stars
of the Trapezium (see Theta-1 (θ^1) Orionis,

above) that lie within it. A northern extension
of the nebula is known as M43.

NGC 1981 ♙ A large, scattered open cluster
visible with binoculars, its brightest stars being
of 6th magnitude. The cluster appears to the
north of the Orion Nebula and lies at about
the same distance from us, 1,400 light years.

The Horsehead Nebula ♛ A dark nebula,
shaped like a chess knight, seen silhouetted
against a strip of brighter nebulosity that
extends south from Zeta (ζ) Orionis. However,
it is too faint to be viewed without a large
telescope, and its shape is most easily seen
on a long-exposure photograph.

THE HORSEHEAD NEBULA
*This distinctively shaped cloud of gas is visible against
a background of brighter hydrogen gas.*

Abbreviation Pav	Genitive Pavonis	Highest in sky at 10 pm July to September

PAVO

Pavo, which represents a peacock, is one of the 12 southern constellations invented in the late 16th century by the Dutch navigators Pieter Dirkszoon Keyser and Frederick de Houtman. The constellation's brightest star, Alpha (α) Pavonis, magnitude 1.9, is also named Peacock. Being a modern constellation, there are no myths associated with it.

THE PEACOCK

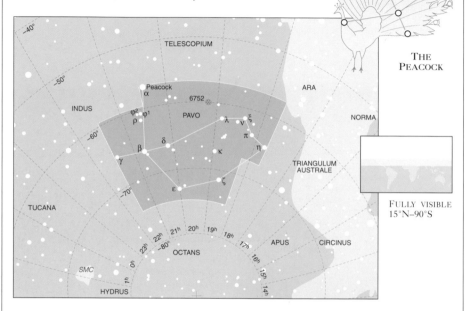

FULLY VISIBLE
15°N–90°S

FEATURES OF INTEREST

Kappa (κ) Pavonis ● A Cepheid variable star. It is a yellow-white supergiant that ranges between magnitudes 3.9 and 4.8 every 9 days 2 hours. It lies about 540 light years away.

Xi (ξ) Pavonis ✱ A close double star with components of unequal brightness. It consists of a red giant of magnitude 4.4 and an 8th-magnitude companion, both about 420 light years away. With a telescope of small aperture, it may be difficult to pick out the fainter star in the glare around the brighter component.

NGC 6752 ♠✱ A globular cluster, just visible to the naked eye and easy to see through binoculars or a small telescope. A telescope with an aperture of 75 mm (3 in) will resolve individual stars. The cluster has an apparent size about half that of the full Moon and lies 14,000 light years away.

NGC 6752
This large globular cluster, one of the brightest in the sky, has many outlying stars.

Width 🖐🖐	Depth 🖐	Area 378 square degrees	Size ranking 44th

Abbreviation Peg	Genitive Pegasi	Highest in sky at 10 pm September to October

PEGASUS

THE WINGED HORSE

This large constellation north of Aquarius and Pisces adjoins Andromeda. It represents the upper body of the winged horse that, in Greek mythology, sprang from the body of Medusa when she was beheaded by Perseus. The most distinctive feature in Pegasus is the Great Square formed by Alpha (α), Beta (β), and Gamma (γ) Pegasi, and Alpha (α) Andromedae. The area inside the square is relatively barren, containing no stars brighter than 4th magnitude.

FULLY VISIBLE
90°N–53°S

M15
This is one of the finest globular clusters in northern skies, appearing through binoculars like a hazy star.

FEATURES OF INTEREST

Beta (β) Pegasi ◕ A variable red giant that forms one corner of the Great Square. It varies unpredictably from magnitude 2.3 to 2.7.

Epsilon (ε) Pegasi (Enif) ♙⚹ A wide double star, which consists of a yellow supergiant of magnitude 2.4 and an 8th-magnitude partner that can be seen with a small telescope or even good binoculars. This star represents Pegasus's muzzle; its popular name is derived from the Arabic word for "nose".

M15 ♙⚹ A globular cluster, clearly visible with binoculars or a small telescope and about one-third the apparent width of the full Moon. It lies about 30,000 light years away.

Width ✋✋	Depth ✋🤏	Area 1,121 square degrees	Size ranking 7th

| Abbreviation Per | Genitive Persei | Highest in sky at 10 pm November to December |

PERSEUS

Perseus represents the mythological Greek hero who
decapitated the fearsome Medusa, whose gaze could turn men
to stone. On his way back from this exploit, Perseus rescued
Andromeda from the jaws of a sea monster. In the sky, Perseus
lies next to Andromeda and her mother, Cassiopeia, forming
part of a great tableau depicting this most famous of Greek
myths. Perseus is represented brandishing his sword in his
right hand, marked by the twin star clusters NGC 869 and
NGC 884, while in his left hand he holds the head of Medusa,
marked by the star Beta (β) Persei, better known as Algol.
A rich part of the Milky Way runs through Perseus, making
it an attractive constellation for binocular users.

PERSEUS

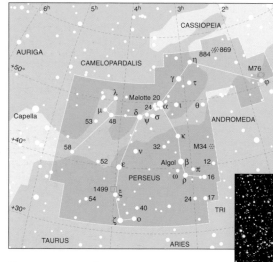

FULLY VISIBLE
90°N–31°S

**NGC 869 AND NGC 884
(THE DOUBLE CLUSTER)**
*These twin star clusters both lie
about 7,300 light years away, in the
Perseus spiral arm of the Galaxy.
NGC 869 is the richer of the two.*

FEATURES OF INTEREST

Alpha (α) Persei 🔭 A yellow-white supergiant of magnitude 1.8, the brightest star in
the constellation. It is the most prominent
member of a large and loose cluster of stars
known as Melotte 20, visible with binoculars,
which lies 550 light years away.

Beta (β) Persei (Algol) 👁 A famous
eclipsing binary star, consisting of a close pair
of stars in orbit around each other. When the
brighter star is eclipsed by the fainter one,
every 2 days 21 hours, the magnitude drops
from 2.1 to 3.4 for about 10 hours.

Rho (ρ) Persei 👁 A variable red giant. Due
to changes in size, it varies from magnitude 3.3
to 4.0 in a cycle lasting about 7 weeks.

M34 🔭 An open cluster, about 1,400 light
years away. It is visible with binoculars or a
small telescope and appears about the same
size as the full Moon. The cluster's brightest
stars are of 7th magnitude.

**NGC 869 and NGC 884 (η and χ Persei,
The Double Cluster)** 🔭 Two open clusters,
just visible to the naked eye and an excellent
sight through binoculars or a small telescope.
Each cluster covers about the same area of sky
as the full Moon.

| Width | Depth | Area 615 square degrees | Size ranking 24th |

Abbreviation Phe	Genitive Phoenicis	Highest in sky at 10 pm October to November

PHOENIX

Phoenix lies near the southern end of Eridanus, close to the bright star Achernar. It is the largest of the 12 constellations invented at the end of the 16th century by the Dutch navigators Pieter Dirkszoon Keyser and Frederick de Houtman, and represents the mythical bird that was supposedly reborn from the dead body of its predecessor. Its brightest star is Alpha (α) Phoenicis, magnitude 2.4.

THE PHOENIX

FEATURES OF INTEREST

Beta (β) Phoenicis ⚹ A double star. The two stars, of magnitudes 4.0 and 4.2, are not easy to divide: a telescope with an aperture of at least 100 mm (4 in) is needed to separate them.

Zeta (ζ) Phoenicis ⊙ ♠ ⚹ A star that is both variable and double. The brighter component, an eclipsing binary of the same type as Algol, ranges between magnitudes 3.9 and 4.4 every 1 day 16 hours. The fainter star, of 8th magnitude, can be seen with a small telescope.

FULLY VISIBLE
32°N–90°S

Width 🖐🖐	Depth 🖐	Area 469 square degrees	Size ranking 37th

Abbreviation Pic	Genitive Pictoris	Highest in sky at 10 pm December to February

PICTOR

Pictor is one of the constellations representing instruments of science and the arts that were introduced in the 18th century by Nicolas Louis de Lacaille. It depicts an easel, and lies due south of Columba between the bright star Canopus in Carina and the Large Magellanic Cloud. Its brightest star is Alpha (α) Pictoris, magnitude 3.2.

THE
PAINTER'S EASEL

FULLY VISIBLE
26°N–90°S

FEATURES OF INTEREST

Beta (β) Pictoris ♄ A blue-white star of magnitude 3.9, lying 63 light years away. Astronomers have found that it is surrounded by a disc of dust, thought to be a planetary system in the early stages of formation.

Iota (ι) Pictoris ⚹ A double star. The two components, of magnitudes 5.6 and 6.4, are easy to separate with a small telescope.

Width 🖐	Depth 🖐	Area 247 square degrees	Size ranking 59th

| Abbreviation Psc | Genitive Piscium | Highest in sky at 10 pm October to November |

PISCES

This constellation of the zodiac, lying between Aquarius and Aries, depicts two fishes whose tails are each tied with cord. The star Alpha (α) Piscium marks a knot that joins the two cords. The constellation originated among the Babylonians of the Middle East, from whom it was inherited by the ancient Greeks. In one Greek myth, the fish represent Aphrodite and her son Eros, who plunged into the Euphrates to escape Typhon, a multi-headed monster. The Sun lies in Pisces from 12 March to 18 April and hence is in the constellation at the March equinox.

THE FISHES

FULLY VISIBLE
83°N–56°S

M74
The structure of this spiral galaxy, which appears face-on to us, can be seen through a large telescope.

FEATURES OF INTEREST

The Circlet ☀ A ring of seven stars of 4th and 5th magnitudes, south of the Great Square of Pegasus, that represents the head of the southernmost of the two fish. It consists of Gamma (γ), Kappa (κ), Lambda (λ), TX (or 19), Iota (ι), Theta (θ), and 7 Piscium.

Alpha (α) Piscium ⚹ A binary star. A telescope with an aperture of 75 mm (3 in) or more is needed to separate the close blue-white components of magnitudes 4.2 and 5.2. The two stars, which lie 140 light years away, have an orbital period of nearly 1,000 years and are currently moving closer together as seen from Earth.

Zeta (ζ) Piscium ⚹ A wide double star. The unrelated components, of magnitudes 5.2 and 6.4, lie 150 and 195 light years away. They can be divided with a small telescope.

Psi-1 (ψ¹) Piscium ⚹ A wide double star, with components of magnitudes 5.3 and 5.5 that can be separated with a small telescope. Both stars lie about 230 light years away.

TX Piscium (19 Piscium) ☀ ♄ A variable red giant that ranges from about magnitude 4.8 to 5.2 with no set period.

M74 ⚹ A spiral galaxy, visible through a small telescope as a rounded misty patch.

| Width 🖐🖐🖐 | Depth 🖐🖐 | Area 889 square degrees | Size ranking 14th |

Abbreviation PsA	Genitive Piscis Austrini	Highest in sky at 10 pm September to October

PISCIS AUSTRINUS

Piscis Austrinus is a small constellation of the southern sky that was known to the ancient Greeks. It depicts a fish into whose mouth Aquarius, represented by the constellation to the north, pours water from his urn. In Greek mythology, this fish was also the parent of the two fish represented by Pisces. The name of the constellation is sometimes given as Piscis Australis.

THE
SOUTHERN
FISH

FULLY VISIBLE
53°N–90°S

**THE MAIN STARS IN
PISCIS AUSTRINUS**
*Fomalhaut, the bright star at centre
left in this photograph, dominates
Piscis Austrinus. The shape of the
fish can just be made out among
the fainter stars to its right.*

FEATURES OF INTEREST

Alpha (α) Piscis Austrini (Fomalhaut) ◉
A blue-white star that lies 25 light years away. At magnitude 1.2, it is not only the brightest star in the constellation but also ranks among the 20 brightest stars in the sky. The name Fomalhaut is derived from an Arabic term that means "fish's mouth", which describes the place the star occupies in the celestial pattern.

Beta (β) Piscis Austrini ⋆ A wide double star, divisible with a small telescope. Its two components are of magnitudes 4.3 and 7.7.

Gamma (γ) Piscis Austrini ⋆ A double star. With a small telescope it is difficult to separate the stars, as the 5th-magnitude primary greatly outshines its close 8th-magnitude neighbour.

Width 〰	Depth 〰 〰	Area 245 square degrees	Size ranking 60th

Abbreviation Pup	Genitive Puppis	Highest in sky at 10pm January to February

PUPPIS

THE STERN

This rich constellation lies in the Milky Way next to Canis Major. It represents the stern of the ship of the Argonauts. Ancient Greek astronomers represented the whole ship as one constellation, Argo Navis. This was later divided into three parts, with Puppis being the largest section. Because it is only part of a once-larger constellation, Puppis has no stars labelled Alpha (α), Beta (β), Gamma (γ), Delta (δ), or Epsilon (ε).

FULLY VISIBLE
39°N–90°S

NGC 2451
This scattered open cluster covers a larger area of sky than the full Moon. The star at the centre of the photograph is c Puppis.

FEATURES OF INTEREST

Zeta (ζ) Puppis (Naos) ◉ The brightest star in the constellation, at magnitude 2.2. It is a hot and luminous blue-white supergiant, lying about 1,400 light years away. Its name is derived from a Greek word meaning "ship".

k Puppis ✶ A double star. A small telescope reveals two similar blue-white stars of almost equal brightness, at magnitudes 4.5 and 4.6.

L Puppis ◉ ♁ A wide pair of unrelated stars, each visible to the naked eye. L^1 Puppis is a blue-white star of magnitude 4.9, while L^2 is a red giant that varies between about 3rd and 6th magnitudes every 5 months or so.

V Puppis ◉ ♁ An eclipsing binary that varies between magnitudes 4.4 and 4.9 every 1 day 11 hours.

M46 ♁ ✶ An open cluster, just visible to the naked eye and appearing the same size as the full Moon. A small telescope resolves its stars. It lies over 5,000 light years away.

M47 ♁ A scattered open cluster, visible to the naked eye and slightly larger than M46 but much closer, about 1,500 light years away. Its brightest stars are of 6th magnitude.

NGC 2451 ◉ ♁ An open cluster, visible to the naked eye and through binoculars. It lies 850 light years away. Its brightest member is an orange giant, c Puppis, of magnitude 3.6.

NGC 2477 ♁ ✶ An open cluster, 4,200 light years away. It is so rich that it resembles a globular cluster when seen through binoculars. A telescope will resolve individual stars.

Width 🖐	Depth 🖐🖐	Area 673 square degrees	Size ranking 20th

Abbreviation Pyx	Genitive Pyxidis	Highest in sky at 10 pm February to March

PYXIS

FULLY VISIBLE
52°N–90°S

This southern constellation lies on the edge of the Milky Way between Hydra and Puppis. Invented by Nicolas Louis de Lacaille in the 18th century, it represents a magnetic compass of the type used by mariners.

FEATURES OF INTEREST

T Pyxidis ♠ A nova that has flared to 6th or 7th magnitude on five known occasions since 1890, the last in 1966.

THE COMPASS

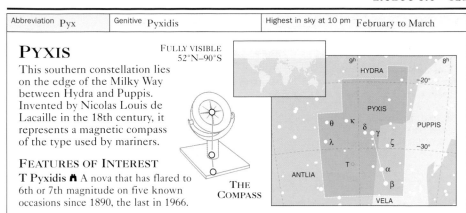

Width 🖑	Depth 🖑	Area 221 square degrees	Size ranking 65th

Abbreviation Ret	Genitive Reticuli	Highest in sky at 10 pm December

RETICULUM

FULLY VISIBLE
23°N–90°S

This small southern constellation near the Large Magellanic Cloud dates from the 18th century. It depicts a device called a grid or reticle, which was used in telescope eyepieces for recording star positions. The brightest star in the constellation is Alpha (α) Reticuli, magnitude 3.3.

THE NET

FEATURES OF INTEREST

Zeta (ζ) Reticuli ◉ ♠ A double star, divisible with the naked eye. The two 5th-magnitude yellow stars, similar to the Sun, both lie 39 light years away.

Width 🖑	Depth 🖑	Area 114 square degrees	Size ranking 82nd

Abbreviation Sge	Genitive Sagittae	Highest in sky at 10 pm August

SAGITTA

THE ARROW   FULLY VISIBLE
90°N–69°S

Although it lies in the Milky Way, with Vulpecula and Cygnus to the north and Aquila to the south, Sagitta contains little that is of interest. The third-smallest constellation, it has been visualized since ancient Greek times as an arrow, with its brightest star, Gamma (γ) Sagittae, magnitude 3.5, marking the arrowhead.

FEATURES OF INTEREST

M71 ♠ ⚹ A small globular cluster, visible with binoculars or a small telescope.

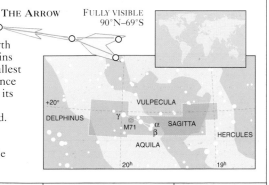

Width 🖑	Depth 🖑	Area 80 square degrees	Size ranking 86th

Abbreviation Sgr	Genitive Sagittarii	Highest in sky at 10 pm July to August

SAGITTARIUS

This constellation of the zodiac lies between Scorpius and Capricornus. It depicts Crotus, the son of the Greek god Pan and the inventor of archery, aiming his bow at a scorpion, represented by the neighbouring constellation of Scorpius. The centre of our Galaxy lies in the same direction as Sagittarius, and binoculars show that the star fields in this part of the Milky Way are particularly dense. The Sun passes through Sagittarius from 18 December to 19 January, a period that includes the December solstice. The constellation's brightest star is Epsilon (ε) Sagittarii, magnitude 1.8.

THE ARCHER

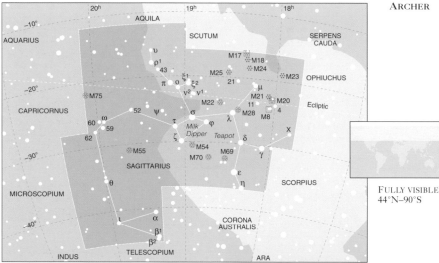

FULLY VISIBLE
44°N–90°S

FEATURES OF INTEREST

The Teapot ◉ A group of eight stars: Gamma (γ), Epsilon (ε), Delta (δ), Lambda (λ), Phi (φ), Zeta (ζ), Sigma (σ), and Tau (τ) Sagittarii. Together, they form the outline of a teapot, with a pointed lid and a large spout. The stars Lambda (λ), Phi (φ), Zeta (ζ), Sigma (σ), and Tau (τ) Sagittarii also form a shape known as the Milk Dipper, so named because it lies in a rich area of the Milky Way.

Beta (β) Sagittarii ◉ ♖ A multiple star, although all the components lie at different distances and are unrelated. The naked eye shows it as a wide double with components of magnitudes 4.0 and 4.3. The brighter star, Beta-1 (β¹), has a 7th-magnitude companion that can be seen through a small telescope.

THE MAIN STARS IN SAGITTARIUS
The Teapot is at the centre in this picture. Also visible are M7 (an open cluster in Scorpius) at centre right, and the arc of Corona Australis below the Teapot.

Width 🖐🖐	Depth 🖐🖑	Area 867 square degrees	Size ranking 15th

M8 (The Lagoon Nebula) ◉ 🔭 A bright nebula, visible to the naked eye and a good target for binoculars. Elongated in shape, it is almost three times the apparent width of the full Moon. A dark lane of dust bisects it: one half contains the cluster NGC 6530, with stars of 7th magnitude and fainter, while the most prominent object in the other half is the 6th-magnitude star 9 Sagittarii. The nebula, and the stars within it, are 5,200 light years away.

M17 (The Omega Nebula) 🔭 A cloud of glowing gas of similar apparent size to the full Moon. It can be seen through binoculars, although a telescope is needed to see its true shape. A small telescope shows a star cluster NGC 6618, within the cloud. The nebula and cluster both lie about 4,900 light years away.

M20 (The Trifid Nebula) 🔭 A nebula with a faint double star at its centre, both visible with a small telescope. Larger apertures, and photographs, show dust lanes trisecting the nebula.

M22 🔭 The third-brightest globular cluster in the sky, 10,000 light years away. It is just visible to the naked eye under good conditions and easy to find with binoculars, which show it as a rounded patch about two-thirds the apparent size of the full Moon. A telescope of moderate aperture resolves its brightest stars.

M23 🔭 A rich open cluster, elongated in shape and almost the same apparent width as the full Moon. It can be seen with binoculars, while a small telescope will resolve its stars. It lies 2,100 light years away.

M24 ◉ 🔭 A large and bright field of stars in the Milky Way, visible to the naked eye and an excellent sight through binoculars. A small telescope reveals a small open cluster, NGC 6603, within it.

M25 🔭 An open cluster, just visible to the naked eye and a good object for observation with binoculars or a small telescope. Its stars, of 7th magnitude and fainter, are scattered over an area of sky the same apparent size as the full Moon. It lies 1,900 light years away.

M17 (THE OMEGA NEBULA)
When viewed with a telescope, this nebula resembles the capital letter Omega (Ω) in the Greek alphabet.

M20 (THE TRIFID NEBULA)
A telescope reveals the three main lanes of dust that cross this nebula and give rise to its popular name.

Abbreviation Sco	Genitive Scorpii	Highest in sky at 10 pm June to July

SCORPIUS

A constellation of the zodiac, Scorpius lies between Libra and
Sagittarius. It depicts the scorpion that, in Greek mythology,
killed Orion with its sting – fittingly, Orion sets as Scorpius
rises. The constellation lies in a rich region of the Milky Way,
in the same direction as the centre of our Galaxy. The Sun
passes through it briefly, from 23 to 29 November. The old
version of its name, Scorpio, is used only in astrology.

THE
SCORPION

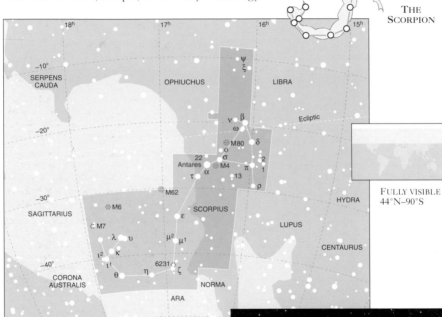

FULLY VISIBLE
44°N–90°S

FEATURES OF INTEREST

Alpha (α) Scorpii (Antares) ◉ ♣ A red
supergiant of variable brightness, ranging
between magnitudes 0.9 and 1.2 in a cycle
lasting approximately 4–5 years. It has a close
blue-white companion of 5th magnitude that
orbits it every 900 years or so and can be seen
with a telescope of moderate aperture. The
name Antares is usually translated as "rival of
Mars", referring to its reddish colour, although
it can also mean "like Mars".

Beta (β) Scorpii ⚹ A double star, which has
components of magnitudes 2.6 and 4.9 that are
easy to separate with a small telescope. The
two stars are unrelated, lying at distances of
530 and 1,100 light years.

THE MAIN STARS IN SCORPIUS
*The stars representing the scorpion's head are at the top
right here. Orange Antares marks the heart, and the
stars in the body and tail curve down and to the left.*

Width 🖐🤚	Depth 🖐🤚	Area 497 square degrees	Size ranking 33rd

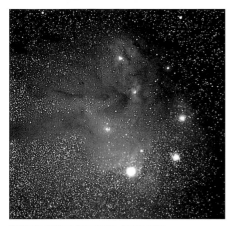

NEBULOSITY AROUND ANTARES
A faint area of nebulosity, visible only on long-exposure photographs, extends northwards from Antares (below centre in this picture) to Rho (ρ) Ophiuchi (top centre).

Zeta (ζ) Scorpii ◉ ♪ A wide pair of unrelated stars, divisible with the naked eye by those with good eyesight. Zeta-1 (ζ¹) is a blue-white supergiant of magnitude 4.7, the brightest star in the cluster NGC 6231 (see below). Zeta-2 (ζ²), a red giant of magnitude 3.6, is much closer at 150 light years away.

Mu (μ) Scorpii ◉ ♪ A double star that can be divided with the naked eye. The brighter component is an eclipsing binary that varies between magnitudes 2.9 and 3.2 every 1 day 10 hours. Its companion is of magnitude 3.6.

Nu (ν) Scorpii ⚹ A multiple star. A small telescope, or even good binoculars, will reveal an optical double, with components of

magnitudes 4.0 and 6.3. The fainter star of the pair has an 8th-magnitude companion that can be seen through a telescope with an aperture of 75 mm (3 in). Larger apertures – 100 mm (4 in) or more – show that the brighter star has an even closer companion, of 5th magnitude. Hence Nu Scorpii is an apparent quadruple.

Xi (ξ) Scorpii ⚹ A multiple star. Like Nu (ν) Scorpii, this is a quadruple. A small telescope reveals a pair of 5th- and 7th-magnitude stars; in the same field of view, a wider pair of 7th- and 8th-magnitude stars can also be seen.

Omega (ω) Scorpii ◉ ♪ A naked-eye double star, with components of magnitudes 3.9 and 4.3, 420 and 260 light years away.

M4 ♪ ⚹ One of the closest globular clusters to us, under 7,000 light years away. It can be seen with binoculars or a small telescope, but a dark sky is needed as its light is spread over a large area, two-thirds the apparent size of the Moon.

M6 ◉ ♪ ⚹ An open cluster, 2,000 light years away. It is visible to the naked eye, and its individual stars can be seen with binoculars. Its brightest star is BM Scorpii, an orange giant that varies between 5th and 7th magnitudes.

M7 ◉ ♪ A large, glorious open cluster, visible with the naked eye and binoculars and more than twice the apparent width of the full Moon. Its brightest stars, of 6th magnitude, are seen against a bright Milky Way background. The cluster is 780 light years away.

NGC 6231 ♪ ⚹ A prominent open cluster, 5,900 light years away. Its individual stars are easy to see with binoculars or a small telescope. The 5th-magnitude star Zeta-1 (ζ¹) Scorpii (see above) is its brightest member.

M4
This globular cluster, between Antares and Sigma (σ) Scorpii, is large but faint and hence difficult to see.

M6 AND M7
M6 is at centre right in this picture, with M7 to its left in front of the bright band of the Milky Way.

Abbreviation Scl	Genitive Sculptoris	Highest in sky at 10 pm October to November

SCULPTOR

SCULPTOR

This faint constellation is to the south of Aquarius and Cetus. It was invented in the 18th century by the French astronomer Nicolas Louis de Lacaille, who visualized it as a sculptor's studio, although its name has since been changed. Its brightest star, Alpha (α) Sculptoris, is of only magnitude 4.3. Sculptor contains the south pole of our Galaxy – the point 90 degrees south of the plane of the Milky Way. In this region, our view into the Universe is uninterrupted by intervening gas and dust in our Galaxy, so many faint and distant galaxies are visible. The north galactic pole lies in Coma Berenices.

FULLY VISIBLE
50°N–90°S

FEATURES OF INTEREST

Epsilon (ε) Sculptoris ⊀ A double star that can be divided with a small telescope. The 5th- and 9th-magnitude components are a true binary pair that orbit each other every 1,200 years or so. They are 89 light years away.

R Sculptoris ♠ A variable red giant that ranges between 6th and 8th magnitudes in a cycle lasting about a year.

NGC 55 ⊀ A spiral galaxy, tilted nearly edge-on to us, so that it appears cigar-shaped when viewed with a small telescope.

NGC 253 ♠⊀ A spiral galaxy. Like NGC 55, it appears to us edge-on but it is brighter and hence visible with binoculars. A telescope of moderate to large aperture shows traces of dark dust clouds silhouetted against its stars.

NGC 253 AND NGC 288
These two objects are in the northern part of Sculptor. NGC 288 (on the left in this picture) is a globular cluster that can be seen through a telescope. The spiral galaxy NGC 253 is on the right.

Width ♘♘	Depth ♘	Area 475 square degrees	Size ranking 36th

Abbreviation Sct	Genitive Scuti	Highest in sky at 10 pm July to August

SCUTUM

Scutum is a small constellation that lies just south of the celestial equator in a rich area of the Milky Way between Aquila and Sagittarius. It was introduced in the late 17th century by the Polish astronomer Johannes Hevelius, who originally termed it Sobieski's Shield in honour of his patron, King John Sobieski. Its brightest star is Alpha (α) Scuti, magnitude 3.9.

THE SHIELD

FULLY VISIBLE
74°N–90°S

M11 (THE WILD DUCK CLUSTER)

The open cluster M11 lies in a bright section of the Milky Way near the border between Aquila and Scutum. On this photograph, taken through a telescope, it is just possible to see the V-shape, with the apex at the top right of the cluster.

FEATURES OF INTEREST

Delta (δ) Scuti ◉ ♠ A pulsating giant, the prototype of a class of variable stars that show very small fluctuations in brightness (a few tenths of a magnitude or less) over short periods of time (no more than a few hours). Delta Scuti itself varies between magnitudes 4.6 and 4.8 over a period of less than 5 hours. It lies 190 light years away.

R Scuti ♠ A pulsating orange supergiant, which varies between magnitudes 4.2 and 8.6 in a 20-week cycle.

M11 (The Wild Duck Cluster) ♠ ☀ A rich open cluster, consisting of hundreds of stars, visible in binoculars as a fuzzy ball nearly half the apparent size of the full Moon. In a small telescope it appears V-shaped, like a flight of ducks, hence its popular name. Near the apex of the V is the cluster's brightest star, of 8th

magnitude. M11 is 5,600 light years away and lies on the northern edge of a particularly bright section of the Milky Way known as the Scutum Star Cloud.

Width 🖐	Depth 🖐	Area 109 square degrees	Size ranking 84th

Abbreviation Ser	Genitive Serpentis	Highest in sky at 10pm June to August

SERPENS

Uniquely, Serpens consists of two separate areas that, taken together, are regarded as one constellation. It depicts a serpent coiled around Ophiuchus, who holds the head (Serpens Caput) in his left hand and the tail (Serpens Cauda) in his right. The constellation's brightest star, Alpha (α) Serpentis, magnitude 2.6, is also known as Unukalhai, a name derived from an Arabic term that means "the serpent's neck".

THE SERPENT

FULLY VISIBLE
74°N–64°S

FEATURES OF INTEREST

Delta (δ) Serpentis ✶ A binary star. The 4th-magnitude primary and its 5th-magnitude partner can be divided with a small telescope and high magnification. Their orbital period is estimated to be several thousand years.

Theta (θ) Serpentis ✶ A wide double star. The components, of magnitudes 4.6 and 5.0, can be separated through a small telescope.

Nu (ν) Serpentis ♏✶ A wide double, with 4th- and 8th-magnitude components that are divisible with binoculars or a small telescope.

Tau-1 (τ¹) Serpentis ♏ The brightest and easternmost member of a triangular field of stars that fans out towards Iota (ι) and Kappa (κ) Serpentis.

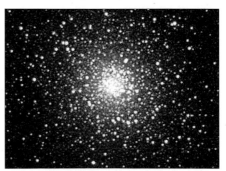

M5
This globular cluster in the southern part of Serpens Caput is visible through binoculars. It is one of the finest objects of its type in northern skies.

Width 🖐🖐🖐	Depth 🖐🖐	Area 637 square degrees	Size ranking 23rd

M5 ♄ ⚹ A globular cluster, about 25,000 light years away. It can be seen through binoculars, appearing about half the size of the full Moon. A telescope of moderate aperture resolves its brightest stars; it also reveals a condensed centre and chains of stars in the outer regions.

M16 ♄ ⚹ An open cluster, visible through binoculars or a small telescope. It appears hazy, since the stars are embedded in the Eagle Nebula, which shows up well only with larger apertures and on photographs. Cluster and nebula are over 8,000 light years away.

◁ THE EAGLE NEBULA
This nebula can be seen through a telescope of large aperture or on a long-exposure photograph.

▽ DARK COLUMNS IN THE EAGLE NEBULA
This close-up, taken by the Hubble Space Telescope, shows dark fingers of dust against areas of brighter gas.

Abbreviation Sex	Genitive Sextantis	Highest in sky at 10 pm March to April

SEXTANS

This faint constellation is on the celestial equator, south of Leo. It was invented in the late 17th century by the Polish astronomer Johannes Hevelius and represents the sextant with which he measured star positions. Its brightest star is Alpha (α) Sextantis, magnitude 4.5.

THE SEXTANT

FULLY VISIBLE
78°N–83°S

FEATURES OF INTEREST

17 and 18 Sextantis ◐ ♄ A wide pair of unrelated stars, detectable with the naked eye by those with good eyesight and easy to divide with binoculars. They are of magnitudes 5.9 and 5.6, and lie 530 and 470 light years away.

NGC 3115 (The Spindle Galaxy) ⚹
An elliptical galaxy, visible through a telescope of small to moderate aperture. Its elongated shape gives rise to its popular name.

Width 🖐	Depth 🖐	Area 314 square degrees	Size ranking 47th

Abbreviation Tau	Genitive Tauri	Highest in sky at 10 pm December to January

TAURUS

This imposing constellation of the zodiac lies between Aries and Gemini. It represents the bull into which the Greek god Zeus transformed himself to abduct Princess Europa of Phoenicia. Zeus then swam to Crete with the princess on his back. The constellation represents the front half of the bull's body – the part visible above the Mediterranean waves. It contains two major star clusters, the Pleiades and Hyades. In mythology, the Pleiades were the seven daughters of Atlas and Pleione, and the cluster is also known as the Seven Sisters; the Hyades were the daughters of Atlas and Aethra. In the sky, the Hyades cluster marks the bull's face, while the red giant star Aldebaran forms the creature's bloodshot eye. The tips of the bull's horns are marked by Beta (β) and Zeta (ζ) Tauri, magnitudes 1.7 and 3.0. The Sun passes through Taurus from 14 May to 21 June.

THE
BULL

FULLY VISIBLE
88°N–58°S

M1 (THE CRAB NEBULA)
This remarkable object is the remains of a massive star that exploded as a supernova.

FEATURES OF INTEREST

Alpha (α) Tauri (Aldebaran) ◉ A red giant star, which varies irregularly in brightness between magnitudes 0.75 and 0.95. Although it appears to be a member of the Hyades cluster, it is actually much closer to us, being 65 light years away.

Theta (θ) Tauri ◉ ♏ A wide double star in the Hyades cluster. Observers with good eyesight can divide the two stars with the naked eye. Theta-1 ($θ^1$) is a yellow giant, magnitude 3.8; Theta-2 ($θ^2$) is a white giant of magnitude 3.4, the brightest member of the Hyades.

Width 👐 👐	Depth 👐 👐	Area 797 square degrees	Size ranking 17th

△ MAGNITUDE KEY

△ THE PLEIADES

△ THE HYADES AND
PLEIADES
*These two outstanding open clusters
lie close together in the sky.*

◁ THE HYADES

Lambda (λ) Tauri ◉ An eclipsing binary
star of the same type as Algol. It ranges
between magnitudes 3.4 and 3.9 in a cycle
lasting just under 4 days.

M1 (The Crab Nebula) ♠ ☈ The remains
of a supernova that was seen from Earth in
AD 1054. Under excellent conditions it can be
found with binoculars or a small telescope, but
a moderate aperture is needed to see it well.
It is elliptical in shape, appearing midway in
size between the disc of a planet and the full
Moon. It lies about 6,500 light years away.

M45 (The Pleiades) ◉ ♠ ☈ A large, bright
open star cluster, easy to see with the naked
eye and a superb sight through binoculars,

appearing almost four times wider than the
full Moon. Its brightest star is Eta (η) Tauri
(Alcyone), a blue-white giant of magnitude
2.9. Those with normal eyesight can see about
six stars, but dozens are visible with binoculars
or a small telescope. The cluster is about 380
light years away. Long-exposure photographs
show nebulosity around the stars, but a large
telescope is needed to see this directly.

The Hyades ◉ ♠ ☈ A large, loose, V-shaped
star cluster, easily visible to the naked eye.
It is best viewed with binoculars because of its
considerable size, being scattered across the
apparent width of 10 full Moons. The cluster
lies about 150 light years away.

Abbreviation Tel	Genitive Telescopii	Highest in sky at 10 pm July to August

TELESCOPIUM

This unremarkable constellation
south of Sagittarius was introduced
by the French astronomer Nicolas
Louis de Lacaille. In its original form,
it represented a large telescope supported
by a winch, but it is a poor tribute to such
an important instrument. Its brightest star
is Alpha (α) Telescopii, magnitude 3.5.

FULLY VISIBLE
33°N–90°S

THE
TELESCOPE

FEATURES OF INTEREST
Delta (δ) Telescopii ◉ ♠ An optical double
star, divisible without optical aid by those with
good eyesight and easy to see with binoculars.
Delta-1 (δ¹), magnitude 4.9, is about 800 light
years away; Delta-2 (δ²) is of magnitude 5.1
and lies more than 1,100 light years away.

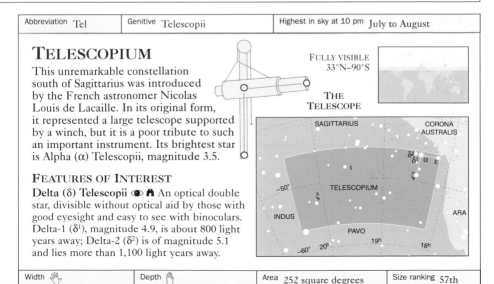

Width 🖐	Depth 🖐	Area 252 square degrees	Size ranking 57th

Abbreviation Tri	Genitive Trianguli	Highest in sky at 10 pm November to December

TRIANGULUM

This small constellation can be found between Andromeda and Aries. It was known to the ancient Greeks, many of whom visualized it as the Nile delta, while for others it represented the island of Sicily. Its brightest star is Beta (β) Trianguli, magnitude 3.0.

THE TRIANGLE

FULLY VISIBLE
90°N–52°S

FEATURES OF INTEREST

6 Trianguli ✶ A binary star. A small telescope is needed to divide the 5th-magnitude primary from its close 7th-magnitude companion.

M33 ♓✶ A spiral galaxy, about 2.6 million light years away and the third-largest member of the Local Group of galaxies. It covers about the same area of sky as the full Moon. Because its light is so spread out, a clear, dark sky is needed to see it. Under good conditions, this galaxy can be detected through binoculars or a small telescope.

Width	Depth	Area 132 square degrees	Size ranking 78th

Abbreviation TrA	Genitive Trianguli Australis	Highest in sky at 10 pm June to July

TRIANGULUM AUSTRALE

Lying in the Milky Way near Alpha (α) and Beta (β) Centauri is the southern counterpart of the northern triangle, Triangulum. Although smaller than Triangulum, it is more prominent because its main stars are brighter. It is the smallest of the 12 constellations introduced at the end of the 16th century by the Dutch navigators Pieter Dirkszoon Keyser and Frederick de Houtman. Its brightest star is Alpha (α) Trianguli Australis, magnitude 1.9.

THE SOUTHERN TRIANGLE

TRIANGULUM AUSTRALE
The three corners of the triangle stand out among the fainter stars in the surrounding Milky Way.

FULLY VISIBLE
19°N–90°S

FEATURES OF INTEREST

NGC 6025 ♓✶ An open cluster in the Milky Way, about one-third the apparent width of the full Moon and easy to see with binoculars or a small telescope, its brightest star being of 7th magnitude. It lies 2,700 light years away.

Width	Depth	Area 110 square degrees	Size ranking 83rd

Abbreviation Tuc	Genitive Tucanae	Highest in sky at 10 pm September to November

TUCANA

This southern constellation, representing a toucan, the large-beaked bird of South and Central America, lies close to the bright star Achernar and south of two other celestial birds, Grus and Phoenix. It was invented in the late 16th century by the Dutch navigators Pieter Dirkszoon Keyser and Frederick de Houtman. Its brightest star is Alpha (α) Tucanae, magnitude 2.9, but its most notable naked-eye object is the Small Magellanic Cloud.

THE
TOUCAN

FULLY VISIBLE
14°N–90°S

NGC 104 (47 TUCANAE)

A telescope of moderate aperture reveals that this spectacular globular cluster has a particularly bright, condensed centre and less dense outer regions.

FEATURES OF INTEREST

Beta (β) Tucanae ◉ ♠ ✷ A multiple star. When seen with the naked eye, or through binoculars, it appears as a double star with components of 4th and 5th magnitudes. A small telescope further divides the primary into components of magnitudes 4.4 and 4.5.

Kappa (κ) Tucanae ✷ A double star, with components of 5th and 8th magnitudes that can be separated through a small telescope.

NGC 104 (47 Tucanae) ◉ ♠ ✷ A globular cluster, rated the second-best of its type in the whole sky. To the naked eye, it appears similar to a hazy star of 4th magnitude. Binoculars or a small telescope show it covering the same area of sky as the full Moon, although an aperture of 100 mm (4 in) is needed to resolve its stars. The cluster lies 15,000 light years away.

NGC 362 ♠ ✷ A globular cluster, visible with binoculars or a small telescope. It appears to

lie near the Small Magellanic Cloud (see below) but is, in fact, only 29,000 light years away and hence is in our own Galaxy.

The Small Magellanic Cloud (SMC)

◉ ♠ ✷ The smaller of the Milky Way's two satellite galaxies. It appears to the naked eye as an elongated patch of light seven times wider than the full Moon, while binoculars or a small telescope resolve individual clusters and nebulae within it. This galaxy is much smaller than our own, having only a few per cent our Galaxy's mass and less than 10 per cent of its diameter. It is about 190,000 light years away.

Width 〰	Depth 〰	Area 295 square degrees	Size ranking 48th

Abbreviation UMa	Genitive Ursae Majoris	Highest in sky at 10 pm February to May

URSA MAJOR

THE GREAT
BEAR

Ursa Major is among the most famous constellations. It is the third-largest in the sky, occupying a much wider area than that covered by the group of seven stars that form the asterism of the Plough (or Big Dipper). Ursa Major represents Callisto, a mortal in Greek myth and a hunting partner of Artemis, who was seduced by Zeus. In different versions of the story, she was turned into a bear either by Zeus's jealous wife, Hera, or by the angry Artemis. Its brightest stars are Alpha (α) and Epsilon (ε) Ursae Majoris, both magnitude 1.8. A line drawn from Beta (β) through Alpha (α) Ursae Majoris points towards Polaris, the north Pole Star, in adjacent Ursa Minor.

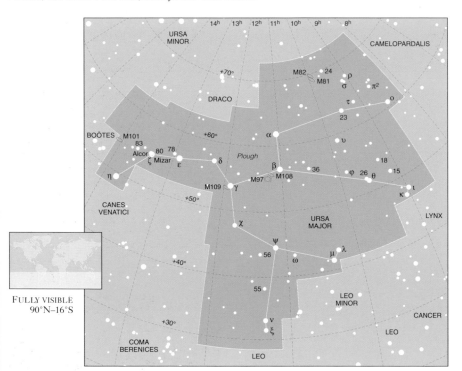

FULLY VISIBLE
90°N–16°S

FEATURES OF INTEREST

The Plough (The Big Dipper) ◉ One of the best-known patterns in the sky, consisting of the naked-eye stars Alpha (α), Beta (β), Gamma (γ), Delta (δ), Epsilon (ε), Zeta (ζ), and Eta (η) Ursae Majoris. The outline that they form is visualized in various cultures as that of a plough, a ladle, a saucepan, and even a wagon. All the stars in the Plough, with the exception of the outermost two (Alpha and Eta), are travelling in the same direction through space and form what is known as a moving cluster.

Zeta (ζ) Ursae Majoris (Mizar) ◉ ♙ ⚹
A multiple star. Observers with good eyesight or using binoculars will see that this star, of

Width 🤚🤚🤚	Depth 🤚🤚	Area 1,280 square degrees	Size ranking 3rd

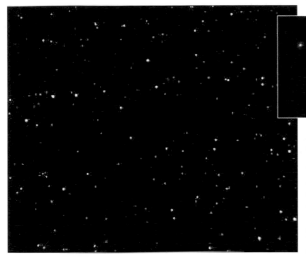

URSA MAJOR (INSET: MIZAR
AND ALCOR)
*The main photograph shows the
whole of the Great Bear, with the
Plough (or Big Dipper) forming
the animal's rump and tail. Mizar,
the second star in the handle of the
Plough (at the right of the inset
picture), forms an optical double
with Alcor (left of inset) and a true
binary with its closer companion.*

magnitude 2.2, has a partner of magnitude 4.0, known as Alcor or 80 Ursae Majoris. Mizar and Alcor are 78 and 81 light years away, so they are not a true binary pair. However, a small telescope reveals that Mizar has a closer 4th-magnitude companion. This pair forms a true binary with a very long orbital period.

Xi (ξ) Ursae Majoris ✶ A binary star, with close components of magnitudes 4.3 and 4.8 that can be separated through a telescope of 75 mm (3 in) aperture. The yellowish stars, similar to the Sun, are 26 light years away and have an orbital period of 60 years.

M81 and M82 ✴✶ Two contrasting galaxies, about 10 million light years away. M81 is a beautiful spiral, visible with binoculars or a small telescope. One Moon diameter to the north is the smaller and fainter M82, a galaxy of peculiar appearance, which is now thought to be a spiral seen edge-on that is passing through a dust cloud.

M101 ✴✶ A spiral galaxy, which appears face-on to us. It covers almost as much sky as the full Moon but it is quite faint, and good conditions are required if it is to be seen with binoculars or a small telescope.

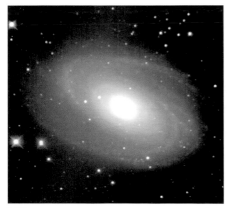

M81
This beautiful spiral galaxy is one of the easiest examples of its type to see with a small telescope.

M101
The arms of this spiral galaxy can be seen with a large telescope or on a long-exposure photograph.

Abbreviation UMi	Genitive Ursae Minoris	Highest in sky at 10 pm May to June

URSA MINOR

Ursa Minor contains the north celestial pole. By chance, there is a moderately bright star, known as Polaris (or the north Pole Star), about 1 degree from the pole. Navigators have long recognized that when looking at Polaris one is facing almost due north. Ursa Minor's main stars form a shape known as the Little Dipper, while the stars Beta (β) and Gamma (γ) Ursae Minoris (Kochab and Pherkad), in the dipper's bowl, are known as the Guardians of the Pole. Ursa Minor is named after a nymph who nursed the infant Zeus, although it is not clear why she is depicted as a bear.

THE LESSER BEAR

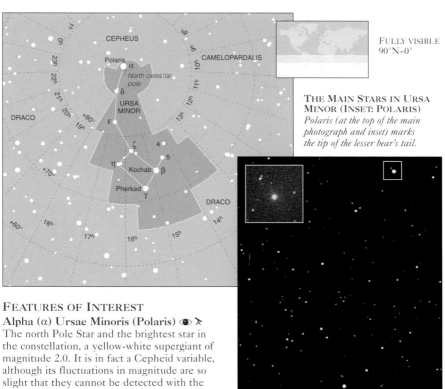

FULLY VISIBLE
90°N–0°

THE MAIN STARS IN URSA MINOR (INSET: POLARIS)
Polaris (at the top of the main photograph and inset) marks the tip of the lesser bear's tail.

FEATURES OF INTEREST

Alpha (α) Ursae Minoris (Polaris) ◉ ⚹

The north Pole Star and the brightest star in the constellation, a yellow-white supergiant of magnitude 2.0. It is in fact a Cepheid variable, although its fluctuations in magnitude are so slight that they cannot be detected with the naked eye. A small telescope shows an unrelated 8th-magnitude companion.

Gamma (γ) Ursae Minoris (Pherkad) ◉ ♙

An optical double star, with components that are divisible with the naked eye or binoculars. Gamma itself is a blue-white giant star of magnitude 3.0, 480 light years away. Its partner, 11 Ursae Minoris, is an orange giant, of magnitude 5.0, 390 light years away.

Eta (η) Ursae Minoris ◉ ♙ An optical

double star. It is a white star of magnitude 5.0, lying 97 light years away. The naked eye and binoculars show a wide companion, 19 Ursae Minoris, of magnitude 5.5, which is almost seven times further away than the primary.

Width 🖐	Depth 🖐🖐	Area 256 square degrees	Size ranking 56th

Abbreviation Vel	Genitive Velorum	Highest in sky at 10 pm February to April

VELA

This is one of the three parts into which the ancient Greek constellation of Argo Navis (the ship of the argonauts) was divided by Nicolas Louis de Lacaille. It represents the sails of the ship. Vela lies in the Milky Way with Carina and Puppis, the other two portions of the ship, on one side, and Centaurus on the other. Since it is only a part of the once-larger constellation, Vela contains no stars labelled Alpha (α) or Beta (β).

THE SAILS

FULLY VISIBLE
32°N–90°S

NGC 3132 (THE EIGHT-BURST NEBULA)
Long-exposure photographs such as this one reveal the loops of gas, intertwined like figures of eight, after which this nebula is named.

FEATURES OF INTEREST

Gamma (γ) Velorum ♠ ⚹ A multiple star. Through a small telescope or even good binoculars, it appears as a wide double star. The primary, Gamma-2 (γ^2), is the brightest star in the constellation, at magnitude 1.8. It is a spectroscopic binary, one component of which is a Wolf–Rayet star, a rare type of ultra-hot star that has lost its outer hydrogen layers. The primary's visible partner, Gamma-1 (γ^1), is an ordinary blue-white star of magnitude 4.3. There are also two wider companions of 8th and 9th magnitudes, which are visible through a small telescope.

NGC 2547 ♠ ⚹ An open cluster, visible with binoculars or a small telescope. It is more than half the apparent size of the full Moon and lies 1,300 light years away.

NGC 3132 (The Eight-Burst Nebula) ⚹ A planetary nebula. Its rounded disc is visible with a small telescope, which may also reveal the 10th-magnitude star at its centre. Photographs show complex loops within the nebula.

IC 2391 ⬤ ♠ ⚹ A large open cluster, visible to the naked eye and an ideal object for binocular observation, covering a greater area of sky than the full Moon. Its brightest star is Omicron (o) Velorum, magnitude 3.6. The cluster lies nearly 600 light years away.

Width	Depth	Area 500 square degrees	Size ranking 32nd

Abbreviation Vir	Genitive Virginis	Highest in sky at 10 pm April to June

VIRGO

This is the largest constellation of the zodiac and the second largest of all the constellations. It lies on the celestial equator between Leo and Libra. The constellation is usually identified as Dike, the Greek goddess of justice, or sometimes as Demeter, the corn goddess. Virgo is of particular interest because it contains the nearest large cluster of galaxies, the Virgo Cluster. The Sun passes through the constellation from 16 September to 31 October.

THE VIRGIN

FULLY VISIBLE
67°N–75°S

FEATURES OF INTEREST

Alpha (α) Virginis (Spica) ● The brightest star in Virgo and, at magnitude 1.0, among the 20 brightest in the sky. It is a blue-white star, 260 light years away. Spica is Latin for "ear of wheat", an object Virgo holds in her left hand.

Gamma (γ) Virginis ⋆ A binary star. To the naked eye, it looks like one star of magnitude 2.7. In fact, there are two yellow-white stars (both of magnitude 3.5) orbiting a common centre of mass every 169 years. This motion affects the stars' appearance: around 2005, when they will be closest to each other as seen from Earth, a 250 mm (10 in) aperture will be needed to divide them. They will then move rapidly apart, coming within range of a 100 mm (4 in) telescope by 2010, and will be divisible with a small aperture for the rest of the century.

M87 ⋆ A famous giant elliptical galaxy near the centre of the Virgo Cluster (see below).

It is probably the easiest member of the cluster to see through a small telescope.

M104 (The Sombrero Galaxy) ⋆ A spiral galaxy that appears almost edge-on to us and looks elongated when seen with a small telescope. Larger apertures show a dark lane of dust in the spiral arms, crossing the central nucleus of stars. The galaxy is not part of the Virgo Cluster, but lies somewhat closer to us.

The Virgo Cluster (The Virgo–Coma Cluster) ⋆ A cluster of 2,000 or more galaxies, about 50 million light years away, that extends from Virgo into Coma Berenices. Its brightest members, notably the elliptical galaxies M49, M60, M84, M86, and M87, are visible with the size of telescope used by amateur observers.

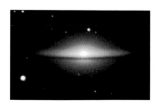

M104 (THE SOMBRERO GALAXY) *This spiral galaxy owes its name to its flattened appearance.*

Width 🖐🖐🖐	Depth 🖐🖐	Area 1,294 square degrees	Size ranking 2nd

Abbreviation Vol	Genitive Volantis	Highest in sky at 10 pm January to March

VOLANS

THE FLYING FISH

This faint southern constellation adjoins Carina. Invented at the end of the 16th century by the Dutch navigators Pieter Dirkszoon Keyser and Frederick de Houtman, it represents the fish of tropical waters that can glide above the waves on its outstretched fins.

FULLY VISIBLE
14°N–90°S

FEATURES OF INTEREST

Gamma (γ) Volantis ✻ An attractive double star. A small telescope reveals its orange and yellow components, of magnitudes 3.8 and 5.7.

Epsilon (ε) Volantis ✻ A double star with 4th- and 7th-magnitude components that can be divided with a small telescope.

Width	Depth	Area 141 square degrees	Size ranking 76th

Abbreviation Vul	Genitive Vulpeculae	Highest in sky at 10 pm August to September

VULPECULA

Vulpecula is in the Milky Way, to the south of Cygnus. When it was introduced in the late 17th century by the Polish astronomer Johannes Hevelius, it was named Vulpecula cum Anser (the Fox and Goose). Its brightest star is Alpha (α) Vulpeculae, magnitude 4.4.

THE FOX

FULLY VISIBLE
90°N–61°S

FEATURES OF INTEREST

M27 (The Dumbbell Nebula) ♠✻ A large planetary nebula, appearing through binoculars as a rounded patch about a quarter the size of the full Moon. Its twin-lobed shape, which explains its popular name, can be seen with a telescope of moderate to large aperture or on a photograph. It is about 1,000 light years away.

Brocchi's Cluster (Collinder 399, The Coathanger) ♠ An unusual open cluster that is easy to find with binoculars. It consists of a line of six stars of 6th and 7th magnitudes, from the centre of which extends a "hook" formed by four other stars, giving it the appearance of a coathanger.

BROCCHI'S CLUSTER
This open cluster lies in the southern part of Vulpecula, within the division in the Milky Way known as the Cygnus Rift.

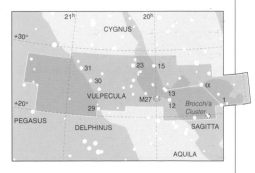

Width	Depth	Area 268 square degrees	Size ranking 55th

MONTHLY SKY GUIDES

HOW THIS SECTION WORKS

THIS SECTION INCLUDES detailed sky charts for every month of the year, with a separate chart for each hemisphere. Each month is introduced by a double-page feature, which looks at interesting celestial phenomena and uses simplified charts to assist in identifying prominent stars and constellations.

USING THE CHARTS

Both the introductory charts (see below) and the whole-sky charts (see opposite) show the night sky as it appears from latitudes 60–20°N (northern hemisphere) and 0–40°S (southern hemisphere). Use the world map (right) to identify your own latitude and associated colour code, then decide which hemisphere map is best for you. You can then use the colour-coded lines and crosses on all charts to identify the viewing horizon and zenith (point overhead) for your latitude. Compared with the whole-sky charts, the introductory charts show a simplified and less detailed view of the night sky.

80°N
60°N
40°N
20°N
0
20°S
40°S
60°S

△ FINDING YOUR COLOUR CODE
Use this map to identify the colour of the latitude line nearest to your geographical location. Bear in mind that 10 degrees difference in latitude will have little effect on the stars you can actually see.

times of sunrise and sunset in mid-month •

photograph of easily recognizable star pattern • *or bright deep-sky object*

key to star • *magnitudes*

clocks indicate times at which charts apply (see panel opposite) •

panel refers to objects shown on whole-sky charts on following pages •

text draws attention to bright stars and prominent constellations visible in the month •

descriptions of stars and deep-sky objects •

charts show all stars brighter than magnitude 3.0 and a selection of constellation patterns •

cross-references to well-placed features described under other months •

colour-coded lines define view from zenith to eastern and western horizons •

description of bright meteor showers (not shown on charts) •

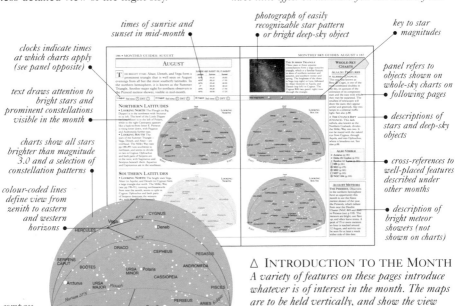

△ INTRODUCTION TO THE MONTH
A variety of features on these pages introduce whatever is of interest in the month. The maps are to be held vertically, and show the view ahead and to the sides, facing north or south.

compass direction •

colour-coded horizon lines •

• *ecliptic*

HOW TO USE THE WHOLE-SKY CHARTS

To view the sky to the south, hold the book flat with the SOUTH *label (at the edge of the chart) nearest your body. Your colour-coded line (around the near edge of the chart) indicates the horizon in front of you; the cross near the chart centre represents the*

zenith (the point directly overhead). The area of the chart beyond your zenith represents the sky to the north; to view this, turn the book around.

when looking south, hold right-hand edge of book nearest to you •

STAR-MOTION DIAGRAMS

N ⟲ S	N ⟲ S
NORTHERN HEMISPHERE	SOUTHERN HEMISPHERE

Next to each whole-sky chart is a diagram showing the direction in which the stars appear to move as the night progresses. The arrows show a general motion from east to west, due to the Earth's rotation, but circumpolar stars (at one end of each chart, as shown by the diagram) rotate around one of the celestial poles without setting.

WHOLE-SKY CHART ▷

chart shows all stars brighter than magnitude 5.0 •

all 88 constellation patterns are plotted on the charts •

symbol for deep-sky object •

colour-coded crosses indicate zeniths from various latitudes •

compass direction •

colour-coded horizon lines for use when facing north •

key to star magnitudes •

• *star-motion diagram (see above)*

• *colour-coded horizon lines for use when facing south*

• *ecliptic (useful for locating planets)*

• *Milky Way*

• *centre of chart shows sky directly overhead*

sides of chart show stars • *visible to east and west*

table shows times when chart is applicable • *(see panel below)*

• *key to deep-sky objects*

TIME

The charts for a particular month show the sky as it appears at 10 PM in mid-month – that is, at 10 PM standard (Std) time for a particular time zone. When daylight-saving time (DST or summer time) is in use, they show the sky as it appears one hour later. The sky will look the same at 11 PM at the start of the month and at 9 PM at the end

of the month as it does at 10 PM in mid-month. If you wish to look at the sky at a different time, you will need to use charts shown under a different month: for every two hours of time before or after 10 PM, go one month backwards or forwards. So, if you want to look at the sky at midnight on 15 January, turn to the chart for February.

JANUARY

JANUARY EVENING SKIES are the most magnificent of the year, with Orion surrounded by a host of bright stars, including Sirius, the brightest of all. From southern latitudes, Canopus, the second-brightest star, and the nearby small galaxy known as the Large Magellanic Cloud add to the richness of the scene.

SUNRISE AND SUNSET ON 15 JANUARY		
Latitude	Sunrise	Sunset
60°N	08.50	15.30
40°N	07.20	17.00
20°N	06.40	17.40
0°	06.10	18.10
20°S	05.30	18.50
40°S	04.50	19.30

1 January Std time 🕐 DST 🕐   15 January Std time 🕐 DST 🕐   30 January Std time 🕐 DST 🕐

NORTHERN LATITUDES

• **LOOKING NORTH** The saucepan shape of the Plough (or Big Dipper) stands on its handle to the right of Polaris, the Pole Star. The W-shape of Cassiopeia is to Polaris's left, with Cepheus beneath it. Capella is almost overhead. Leo rises in the northeast, while the Great Square of Pegasus sets in the northwest.

• **LOOKING SOUTH** Magnificent Orion commands centre stage, to the right of his dogs, marked by Sirius (in Canis Major) and Procyon (in Canis Minor). Aldebaran glints above and to the right of Orion, with the Pleiades cluster (see p.147) higher and further to the right. Nearly overhead are Castor and Pollux, along with Capella.

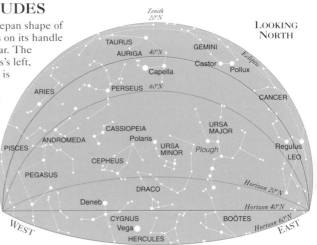

SOUTHERN LATITUDES

• **LOOKING NORTH** Orion stands high, with Capella and the other stars of Auriga closer to the northern horizon. Brilliant Sirius and Procyon are visible to Orion's right. Aldebaran and the stars of Taurus are to the lower left of Orion, with Castor and Pollux to Orion's lower right, in the northeast. Perseus sets in the northwest.

• **LOOKING SOUTH** Canopus is high in the south, with Sirius above it, almost overhead. Lower down, to the southwest, Achernar marks the end of the celestial river, Eridanus. Just below Canopus is the Large Magellanic Cloud (LMC); the Small Magellanic Cloud (SMC) is to its lower right (see p.149).

ORION'S BELT
The three stars at the centre of this picture form a distinctive line that marks the belt of Orion, the hunter (pp.114–15). They are (from left to right): Delta (δ) Orionis (also known as Mintaka), Epsilon (ε) Orionis (Alnilam), and Zeta (ζ) Orionis (Alnitak).

Star magnitudes	−1	0	1	2	3

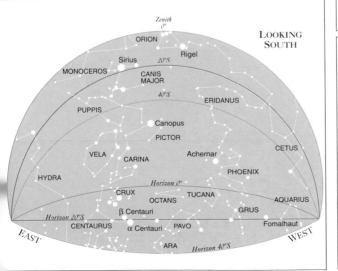

WHOLE-SKY CHARTS

JANUARY FEATURES

☐ **M42 (ORION).** This diffuse nebula forms part of the sword that hangs from Orion's belt. It is one of the most celebrated objects in the entire sky and the most prominent of all nebulae, being visible to the naked eye under good conditions as a hazy, milky white or greenish patch, although it is better seen with binoculars. A huge cloud of dust and gas, M42 consists mainly of hydrogen gas, which shows as a reddish colour on photographs. It glows by the light of a star that formed within it, Theta-1 (θ¹) Orionis, also called the Trapezium since it in fact consists of four stars, visible through a small telescope. See also pp.114–15.

ALSO VISIBLE

- **Castor** (p.151)
- ✣ **M36, M37, and M38** (p.211)
- ✣ **M41** (p.151)
- ✣ **M44** (p.157)
- ☐ **NGC 2244** (p.151)
- **The Hyades and Pleiades** (p.211)

JANUARY METEORS

THE QUADRANTIDS. This shower, visible to northern-hemisphere observers only, appears in the first week of January, radiating from northern Boötes, near the handle of the Plough. This area was once known as the constellation of Quadrans, hence the shower's name. Activity reaches about 100 meteors an hour on 3 and 4 January, but the peak is short-lived, the meteors are usually faint, and the radiant does not rise very high until after midnight.

WHOLE-SKY CHART

Northern Latitudes

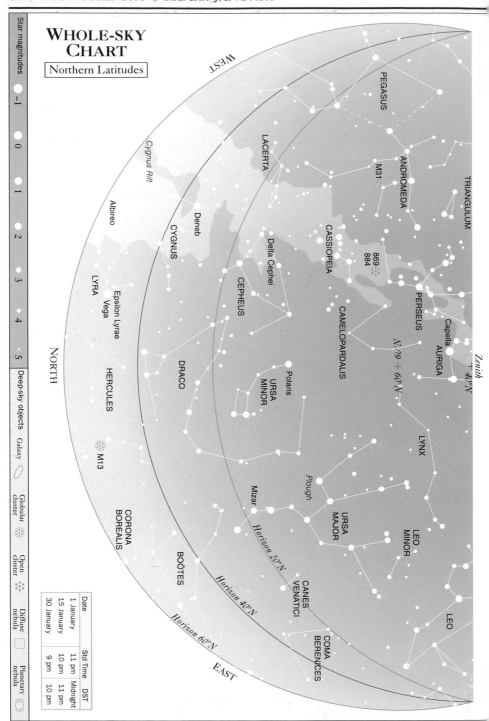

WEST

PEGASUS

LACERTA

M31

ANDROMEDA

TRIANGULUM

Cygnus Rift

Deneb

CASSIOPEIA

869
884

PERSEUS

Capella

AURIGA

Albireo

CYGNUS

Delta Cephei

CEPHEUS

CAMELOPARDALIS

Zenith
40° N

LYRA

Epsilon Lyrae
Vega

DRACO

Polaris
URSA
MINOR

Lat. 60° N

LYNX

NORTH

HERCULES

Plough

URSA
MAJOR

LEO
MINOR

M13

Mizar

Horizon 20° N

CANES
VENATICI

LEO

CORONA
BOREALIS

BOÖTES

Horizon 40° N

COMA
BERENICES

Horizon 60° N

EAST

Date	Std Time	DST
1 January	11 pm	Midnight
15 January	10 pm	11 pm
30 January	9 pm	10 pm

Star magnitudes

–1	0	1	2	3	4	5

Deep-sky objects	Galaxy	Globular cluster	Open cluster	Diffuse nebula	Planetary nebula

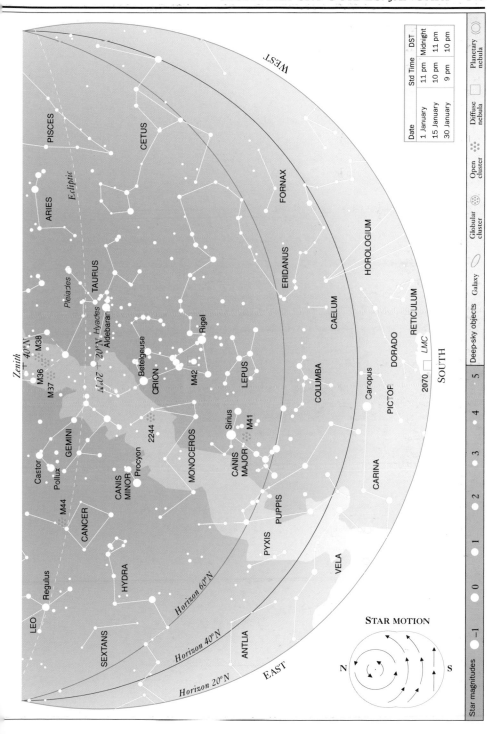

WEST

PISCES

CETUS

ARIES

Ecliptic

FORNAX

Pleiades

TAURUS

ERIDANUS

HOROLOGIUM

Hyades

40°N

20°N Aldebaran

Rigel

CAELUM

Zenith

M38

M36

M37

Betelgeuse

ORION

M42

LEPUS

RETICULUM

DORADO

LMC

2070

SOUTH

Castor

GEMINI

Pollux

CANIS

MINOR

Procyon

M44

2244

MONOCEROS

Sirius

CANIS

MAJOR M41

COLUMBA

Caropus

PICTOR

CARINA

CANCER

PUPPIS

LEO

Regulus

HYDRA

PYXIS

VELA

SEXTANS

ANTLIA

Horizon 60°N

Horizon 40°N

EAST

Horizon 20°N

Date	Std Time	DST
1 January	11 pm	Midnight
15 January	10 pm	11 pm
30 January	9 pm	10 pm

Planetary nebula						
Diffuse nebula						
Open cluster						
Globular cluster						
Galaxy						
Deep-sky objects						

STAR MOTION

N   S

| Star magnitudes | −1 | 0 | 1 | 2 | 3 | 4 | 5 |

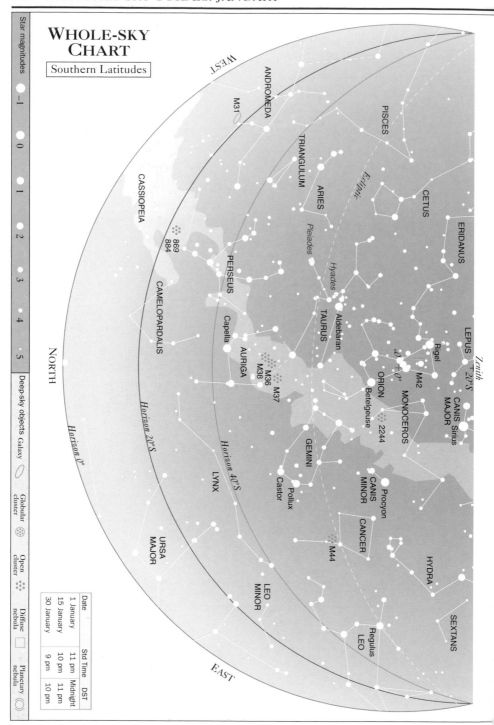

WHOLE-SKY CHART

Southern Latitudes

Star magnitudes

-1 0 1 2 3 4 .5

NORTH

Deep-sky objects: Galaxy ◯ | Globular cluster ◉ | Open cluster ⦂⦂ | Diffuse nebula ▢ | Planetary nebula ◎

Date	Std Time	DST
1 January	11 pm	Midnight
15 January	10 pm	11 pm
30 January	9 pm	10 pm

WEST

ANDROMEDA

M31

PISCES

TRIANGULUM

CETUS

ARIES

CASSIOPEIA

ERIDANUS

869
884

PERSEUS

Pleiades

Hyades

LEPUS

Zenith

20°S

CAMELOPARDALIS

Capella

TAURUS

Aldebaran

Rigel

CANIS
MAJOR Sirius

AURIGA

M38
M36

M37

Betelgeuse

ORION

M42

0°

MONOCEROS

2244

Horizon 20°S

GEMINI

CANIS
MINOR Procyon

Horizon 40°S

LYNX

Castor

Pollux

CANCER

HYDRA

Horizon 0°

URSA
MAJOR

M44

SEXTANS

LEO
MINOR

LEO Regulus

EAST

Ecliptic

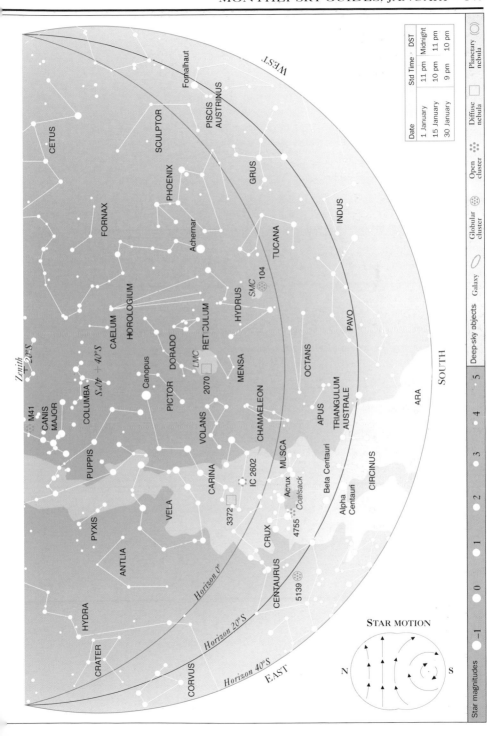

Date	Std Time • DST	
1 January	11 pm	Midnight
15 January	10 pm	11 pm
30 January	9 pm	10 pm

STAR MOTION

N   S

Star magnitudes   −1   0   1   2   3   4   5

Deep-sky objects   Galaxy   Globular cluster   Open cluster   Diffuse nebula   Planetary nebula

SOUTH

WEST

EAST

Zenith

Horizon 0°

Horizon 20°S

Horizon 40°S

CETUS
CANIS MAJOR
M41
COLUMBA
PUPPIS
PYXIS
ANTLIA
HYDRA
CRATER
CORVUS
VELA
CARINA
CRUX
CENTAURUS
5139
4755
Coalsack
Acrux
MUSCA
Beta Centauri
Alpha Centauri
CIRCINUS
IC 2602
3372
VOLANS
CHAMAELEON
APUS
TRIANGULUM AUSTRALE
ARA
CIRCINUS
PICTOR
Canopus
CAELUM
HOROLOGIUM
DORADO
LMC
2070
RETICULUM
MENSA
OCTANS
PAVO
FORNAX
SCULPTOR
PHOENIX
Achernar
HYDRUS
SMC
104
TUCANA
INDUS
PISCIS AUSTRINUS
Fomalhaut
GRUS

S 20°S
S 40° + 40°S

FEBRUARY

SIRIUS, the brightest star, is visible in the evening sky at all latitudes, while observers in the south can also see Canopus, the second-brightest star. High in southern skies are the three constellations – Carina, Puppis, and Vela – that the ancient Greeks regarded as one: Argo Navis, the ship of Jason and the Argonauts.

SUNRISE AND SUNSET ON 15 FEBRUARY		
Latitude	Sunrise	Sunset
60°N	07.40	16.50
40°N	06.50	17.40
20°N	06.30	18.00
0°	06.10	18.20
20°S	05.50	18.40
40°S	05.30	19.00

1 February Std time 🕐 DST 🕐 | 15 February Std time 🕐 DST 🕐 | 1 March Std time 🕐 DST 🕐

NORTHERN LATITUDES

• **LOOKING NORTH** Perseus and Cassiopeia are easy to find in the northwest, with the bright star Capella in Auriga above them. The familiar seven-star outline of the Plough (or Big Dipper) is the main feature in the northeast. Due north, the faint constellations Cepheus and Draco skim the horizon.

• **LOOKING SOUTH** Orion and Taurus are prominent in the southwest. Sirius, the brightest star in the sky, lies almost due south, with Procyon above and slightly to its left. Castor and Pollux, the two brightest stars in Gemini, are overhead, with Cancer to their left. In the southeast, the distinctive shape of Leo is becoming well placed.

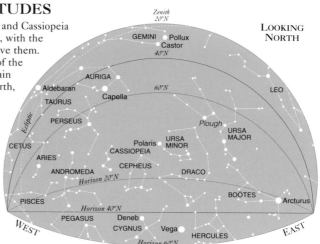

SOUTHERN LATITUDES

• **LOOKING NORTH** Castor and Pollux in Gemini lie due north, with Procyon in Canis Minor above them. Sirius shines near the zenith. The stars of Orion and Taurus are prominently placed in the northwest, while Leo follows Cancer into the northeastern sky.

• **LOOKING SOUTH** The three parts of Argo Navis, the ship of the Argonauts, are easily seen: Carina, the keel (with its brightest star Canopus); Puppis, the stern; and Vela, the sails, in between them. Achernar, in Eridanus, lies in the southwest with the Magellanic Clouds close by (see p.155). In the southeast, Centaurus and Crux (the Southern Cross) are rising.

THE WINTER TRIANGLE
Three brilliant stars in separate
constellations form an equilateral
triangle in the skies of northern
winter and southern summer.
Sirius in Canis Major forms the
southern apex, while Betelgeuse
(top right) in Orion and Procyon
(top left) in Canis Minor complete
the figure. The Winter Triangle
straddles the celestial equator, and
is clearly visible from all latitudes.

WHOLE-SKY CHARTS

FEBRUARY FEATURES

● CASTOR (GEMINI). This
star, also known as Alpha
(α) Geminorum, can be seen
as a close double through a
telescope with magnification
of about 100 times. The two
stars orbit each other about
every 470 years. There are
other stars connected to
Castor by gravity, too,
completing a family of six
stars in all, including a pair of
faint red dwarfs. All six stars
formed from the same cloud
of gas. See also p.96.

⁘ M41 (CANIS MAJOR).
Observers in high northern
latitudes often overlook this
open cluster four degrees
south of Sirius because from
their locations it lies close to
the horizon. However, it is
easy to see with binoculars
and can be detected with the
naked eye under favourable
conditions. See also p.74.

⁘ NGC 2244
(MONOCEROS). The
brightest members of this
large open cluster are easily
visible through binoculars.
The stars are arranged in a
rectangle, but the brightest
of them, 6th-magnitude 12
Monocerotis, is a foreground
object. The cluster lies at the
centre of the Rosette Nebula
(NGC 2237), a flower-like
loop of gas that shows up
well only on photographs.
See also pp.110–11.

Star magnitudes	●−1	●0	●1	•2	·3

Zenith
60°N

LOOKING SOUTH

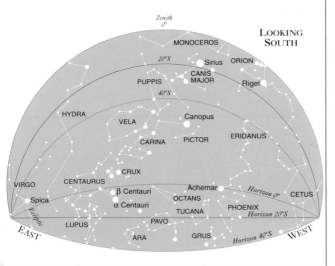

Zenith
0°

LOOKING SOUTH

ALSO VISIBLE	
⁘ M36, M37, and M38 (p.211)	
☐ M42 (p.145)	
⁘ M44 (p.157)	
☐ NGC 3372 (p.157)	
⁘ IC 2602 (p.157)	
● The Hyades and Pleiades (p.211)	

WHOLE-SKY CHART

Northern Latitudes

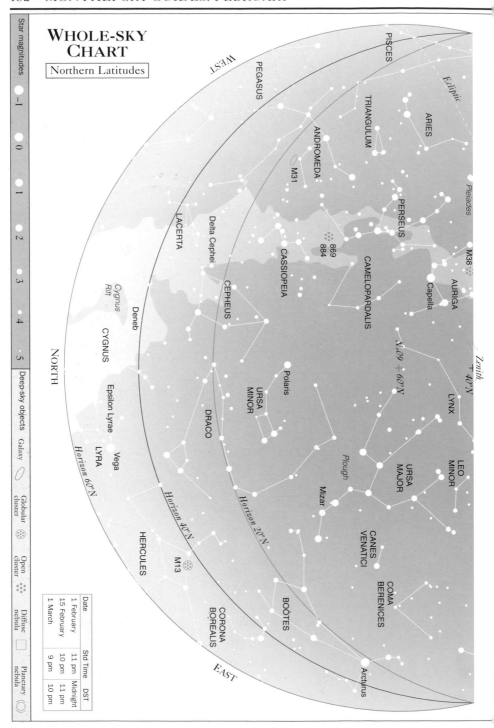

Star magnitudes
-1
0
1
2
3
4
5

Deep-sky objects
Galaxy
Globular cluster
Open cluster
Diffuse nebula
Planetary nebula

Date	Std Time	DST
1 February	11 pm	Midnight
15 February	10 pm	11 pm
1 March	9 pm	10 pm

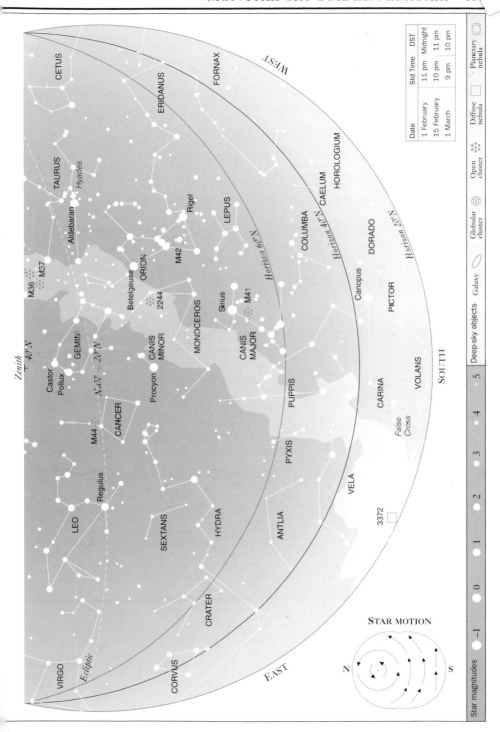

Date	Std Time	DST
1 February	11 pm	Midnight
15 February	10 pm	11 pm
1 March	9 pm	10 pm

Deep-sky objects

Galaxy — Globular cluster — Open cluster — Diffuse nebula — Planetary nebula

Star magnitudes

−1 0 1 2 3 4 5

STAR MOTION

N   S

SOUTH

EAST

WEST

Zenith
+40°N

Noon +20°N

Horizon 20°N

Horizon 40°N

Horizon 60°N

CETUS
ERIDANUS
FORNAX
TAURUS
Hyades
Aldebaran
CAELUM
HOROLOGIUM
LEPUS
Rigel
M42
ORION
Betelgeuse
COLUMBA
DORADO
Canopus
PICTOR
CARINA
VOLANS
M36
M37
2244
GEMINI
Castor
Pollux
Sirius
M41
CANIS
MAJOR
MONOCEROS
CANIS
MINOR
Procyon
CANCER
M44
PUPPIS
False
Cross
VELA
PYXIS
ANTLIA
3372
LEO
Regulus
SEXTANS
HYDRA
CRATER
CORVUS
VIRGO
Ecliptic
Vela

WHOLE-SKY CHART

Southern Latitudes

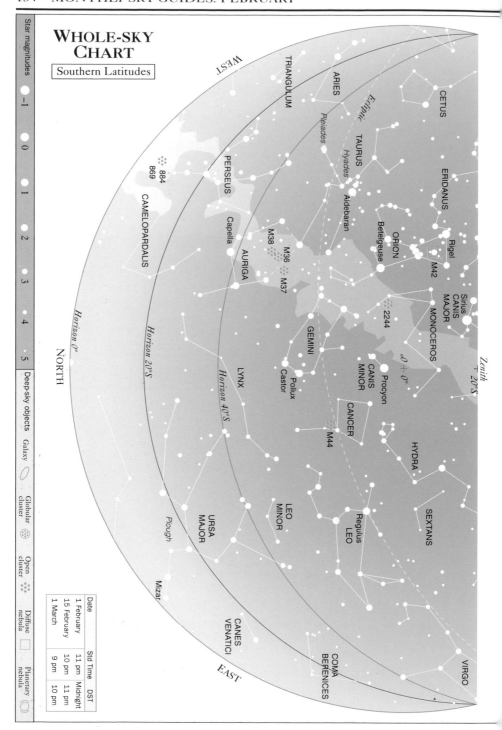

Star magnitudes

- −1
- 0
- 1
- 2
- 3
- 4
- 5

NORTH

Deep-sky objects

Galaxy

Globular cluster

Open cluster

Diffuse nebula

Planetary nebula

Date	Std Time	DST
1 February	11 pm	Midnight
15 February	10 pm	11 pm
1 March	9 pm	10 pm

WEST

TRIANGULUM

ARIES

CETUS

Pleiades

Ecliptic

TAURUS

ERIDANUS

Hyades

PERSEUS

884
869

Aldebaran

ORION

Rigel

CAMELOPARDALIS

Capella

M38

Betelgeuse

M42

Sirius
CANIS
MAJOR

M36

AURIGA

M37

2244

MONOCEROS

Horizon 0°

GEMINI

CANIS
MINOR

Procyon

0 + 0°

LYNX

Castor
Pollux

Horizon 20°S

CANCER

Zenith
−20°S

M44

HYDRA

Horizon 40°S

LEO
MINOR

SEXTANS

URSA
MAJOR

Regulus
LEO

Plough

COMA
BERENICES

Mizar

CANES
VENATICI

VIRGO

EAST

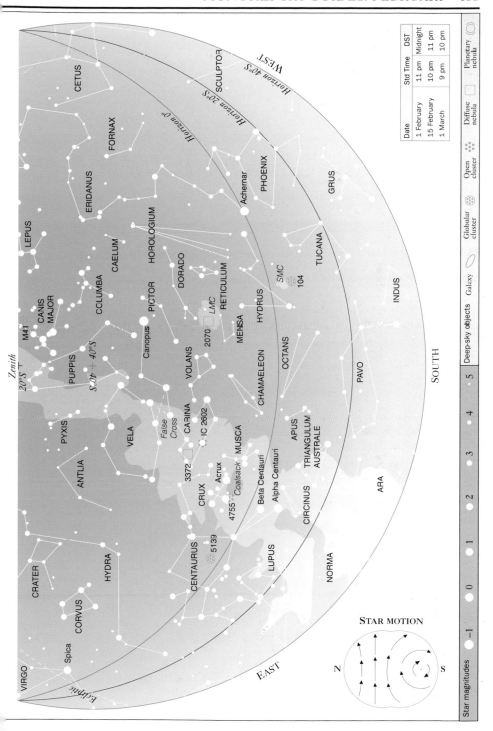

Date	Std Time	DST
1 February	11 pm	Midnight
15 February	10 pm	11 pm
1 March	9 pm	10 pm

Deep-sky objects

Galaxy · Globular cluster · Open cluster · Diffuse nebula · Planetary nebula

Star magnitudes

−1 · 0 · 1 · 2 · 3 · 4 · 5

STAR MOTION

N · S

WEST

SOUTH

EAST

Zenith

20°S

SCULPTOR
CETUS
FORNAX
ERIDANUS
LEPUS
M41
CANIS MAJOR
PUPPIS
PYXIS
ANTLIA
HYDRA
CRATER
CORVUS
VIRGO
Spica
Ecliptic
CRUX
CENTAURUS
5139
LUPUS
NORMA
CIRCINUS
TRIANGULUM AUSTRALE
APUS
ARA
PAVO
OCTANS
INDUS
GRUS
TUCANA
104
SMC
PHOENIX
Achernar
HYDRUS
MENSA
LMC
2070
RETICULUM
HOROLOGIUM
DORADO
PICTOR
CAELUM
COLUMBA
CHAMAELEON
VOLANS
CARINA
IC 2602
3372
False Cross
Coalsack
MUSCA
4755
Acrux
Beta Centauri
Alpha Centauri
Canopus
VELA
S 40° + 40°S
20°S + 40°S
Horizon 0°
Horizon 20°S
Horizon 40°S

MARCH

D AY AND NIGHT become nearly equal in length the world over as the equinox approaches, around 21 March, the start of northern spring and southern autumn. Orion and the bright stars around it are in the west, while from southern latitudes rich fields of stars, from Carina to Centaurus, lie south and southeast.

SUNRISE AND SUNSET ON 15 MARCH		
Latitude	Sunrise	Sunset
60°N	06.20	18.00
40°N	06.10	18.10
20°N	06.10	18.10
0°	06.10	18.10
20°S	06.00	18.20
40°S	06.00	18.20

1 March Std time 🕐 DST 🕐	15 March Std time 🕐 DST 🕐	30 March Std time 🕐 DST 🕐

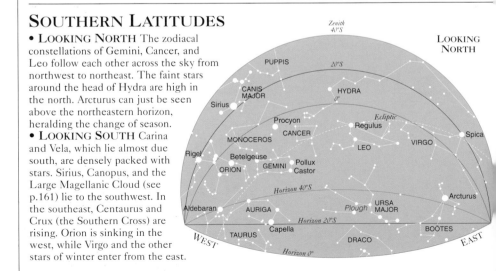

NORTHERN LATITUDES

• LOOKING NORTH The Plough (or Big Dipper) stands high in the northeast. Its bowl opens downwards, towards Polaris, while its handle points east to Arcturus, whose rising signals the arrival of spring. Capella is the most prominent star in the northwest, with Perseus and Cassiopeia now sinking low towards the western horizon.
• LOOKING SOUTH Leo, shaped like a crouching lion, lies due south, with the fainter stars of Cancer to its right. Virgo, with its brightest star Spica, is rising in the southeast, while Orion and the other stars of winter depart in the southwest. Sirius appears to twinkle above the southwestern horizon.

SOUTHERN LATITUDES

• LOOKING NORTH The zodiacal constellations of Gemini, Cancer, and Leo follow each other across the sky from northwest to northeast. The faint stars around the head of Hydra are high in the north. Arcturus can just be seen above the northeastern horizon, heralding the change of season.
• LOOKING SOUTH Carina and Vela, which lie almost due south, are densely packed with stars. Sirius, Canopus, and the Large Magellanic Cloud (see p.161) lie to the southwest. In the southeast, Centaurus and Crux (the Southern Cross) are rising. Orion is sinking in the west, while Virgo and the other stars of winter enter from the east.

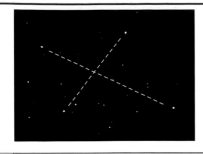

THE FALSE CROSS
Four stars in the adjacent constellations Carina and Vela form the False Cross, sometimes mistaken for the smaller but brighter true Southern Cross. The stars are Kappa (κ) and Delta (δ) Velorum (top left and right) and Iota (ι) and Epsilon (ε) Carinae (bottom left and right).

Star magnitudes ● −1 ● 0 ● 1 ● 2 · 3

LOOKING SOUTH

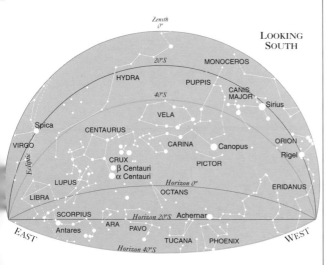

LOOKING SOUTH

WHOLE-SKY CHARTS

MARCH FEATURES

✵ **M44 (CANCER).** Cancer, the faintest constellation of the zodiac, contains a major attraction: the open cluster M44, popularly known as Praesepe or the Beehive. Binoculars show it as a rounded patch of faint stars, resembling a swarm of bees. It can be detected with the naked eye in country skies. The stars Gamma (γ) and Delta (δ) Cancri, to the north and south of the cluster, were visualized in ancient times as donkeys feeding at a manger. See also p.72.

☐ **NGC 3372 (CARINA).** This diffuse nebula, which contains the 5th-magnitude star Eta (η) Carinae, is commonly known as the Eta Carinae Nebula. On dark nights it can be seen with the naked eye, appearing as a particularly bright patch in the Milky Way. Its large size makes it ideal for observation through binoculars. A dark, V-shaped lane of dust runs through it. See also pp.76–77.

✵ **IC 2602 (CARINA).** This bright open star cluster, popularly termed the Southern Pleiades, consists of a handful of naked-eye stars, the brightest of which is Theta (θ) Carinae, magnitude 2.7. Binoculars show about two dozen stars. See also pp.76–77.

ALSO VISIBLE

● **Acrux** (p.163)
● **Castor** (p.151)
✵ **M36, M37, and M38** (p.211)
✵ **M41** (p.151)
☐ **M42** (p.145)
☐ **NGC 2244** (p.151)
✵ **NGC 4755** (p.163)

WHOLE-SKY CHART

Northern Latitudes

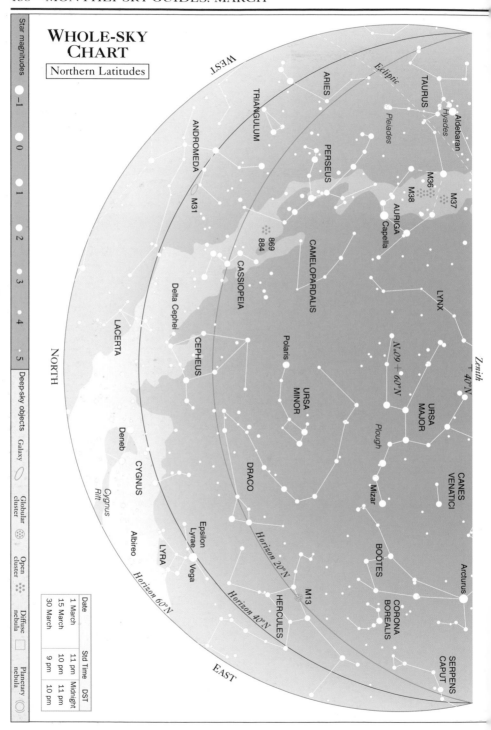

WEST

Ecliptic

ARIES

TRIANGULUM

TAURUS

Hyades

Aldebaran

Pleiades

ANDROMEDA

M31

PERSEUS

M36

M38

M37

AURIGA

Capella

869
884

CAMELOPARDALIS

LYNX

CASSIOPEIA

Delta Cephei

$N.09 + 60°N$

URSA MAJOR

40°N

Zenith

LACERTA

CEPHEUS

Polaris

URSA MINOR

Plough

CANES VENATICI

NORTH

Deneb

DRACO

Mizar

Arcturus

CYGNUS

Cygnus Rift

M13

BOÖTES

Albireo

LYRA

Epsilon Lyrae

Vega

Horizon 20°N

HERCULES

CORONA BOREALIS

Horizon 40°N

Horizon 60°N

EAST

SERPENS CAPUT

Date	Std Time	DST
1 March	11 pm	Midnight
15 March	10 pm	11 pm
30 March	9 pm	10 pm

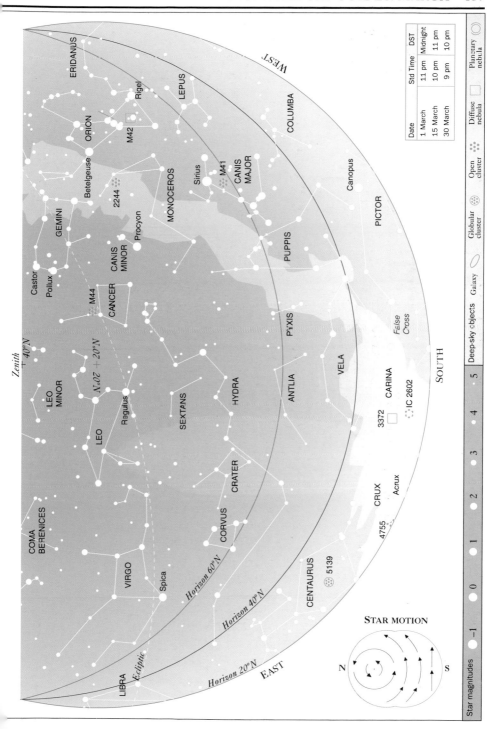

Date	Std Time	DST
1 March	11 pm	Midnight
15 March	10 pm	11 pm
30 March	9 pm	10 pm

Deep-sky objects

Galaxy
Globular cluster
Open cluster
Diffuse nebula
Planetary nebula

WEST

ERIDANUS
LEPUS
COLUMBA
Rigel
ORION
M42
Betelgeuse
Sirius
M41
CANIS MAJOR
Canopus
GEMINI
2244
MONOCEROS
PICTOR
Castor
Pollux
Procyon
CANIS MINOR
PUPPIS
Zenith 40°N
M44
CANCER
PYXIS
VELA
LEO MINOR
20°N + 20°N
Regulus
SEXTANS
HYDRA
ANTLIA
False Cross
CARINA
LEO
3372
IC 2602
COMA BERENICES
CRATER
CRUX
4755
Acrux
VIRGO
CORVUS
Horizon 60°N
CENTAURUS
5139
Spica
Horizon 40°N
LIBRA
Ecliptic
Horizon 20°N
EAST

SOUTH

Star magnitudes
−1 0 1 2 3 4 5

STAR MOTION

N   S

WHOLE-SKY CHART

Southern Latitudes

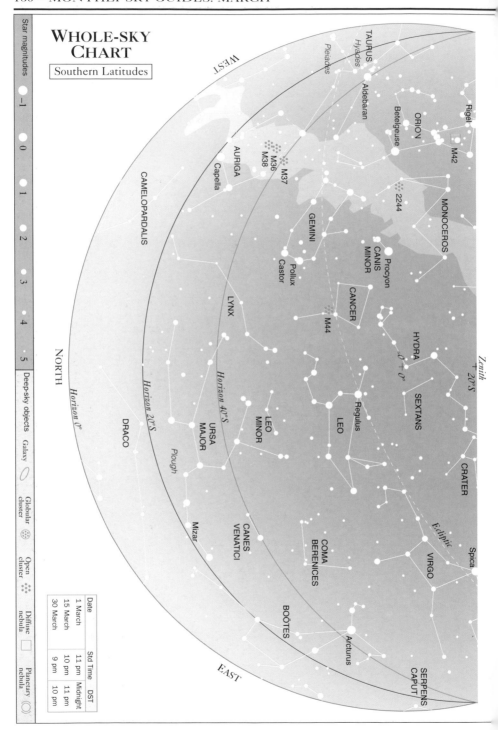

Star magnitudes

- −1
- 0
- 1
- 2
- 3
- 4
- 5

Deep-sky objects

Galaxy

Globular cluster

Open cluster

Diffuse nebula

Planetary nebula

Date	Std Time	DST
1 March	11 pm	Midnight
15 March	10 pm	11 pm
30 March	9 pm	10 pm

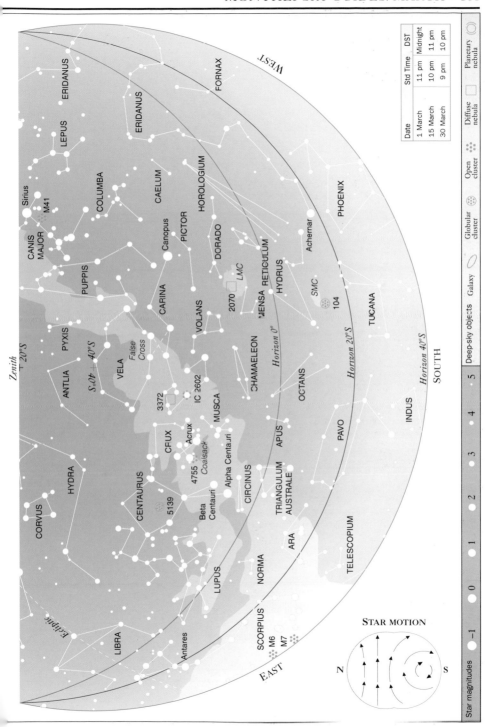

Date	Std Time	DST
1 March	11 pm	Midnight
15 March	10 pm	11 pm
30 March	9 pm	10 pm

Deep-sky objects

Planetary nebula

Diffuse nebula

Open cluster

Globular cluster

Galaxy

STAR MOTION

N   S

Star magnitudes −1 0 1 2 3 4 5

WEST

SOUTH

EAST

Zenith
20°S

Horizon 0°

Horizon 20°S

Horizon 40°S

S of 40°S

ERIDANUS
LEPUS
ERIDANUS
FORNAX
Sirius
M41
CANIS MAJOR
COLUMBA
CAELUM
HOROLOGIUM
PHOENIX
PUPPIS
Canopus
PICTOR
DORADO
Achernar
RETICULUM
MENSA
LMC
2070
HYDRUS
SMC
104
TUCANA
CARINA
VOLANS
CHAMAELEON
OCTANS
PYXIS
VELA
False Cross
3372
IC 2602
MUSCA
APUS
INDUS
PAVO
ANTLIA
CRUX
Acrux
4755
Coalsack
Alpha Centauri
CIRCINUS
TRIANGULUM AUSTRALE
TELESCOPIUM
HYDRA
CENTAURUS
5139
Beta Centauri
NORMA
ARA
CORVUS
LUPUS
SCORPIUS
M6
M7
Antares
Ecliptic
LIBRA

APRIL

D AYLIGHT-SAVING TIME is in use in most northern latitudes, while darkness now arrives earlier in the south. The Plough (or Big Dipper) is high in the northern sky, Leo is prominent from all latitudes, and the Milky Way, containing a wealth of bright stars, is well placed for observers in the southern hemisphere.

SUNRISE AND SUNSET ON 15 APRIL

Latitude	Sunrise	Sunset
60°N	04.40	19.20
40°N	05.20	18.40
20°N	05.40	18.20
0°	06.00	18.00
20°S	06.10	17.50
40°S	06.30	17.30

1 April Std time 🕐 DST 🕐   15 April Std time 🕐 DST 🕐   30 April Std time 🕐 DST 🕐

NORTHERN LATITUDES

• LOOKING NORTH The familiar shape of the Plough (or Big Dipper) is almost overhead, the stars in its bowl pointing downwards to Polaris. Capella is in the northwest, while to its right the constellations Perseus and Cassiopeia sink low. In the east, Vega and Deneb lead the stars of summer into view.
• LOOKING SOUTH Leo is high in the south. Beneath it is the relatively blank area of sky around Hydra. Left of Leo, in the southeast, the bright star Arcturus is prominently placed, with Spica in Virgo closer to the horizon. Above the western horizon, Castor and Pollux, in Gemini, are still visible, with Procyon just beneath them.

SOUTHERN LATITUDES

• LOOKING NORTH Due north, Leo resembles a lion lying on its back, while Arcturus is prominent in the east, with Spica high above. Procyon remains on view in the northwest, as Castor and Pollux, in Gemini, set beneath it. The large but faint constellation of Hydra arches overhead from northwest to northeast.
• LOOKING SOUTH Crux (the Southern Cross) is high in the south with Vela and Carina to its right and Alpha (α) and Beta (β) Centauri to its left. Canopus is in the southwest, the Large Magellanic Cloud (LMC) to its lower left (see p.167). Sirius is almost due west, while Scorpius lies southeast.

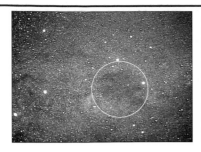

THE COALSACK (CRUX)
What appears to be a hole in the Milky Way next to Crux (the Southern Cross) is in fact a huge cloud of dust that blots out light from the stars behind it. This dark nebula, known as the Coalsack, is about 60 light years in diameter, and is thought to lie about 600 light years from us.

Star magnitudes   ●−1   ●0   ●1   ●2   ●3

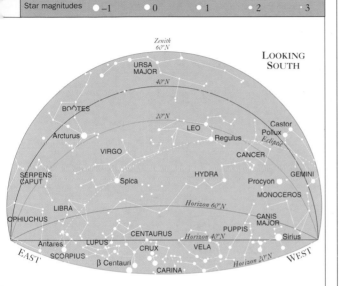

Zenith
60°N

LOOKING
SOUTH

URSA MAJOR
40°N
BOÖTES
20°N
Arcturus   LEO   Castor
Pollux
Regulus   Eclipse
VIRGO
CANCER
SERPENS CAPUT   HYDRA   GEMINI
Spica   Procyon
MONOCEROS
LIBRA   Horizon 60°N
OPHIUCHUS   CANIS MAJOR
CENTAURUS   PUPPIS
Horizon 40°N   Sirius
Antares   LUPUS   CRUX   VELA
EAST   SCORPIUS   β Centauri   Horizon 20°N   WEST
CARINA

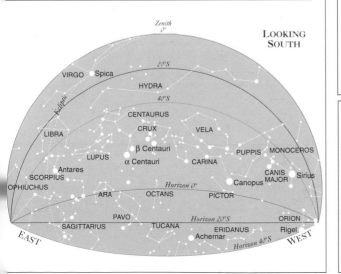

Zenith
0°

LOOKING
SOUTH

20°S
VIRGO   Spica
HYDRA
40°S
Eclipse
CENTAURUS
CRUX   VELA
LIBRA
β Centauri   PUPPIS   MONOCEROS
LUPUS   α Centauri   CARINA
Antares
SCORPIUS   CANIS   Sirius
OPHIUCHUS   Canopus   MAJOR
Horizon 0°
ARA   OCTANS   PICTOR
PAVO   Horizon 20°S   ORION
EAST   SAGITTARIUS   TUCANA   ERIDANUS   Rigel
Achernar
Horizon 40°S   WEST

WHOLE-SKY CHARTS

APRIL FEATURES

● **ACRUX (CRUX).** The brightest star in the Southern Cross, known as Acrux or Alpha (α) Crucis, is in fact a close double star. A small telescope will divide it into two sparkling points. A fainter star, which is not related to the main pair, can be seen through binoculars. See also pp.86–87.

✵ **NGC 4755 (CRUX).** This open cluster, popularly known as the Jewel Box, is visible to the naked eye as a hazy star, and is best viewed through binoculars or a small telescope. The English astronomer Sir John Herschel described it in the 1830s as resembling "a casket of variously coloured precious stones". Although it appears to lie next to the Coalsack (see photograph, above), it is in fact over 12 times more distant. See also pp.86–87.

ALSO VISIBLE

● **Alpha (α) Centauri** (p.169)
● **Mizar** (p.169)
✵ **M44** (p.157)
✵ **NGC 2244** (p.151)
☐ **NGC 3372** (p.157)
✵ **NGC 5139** (p.169)
✵ **IC 2602** (p.157)

APRIL METEORS

THE LYRIDS. The Lyrid meteor shower, most easily seen from northern latitudes, reaches its peak around 21 April. It is one of the poorer showers, with a maximum rate of only about 10 meteors an hour, but the meteors are fast, bright, and often leave trains. The radiant is in the constellation Lyra, close to the bright star Vega.

WHOLE-SKY CHART

Northern Latitudes

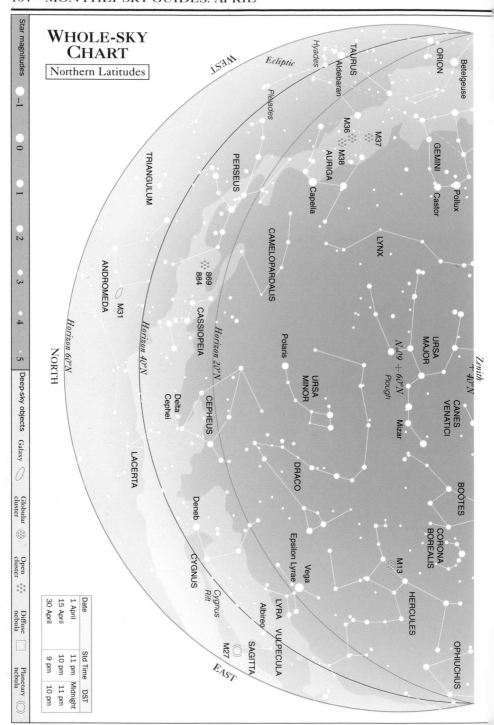

NORTH

WEST

EAST

Zenith +40°N

Ecliptic

Hyades

Pleiades

TAURUS
Aldebaran

ORION

Betelgeuse

GEMINI

Pollux

Castor

M36
M37
M38
AURIGA
Capella

PERSEUS

TRIANGULUM

ANDROMEDA

M31

869
884

CAMELOPARDALIS

LYNX

URSA MAJOR

CANES VENATICI

N.09 + 60°N
Plough
Mizar

CASSIOPEIA

Polaris

URSA MINOR

BOÖTES

CORONA BOREALIS

M13

HERCULES

CEPHEUS

Delta Cephei

DRACO

LACERTA

Deneb

Epsilon Lyrae

Vega

LYRA

Albireo

Cygnus Rift

CYGNUS

VULPECULA

SAGITTA

M27

OPHIUCHUS

Horizon 60°N

Horizon 40°N

Horizon 20°N

Star magnitudes

-1	●
0	●
1	●
2	●
3	●
4	·
5	·

Deep-sky objects

Galaxy ⬭

Globular cluster ⬤

Open cluster ⁂

Diffuse nebula ▢

Planetary nebula ◎

Date	Std Time	DST
1 April	11 pm	Midnight
15 April	10 pm	11 pm
30 April	9 pm	10 pm

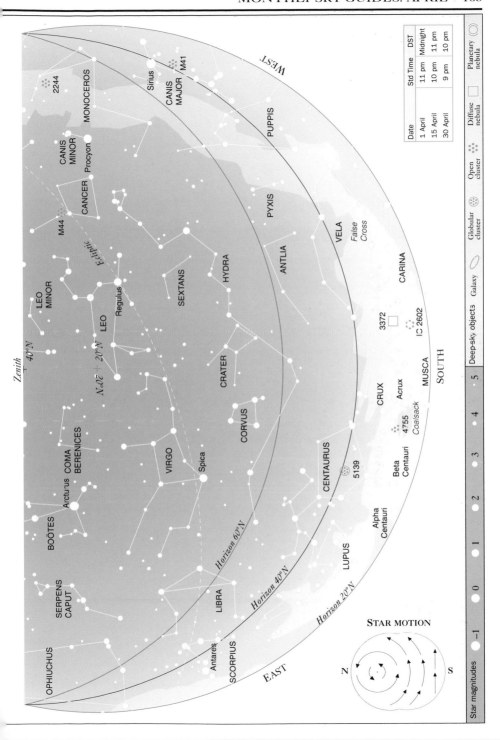

Date	Std Time	DST
1 April	11 pm	Midnight
15 April	10 pm	11 pm
30 April	9 pm	10 pm

WEST

Zenith

40°N

Lat. 20°N

Lat. 40°N + 20°N

OPHIUCHUS

SERPENS CAPUT

BOÖTES

Arcturus COMA BERENICES

LEO MINOR

Regulus

LEO

Ecliptic

M44

CANCER

CANIS MINOR

Procyon

MONOCEROS

2244

CANIS MAJOR

Sirius

M41

PUPPIS

VIRGO

Spica

CORVUS

CRATER

SEXTANS

HYDRA

PYXIS

ANTLIA

VELA

False Cross

CARINA

3372

IC 2602

LIBRA

Antares

SCORPIUS

LUPUS

Alpha Centauri

CENTAURUS

5139

Beta Centauri

4755

Coalsack

CRUX

Acrux

MUSCA

Horizon 20°N

Horizon 40°N

Horizon 60°N

EAST

SOUTH

STAR MOTION

N   S

Deep-sky objects

Galaxy   Globular cluster   Open cluster   Diffuse nebula   Planetary nebula

Star magnitudes

−1   0   1   2   3   4   5

WHOLE-SKY CHART

Southern Latitudes

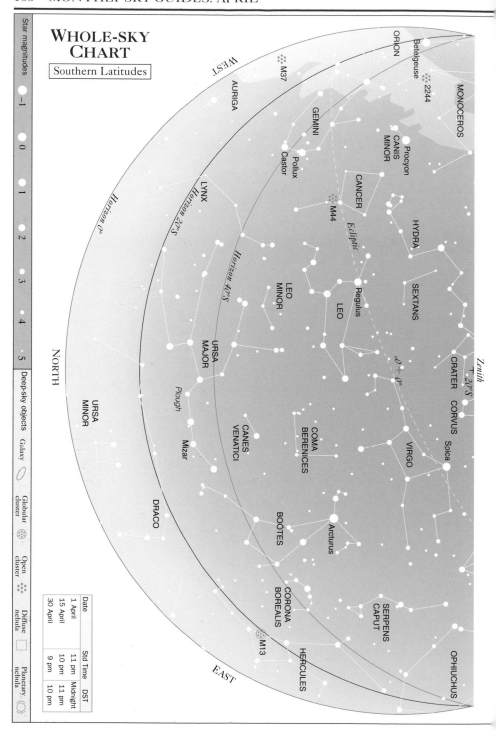

Star magnitudes

● −1
● 0
● 1
● 2
• 3
• 4
· 5

NORTH

Deep-sky objects

Galaxy ⬭
Globular cluster ◉
Open cluster ⁘
Diffuse nebula ▢
Planetary nebula ◎

Date	Std Time	DST
1 April	11 pm	Midnight
15 April	10 pm	11 pm
30 April	9 pm	10 pm

WEST

ORION

Betelgeuse

⁘ M37

2244

MONOCEROS

AURIGA

GEMINI

Procyon

CANIS MINOR

Pollux

Castor

CANCER

⁘ M44

HYDRA

LYNX

Ecliptic

SEXTANS

Horizon 0°

Horizon 20°S

Horizon 40°S

LEO MINOR

Regulus

LEO

Zenith

20°S

CRATER

CORVUS

VIRGO

Spica

URSA MAJOR

URSA MINOR

Plough

Mizar

CANES VENATICI

COMA BERENICES

Arcturus

BOÖTES

SERPENS CAPUT

DRACO

CORONA BOREALIS

M13 ⁘

HERCULES

OPHIUCHUS

EAST

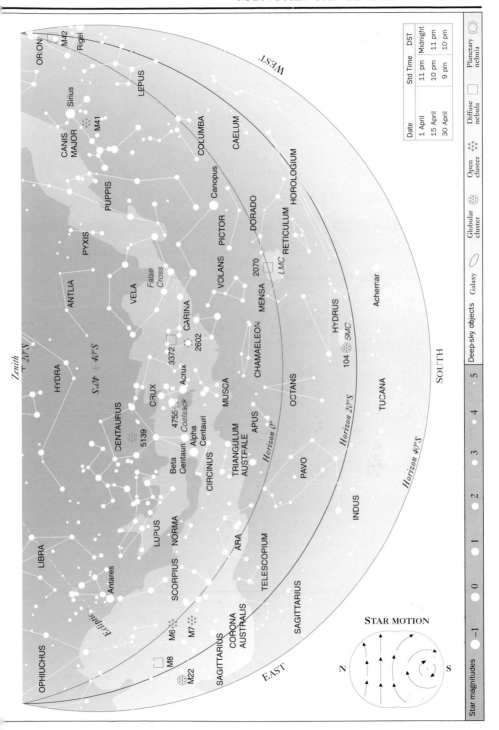

Date	Std Time	DST
1 April	11 pm	Midnight
15 April	10 pm	11 pm
30 April	9 pm	10 pm

STAR MOTION

N ← → S

Star magnitudes −1 0 1 2 3 4 5

Deep-sky objects

Galaxy Globular cluster Open cluster Diffuse nebula Planetary nebula

OPHIUCHUS
LIBRA
Antares
SCORPIUS
LUPUS
NORMA
ARA
TELESCOPIUM
CORONA AUSTRALIS
SAGITTARIUS
M6
M7
M8
M22
Ecliptic
EAST

HYDRA
CENTAURUS
5139
Beta Centauri
Alpha Centauri
4755
Coalsack
CRUX
CIRCINUS
TRIANGULUM AUSTRALE
APUS
MUSCA
PAVO
INDUS
Horizon 0°
Horizon 20°S

ANTLIA
VELA
False Cross
3372
Acrux
2602
CARINA
CHAMAELEON
OCTANS
TUCANA
104 SMC
HYDRUS
Horizon 40°S
SOUTH

Zenith
Lat 20°S
Lat 40°S

PYXIS
PUPPIS
Canopus
VOLANS
MENSA
2070
LMC
DORADO
PICTOR
RETICULUM
Achernar

CANIS MAJOR
Sirius
M41
LEPUS
COLUMBA
CAELUM
HOROLOGIUM

ORION
M42
Rigel
WEST

MAY

L ENGTHENING TWILIGHT can make early evening observing more difficult in northern latitudes, where the sparkling stars of winter are being replaced by those of summer. In the southern hemisphere, this is the best time of year to see Crux (the Southern Cross) and its "pointers", Alpha and Beta Centauri.

SUNRISE AND SUNSET ON 15 MAY		
Latitude	Sunrise	Sunset
60°N	03.20	20.30
40°N	04.40	19.10
20°N	05.20	18.30
0°	05.50	18.00
20°S	06.20	17.30
40°S	07.00	17.00

1 May Std time ⊕ DST ⊕	15 May Std time ⊕ DST ⊕	30 May Std time ⊕ DST ⊕

NORTHERN LATITUDES

• **LOOKING NORTH** The Plough (or Big Dipper) stands almost overhead, while Cygnus and the bright star Vega climb higher in the northeast as a foretaste of summer. The faint constellation of Cepheus is between Polaris and the northern horizon. Gemini is the last of the winter constellations to sink below the northwestern horizon.

• **LOOKING SOUTH** The bright stars Arcturus in Boötes and Spica in Virgo are high in the south. Ophiuchus and both halves of Serpens occupy much of the southeastern sky, with Hercules above them. Leo dominates the southwest, with the largely blank area of sky occupied by Hydra beneath it.

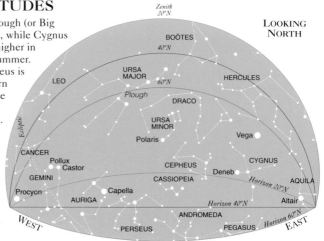

SOUTHERN LATITUDES

• **LOOKING NORTH** Arcturus, in Boötes, glitters in the north, with Spica, in Virgo, nearly overhead. Hercules is close to the northeastern horizon, to the lower right of Arcturus, while Ophiuchus and the two halves of Serpens cover much of the eastern sky. Leo is prominent in the northwest.

• **LOOKING SOUTH** Centaurus and its adjoining constellations dominate the southern sky, with Alpha (α) and Beta (β) Centauri pointing towards Crux (the Southern Cross). While Canopus sets in the southwest, the well-stocked constellations Sagittarius and Scorpius are rising in the south-east, a sign that winter is on its way.

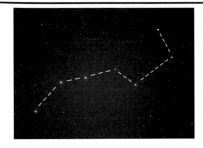

THE PLOUGH
The familiar shape of the Plough (or Big Dipper), formed by seven stars in Ursa Major (pp.136–37), is a prominent sight in northern skies in spring. The second star in the handle, called Mizar, has a fainter partner, visible to observers with normal eyesight (see panel, right).

Star magnitudes ● –1   ● 0   ● 1   • 2   • 3

Zenith
60°N

LOOKING
SOUTH

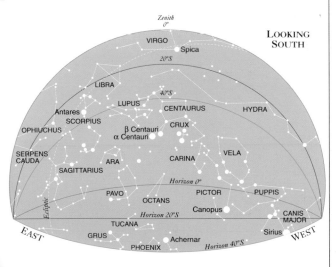

Zenith
0°

LOOKING
SOUTH

WHOLE-SKY CHARTS

MAY FEATURES

● **ALPHA (α) CENTAURI.** A mere 4.3 light years away, this is the closest star to the Earth after the Sun. A small telescope reveals two yellow stars, the brighter of which is similar in temperature and brightness to the Sun. A third member of the family, Proxima Centauri, is much fainter. See also p.79.

● **MIZAR (URSA MAJOR).** The second star in the handle of the Plough, known as Mizar or Zeta (ζ) Ursae Majoris, is a wide double. Its companion, Alcor, is visible to the naked eye, while a small telescope shows another star, closer to Mizar. See also pp.136–37.

⊛ **NGC 5139 (CENTAURUS).** The largest and brightest globular cluster in the sky, also called Omega (ω) Centauri, is visible to the naked eye as a hazy star. It is clearer through binoculars, and a small telescope shows the brightest of its 100,000 or more stars. See also p.79.

ALSO VISIBLE

● Acrux (p.163)
∷ M6 and M7 (p.175)
⊛ M13 (p.175)
∷ M44 (p.157)
∷ NGC 4755 (p.163)

MAY METEORS

THE ETA AQUARIDS. These fast-moving, bright meteors, caused by dust from Halley's Comet, radiate from a point near the "water jar" in Aquarius, and are best seen from southern latitudes. Activity begins in late April, peaks at about 35 meteors an hour in the first week of May, and ends in late May.

WHOLE-SKY CHART

Northern Latitudes

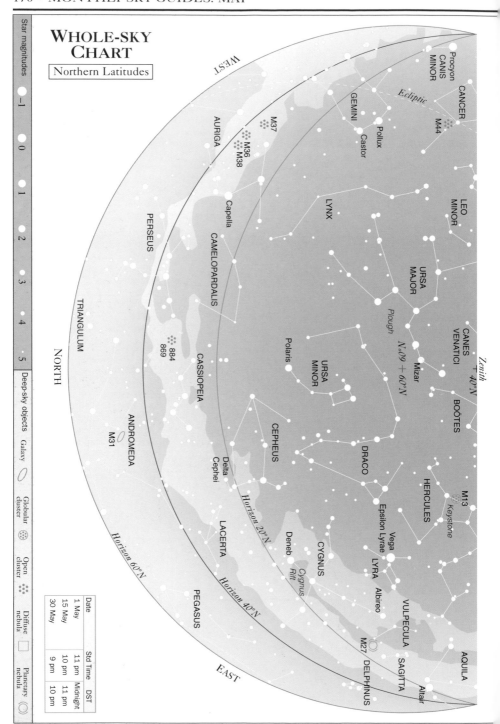

WEST

Procyon
CANIS MINOR
CANCER
M44
Ecliptic
GEMINI
Pollux
Castor
M37
AURIGA
M36
M38
Capella
LEO MINOR
LYNX
URSA MAJOR
CANES VENATICI
Plough
$N_{o}09 + 60°N$
Mizar
PERSEUS
CAMELOPARDALIS
BOÖTES
TRIANGULUM
884
869
CASSIOPEIA
Polaris
URSA MINOR
HERCULES
M13
Keystone
ANDROMEDA
M31
CEPHEUS
DRACO
Vega
Epsilon Lyrae
Delta Cephei
Deneb
LYRA
Albireo
VULPECULA
LACERTA
CYGNUS
Cygnus Rift
SAGITTA
M27
DELPHINUS
PEGASUS
AQUILA
Altair
Zenith 40°N
Horizon 20°N
Horizon 40°N
Horizon 60°N
NORTH
EAST

Star magnitudes

−1	0
1	2
3	4
5	

Deep-sky objects

Galaxy
Globular cluster
Open cluster
Diffuse nebula
Planetary nebula

Date	Std Time	DST
1 May	11 pm	Midnight
15 May	10 pm	11 pm
30 May	9 pm	10 pm

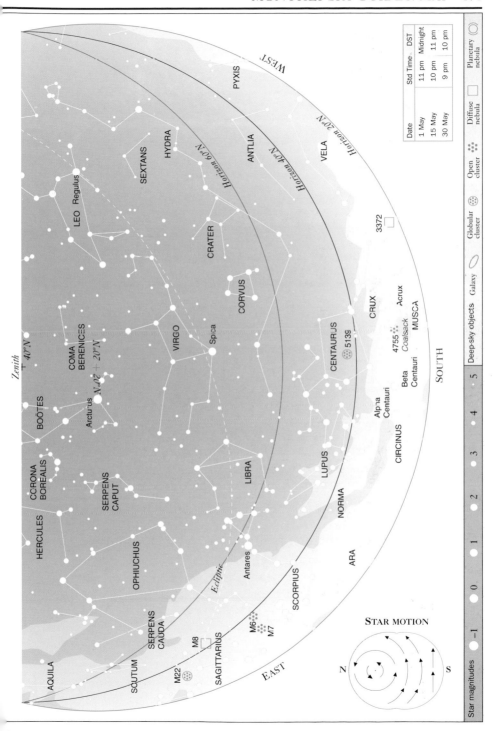

Date	Std Time	DST
1 May	11 pm	Midnight
15 May	10 pm	11 pm
30 May	9 pm	10 pm

Deep-sky objects: Galaxy, Globular cluster, Open cluster, Diffuse nebula, Planetary nebula

STAR MOTION

Star magnitudes: -1 0 1 2 3 4 5

WHOLE-SKY CHART

Southern Latitudes

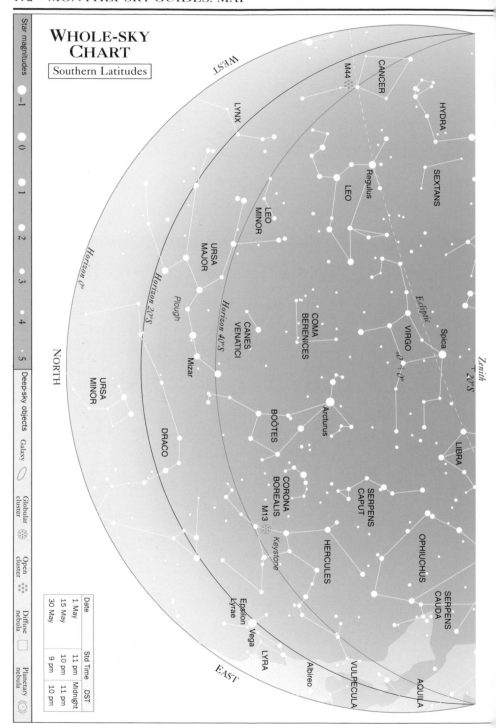

Star magnitudes

-1
0
1
2
3
4
5

Deep-sky objects

Galaxy

Globular cluster

Open cluster

Diffuse nebula

Planetary nebula

WEST

M44

CANCER

HYDRA

LYNX

SEXTANS

Regulus

LEO

LEO MINOR

URSA MAJOR

Plough

Horizon 0°

Horizon 20°S

Horizon 40°S

CANES VENATICI

COMA BERENICES

Ecliptic

VIRGO

Spica

Zenith

20°S

Mizar

BOÖTES

Arcturus

LIBRA

URSA MINOR

DRACO

CORONA BOREALIS

M13

Keystone

SERPENS CAPUT

OPHIUCHUS

SERPENS CAUDA

HERCULES

NORTH

Epsilon Lyrae

Vega

LYRA

Albireo

VULPECULA

AQUILA

EAST

Date	Std Time	DST
1 May	11 pm	Midnight
15 May	10 pm	11 pm
30 May	9 pm	10 pm

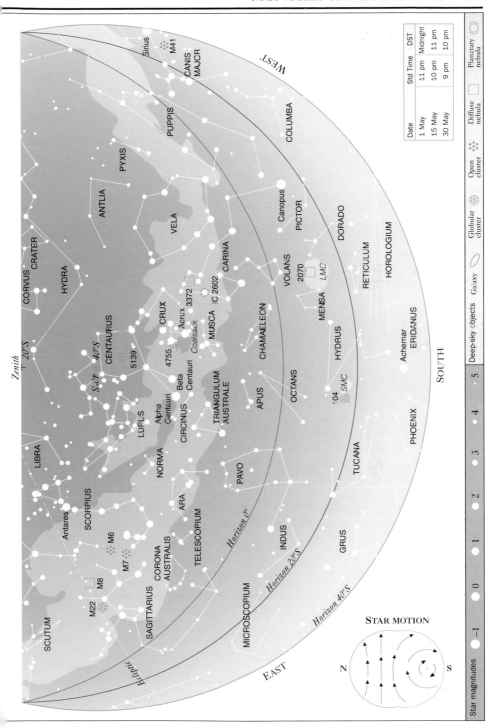

Zenith

WEST

20°S

S 40°

40°S

SCUTUM

SAGITTARIUS

M22

M8

SCORPIUS

Antares

M6

M7

LIBRA

CORONA
AUSTRALIS

TELESCOPIUM

ARA

NORMA

LUPUS

Alpha
Centauri

Beta
Centauri

CIRCINUS

TRIANGULUM
AUSTRALE

CENTAURUS

5139

4755

CRUX

Acrux

Coalsack

MUSCA

3372

IC 2602

CARINA

CHAMAELEON

APUS

PAVO

MICROSCOPIUM

INDUS

OCTANS

TUCANA

GRUS

PHOENIX

HYDRUS

SMC

04

MENSA

VOLANS

2070

LMC

PICTOR

Canopus

COLUMBA

Achernar

ERIDANUS

RETICULUM

HOROLOGIUM

DORADO

MENSA

CANIS
MAJOR

Sirius

M41

PUPPIS

PYXIS

ANTLIA

VELA

HYDRA

CRATER

CORVUS

SOUTH

EAST

Ecliptic

Horizon 0°

Horizon 20°S

Horizon 40°S

STAR MOTION

N

S

Date	Std Time	DST
1 May	11 pm	Midnight
15 May	10 pm	11 pm
30 May	9 pm	10 pm

Deep-sky objects Galaxy Globular cluster Open cluster Diffuse nebula Planetary nebula

Star magnitudes −1 0 1 2 3 4 5

JUNE

NIGHTS ARE AT THEIR SHORTEST and days at their longest in northern latitudes in June, and vice versa in the southern hemisphere. In the far north, twilight is now permanent throughout the night, while the winter skies of the south are dominated by a band of prominent constellations lying in the Milky Way.

SUNRISE AND SUNSET ON 15 JUNE

Latitude	Sunrise	Sunset
60°N	02.40	21.20
40°N	04.30	19.30
20°N	05.20	18.40
0°	06.00	18.00
20°S	06.30	17.30
40°S	07.20	16.40

1 June Std time ⏰ DST ⏰   15 June Std time ⏰ DST ⏰   30 June Std time ⏰ DST ⏰

NORTHERN LATITUDES
• **LOOKING NORTH** Ursa Minor (the Little Bear) stands on its tail, and Draco arches above the north celestial pole, marked by Polaris. The Plough (or Big Dipper) is high in the northwest. Towards the east, the stars that form the Summer Triangle are in view: Vega, Deneb in Cygnus, and Altair in Aquila (far left of Looking South map).
• **LOOKING SOUTH** Hercules is high in the south-east, with Vega to its left and Arcturus, in Boötes, to its right. Ophiuchus, Virgo, and both halves of Serpens are below them. Antares, in Scorpius, glints red above the southern horizon, the faint stars of Libra to its right. Leo is setting in the west.

SOUTHERN LATITUDES
• **LOOKING NORTH** Boötes and Hercules are prominently placed almost due north, with Virgo, Ophiuchus, and both parts of Serpens above them. Antares (in Scorpius) is overhead. Altair (in Aquila) and Vega are the most prominent stars in the northeast. Leo is setting in the northwest.
• **LOOKING SOUTH** The constellations Sagittarius, Ara, Scorpius, Lupus, Centaurus, Crux (the Southern Cross), Carina, and Vela form a bright band, from southeast to southwest, against dense star fields in the Milky Way. The brightest stars along this band are Antares, Alpha (α) and Beta (β) Centauri, and Acrux (see also p.179).

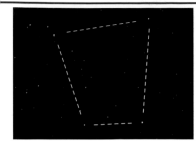

THE KEYSTONE (HERCULES)
Four stars form a shape known as the Keystone that represents the pelvis of Hercules (pp.98–99). Clockwise from top left, they are Pi (π), Eta (η), Zeta (ζ), and Epsilon (ε) Herculis. The star cluster M13 (see panel, right) lies between Eta and Zeta.

WHOLE-SKY CHARTS

JUNE FEATURES

✣ **M6 (SCORPIUS).** This open cluster and the nearby M7 lie near the "sting" in the tail of Scorpius, the scorpion. M6 can be seen with the naked eye and is an impressive sight through binoculars. It is sometimes called the Butterfly Cluster because its stars are arranged in the shape of a butterfly with open wings. See also pp.126–27.

✣ **M7 (SCORPIUS).** This open cluster appears to the naked eye as a bright patch in front of dense fields of stars in the Milky Way, and is a superb sight when seen through binoculars. It is larger and brighter than its neighbour M6, being less than half the distance from us (800 light years, compared with 2,000 light years for M6). See also pp.126–27.

✥ **M13 (HERCULES).** This is the most prominent globular cluster in northern skies; even so, it is barely visible to the naked eye, and from urban areas it can be seen only with the aid of binoculars, through which it resembles a glowing ball with a bright centre. It lies on one side of the Keystone of Hercules (see photograph, above), one-third the way between Eta (η) and Zeta (ζ) Herculis. See also pp.98–99.

Star magnitudes   ● −1   ● 0   ● 1   · 2   · 3

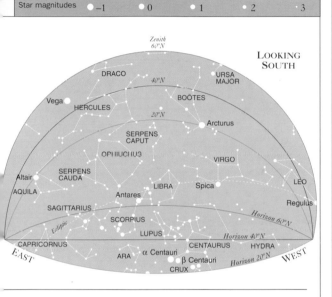

LOOKING SOUTH

Zenith 60°N

DRACO · 40°N · URSA MAJOR · BOÖTES · Vega · HERCULES · 20°N · SERPENS CAPUT · Arcturus · OPHIUCHUS · VIRGO · Altair · SERPENS CAUDA · AQUILA · LIBRA · Spica · LEO · Antares · Regulus · SAGITTARIUS · Ecliptic · SCORPIUS · *Horizon 60°N* · CAPRICORNUS · LUPUS · *Horizon 40°N* · EAST · CENTAURUS · HYDRA · ARA · α Centauri · β Centauri · *Horizon 20°N* · WEST · CRUX

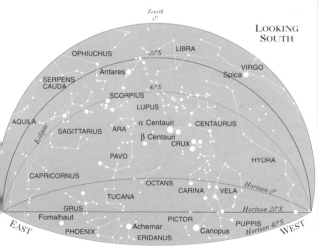

LOOKING SOUTH

Zenith 0°

OPHIUCHUS · 20°S · LIBRA · Antares · VIRGO · SERPENS CAUDA · Spica · 40°S · SCORPIUS · LUPUS · AQUILA · α Centauri · CENTAURUS · Ecliptic · SAGITTARIUS · ARA · β Centauri · CRUX · PAVO · HYDRA · CAPRICORNUS · OCTANS · *Horizon 0°* · TUCANA · CARINA · VELA · GRUS · *Horizon 20°S* · Fomalhaut · PICTOR · EAST · Achernar · PUPPIS · *Horizon 40°S* · WEST · PHOENIX · Canopus · ERIDANUS

ALSO VISIBLE

- ● Albireo (p.187)
- ● Alpha (α) Centauri (p.169)
- ● Antares (p.181)
- ● Epsilon (ε) Lyrae (p.181)
- ● Mizar (p.169)
- □ M8 (p.181)
- ✥ M22 (p.181)
- ○ M27 (p.193)
- ✥ NGC 5139 (p.169)

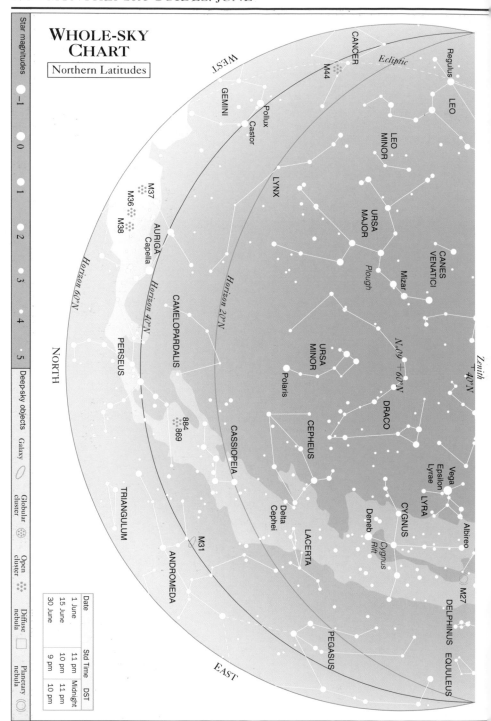

WHOLE-SKY CHART

Northern Latitudes

Star magnitudes

●−1 ● 0 ● 1 ● 2 ● 3 ● 4 · 5

Deep-sky objects

Galaxy ⬭

Globular cluster ❊

Open cluster ❊

Diffuse nebula ▫

Planetary nebula ◎

NORTH

WEST

EAST

Zenith 40°N

Horizon 60°N

Horizon 40°N

Horizon 20°N

Ecliptic

CANCER

M44

GEMINI

Pollux

Castor

LYNX

LEO

Regulus

LEO MINOR

URSA MAJOR

Plough

CANES VENATICI

Mizar

N,ν + 60°N

URSA MINOR

Polaris

DRACO

Vega

Epsilon Lyrae

LYRA

CYGNUS

Deneb

Cygnus Rift

Albireo

DELPHINUS EQUULEUS

M27

CEPHEUS

Delta Cephei

LACERTA

PEGASUS

CASSIOPEIA

884 869

CAMELOPARDALIS

AURIGA

Capella

M37

M36

M38

PERSEUS

TRIANGULUM

ANDROMEDA

M31

Date	Std Time	DST
1 June	11 pm	Midnight
15 June	10 pm	11 pm
30 June	9 pm	10 pm

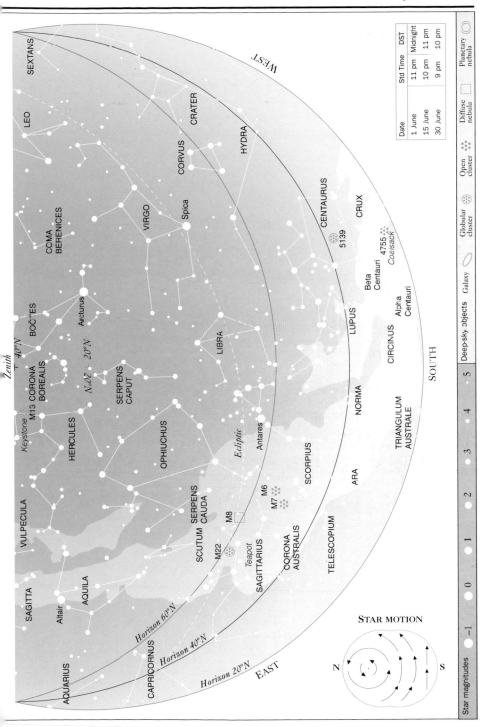

Zenith

⊕ 40°N

WEST

SEXTANS

LEO

CRATER

CORVUS

HYDRA

COMA BERENICES

VIRGO

Spica

CENTAURUS

5139

CRUX

Beta Centauri

4755

Coalsack

Alpha Centauri

BOÖTES

Arcturus

N₀0Z ~ 20°N

CORONA BOREALIS

M13

LIBRA

LUPUS

CIRCINUS

Keystone

HERCULES

SERPENS CAPUT

OPHIUCHUS

Ecliptic

Antares

NORMA

SOUTH

ARA

TRIANGULUM AUSTRALE

VULPECULA

SERPENS CAUDA

M8

SCUTUM

M6

M7

SCORPIUS

SAGITTA

AQUILA

M22

Teapot

SAGITTARIUS

CORONA AUSTRALIS

TELESCOPIUM

Altair

AQUARIUS

CAPRICORNUS

Horizon 60° N

Horizon 40° N

Horizon 20° N

EAST

STAR MOTION

N

S

Date	Std Time	DST
1 June	11 pm	Midnight
15 June	10 pm	11 pm
30 June	9 pm	10 pm

Deep-sky objects

Galaxy

Globular cluster

Open cluster

Planetary nebula

Diffuse nebula

Star magnitudes   −1   0   1   2   3   4   5

WHOLE-SKY CHART

Southern Latitudes

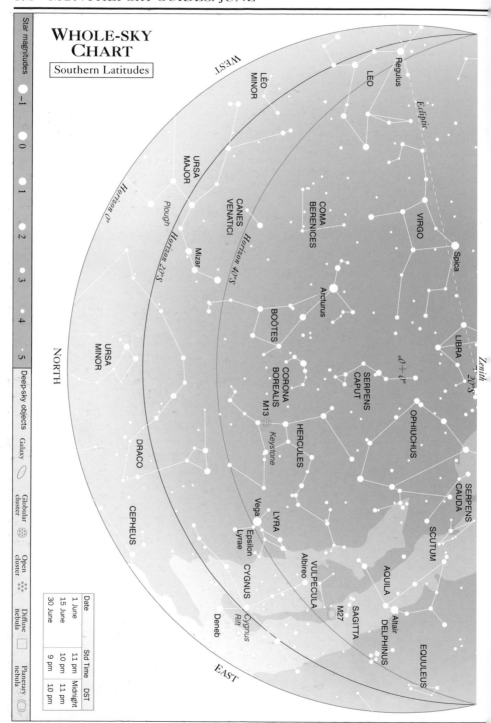

WEST

Ecliptic

LEO MINOR

LEO

Regulus

Horizon 0°

URSA MAJOR

Plough

Horizon 20°S

CANES VENATICI

Horizon 40°S

COMA BERENICES

VIRGO

Spica

Mizar

Arcturus

BOÖTES

CORONA BOREALIS

SERPENS CAPUT

0 + 0°

LIBRA

Zenith

20°S

URSA MINOR

M13

Keystone

HERCULES

OPHIUCHUS

NORTH

DRACO

Vega

LYRA

SERPENS CAUDA

SCUTUM

CEPHEUS

Epsilon Lyrae

CYGNUS

Albireo

VULPECULA

AQUILA

Altair

SAGITTA

DELPHINUS

EQUULEUS

Deneb

Cygnus Rift

M27

EAST

Star magnitudes

- -1
- 0
- 1
- 2
- 3
- 4
- 5

Deep-sky objects

- Galaxy
- Globular cluster
- Open cluster
- Diffuse nebula
- Planetary nebula

Date	Std Time	DST
1 June	11 pm	Midnight
15 June	10 pm	11 pm
30 June	9 pm	10 pm

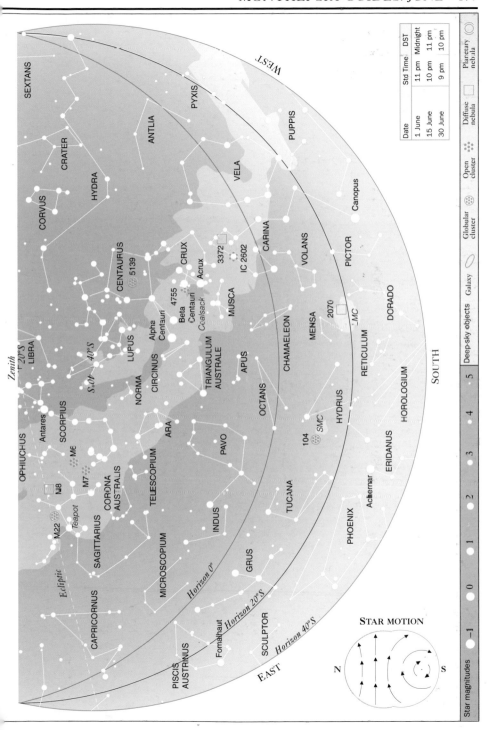

SEXTANS

WEST

PYXIS

ANTLIA

CRATER

CORVUS

HYDRA

VELA

PUPPIS

CENTAURUS
5139

CARINA

Canopus

CRUX
3372
Acrux
IC 2602
VOLANS
PICTOR

4755
Beta
Centauri
Coalsack
MUSCA
2070
_MC
DORADO

Alpha
Centauri
LUPUS
CHAMAELEON
MENSA

20°S
Zenith
LIBRA
Sth 40°S
CIRCINUS
NORMA
TRIANGULUM
AUSTRALE
APUS
OCTANS
RETICULUM
HOROLOGIUM

OPHIUCHUS
Antares
SCORPIUS
M6
ARA
PAVO
HYDRUS
104
SMC
ERIDANUS
Achernar

M7
CORONA
AUSTRALIS
TELESCOPIUM
INDUS
TUCANA
PHOENIX

M8
Teapot
M22
SAGITTARIUS
MICROSCOPIUM
GRUS
Horizon 0°
Horizon 20°S
Horizon 40°S

Ecliptic
CAPRICORNUS
PISCIS
AUSTRINUS
Fomalhaut
SCULPTOR
EAST

SOUTH

Date	Std Time	DST
1 June	11 pm	Midnight
15 June	10 pm	11 pm
30 June	9 pm	10 pm

| Deep-sky objects | Galaxy | Globular cluster | Open cluster | Diffuse nebula | Planetary nebula |

STAR MOTION

N   S

Star magnitudes   −1   0   1   2   3   4   5

JULY

T HIS IS THE BEST TIME for northern observers to see the rich southern constellations Sagittarius and Scorpius. The centre of our Galaxy is in Sagittarius, so the Milky Way star fields are particularly dense in this region. For southern observers, these constellations are almost overhead and dominate the scene.

SUNRISE AND SUNSET ON 15 JULY		
Latitude	Sunrise	Sunset
60°N	03.00	21.10
40°N	04.40	19.30
20°N	05.30	18.40
0°	06.00	18.10
20°S	06.40	17.40
40°S	07.20	16.50

1 July Std time 🕐 DST 🕐   15 July Std time 🕐 DST 🕐   30 July Std time 🕐 DST 🕐

NORTHERN LATITUDES
• **LOOKING NORTH** Ursa Minor (the Little Bear) remains well placed, with Draco coiled around it. The Plough (or Big Dipper) is in the northwest, with Cassiopeia and Cepheus in the northeast. The Great Square of Pegasus is rising in the east, while Arcturus, in Boötes, remains high in the west.
• **LOOKING SOUTH** Due south, Ophiuchus is entwined by both halves of Serpens with Hercules above it. In the east, the Summer Triangle of Vega, Deneb, and Altair is well placed. Antares in Scorpius is near the southern horizon, with Sagittarius visible to its left for observers in southerly locations. Virgo is setting in the far west.

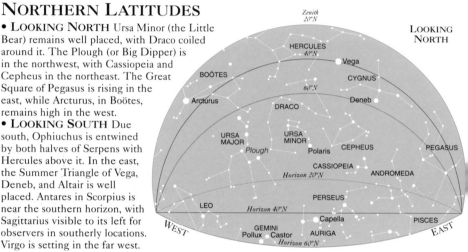

SOUTHERN LATITUDES
• **LOOKING NORTH** Ophiuchus and both parts of Serpens are centrally placed, with Aquila to their right. Hercules is closer to the northern horizon, midway between reddish Arcturus in the northwest and blue-white Vega in the north. To the right of Vega, Cygnus is rising.
• **LOOKING SOUTH** Scorpius, shaped like a fish hook, and Sagittarius are almost overhead, containing dense fields of stars near the centre of our Galaxy. To the southwest, along the star trail of the Milky Way (see pp.184–85), are Centaurus and Crux (the Southern Cross); Virgo is setting further west. In the east, Capricornus, Aquarius, and the star Fomalhaut are rising.

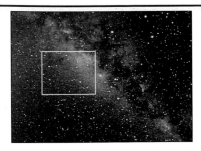

THE GALACTIC
CENTRE (SAGITTARIUS)
From southern latitudes
on July evenings, the
centre of our Galaxy lies
overhead, among dense
Milky Way star fields in
Sagittarius. Eight stars
in Sagittarius (enclosed
here in a rectangle) form
a shape known as the
Teapot (see pp.124–25).

WHOLE-SKY CHARTS

JULY FEATURES

● **ANTARES (SCORPIUS).**
Also known as Alpha (α)
Scorpii, this is one of the
largest stars visible to the
naked eye. It is a red supergiant, around 500 times
larger than the Sun. If it
were placed where our Sun
is, it would engulf the orbit
of Mars. See also pp.126–27.

● **EPSILON (ε) LYRAE.**
Near the bright star Vega lies
this remarkable multiple star.
Binoculars, or even sharp
eyesight, show that it is
double. Through a telescope,
each of these stars is itself
seen to be a close double,
hence this star's popular
name, the Double Double.
See also p.100.

☐ **M8 (SAGITTARIUS).**
This diffuse nebula is visible
to the naked eye in country
skies and is easy to find with
binoculars. It is elongated in
shape and is also called the
Lagoon Nebula, the lagoon
being a dark lane of dust
that crosses its centre. M8
contains NGC 6530, a cluster
visible through binoculars.
See also pp.124–25.

⊛ **M22 (SAGITTARIUS).**
This globular cluster, which
lies near the lid of the
Teapot in Sagittarius, is rated
the third best of its kind in
the sky, after Omega (ω)
Centauri and 47 Tucanae.
It can be seen as a hazy star
with the naked eye, and is
easy to find with binoculars.
See also pp.124–25.

ALSO VISIBLE

● **Albireo** (p.187)
✲ **M6 and M7** (p.175)
⊛ **M13** (p.175)
⊛ **M27** (p.193)
● **The Cygnus Rift** (p.187)

Star magnitudes −1 0 1 2 3

LOOKING
SOUTH

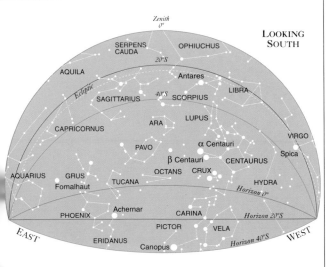

LOOKING
SOUTH

WHOLE-SKY CHART

Northern Latitudes

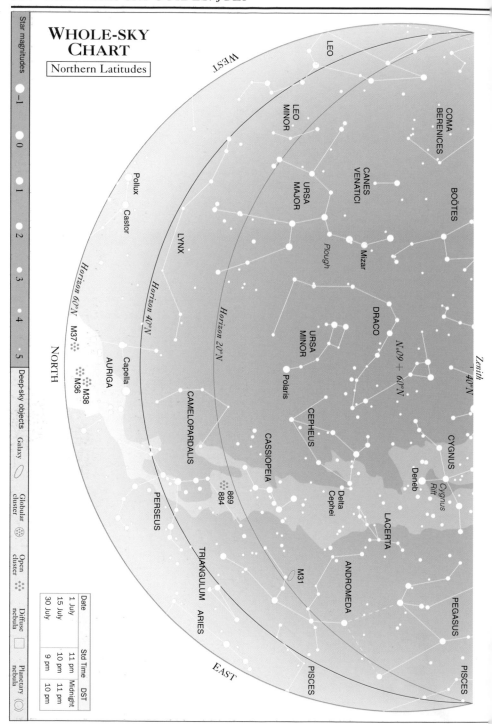

Star magnitudes

−1	
0	
1	
2	
3	
4	
5	

NORTH

Deep-sky objects

Galaxy

Globular cluster

Open cluster

Diffuse nebula

Planetary nebula

LEO

COMA BERENICES

LEO MINOR

CANES VENATICI

URSA MAJOR

BOÖTES

Pollux

Castor

LYNX

Plough

Mizar

Horizon 60°N

Horizon 40°N

Horizon 20°N

M37

M38

M36

AURIGA

Capella

CAMELOPARDALIS

URSA MINOR

Polaris

DRACO

$N°09 + 60°N$

CYGNUS

Cygnus Rift

Deneb

Zenith 40°N

CEPHEUS

CASSIOPEIA

Delta Cephei

LACERTA

PERSEUS

869 884

ANDROMEDA

PEGASUS

M31

TRIANGULUM

ARIES

PISCES

PISCES

WEST

EAST

Date	Std Time	DST
1 July	11 pm	Midnight
15 July	10 pm	11 pm
30 July	9 pm	10 pm

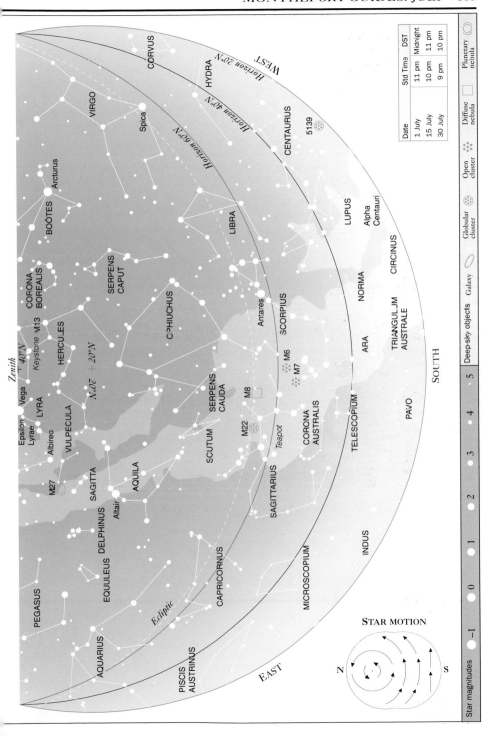

Date	Std Time	DST
1 July	11 pm	Midnight
15 July	10 pm	11 pm
30 July	9 pm	10 pm

Deep-sky objects

⬭ Galaxy

◎ Globular cluster

✸ Open cluster

◻ Diffuse nebula

◉ Planetary nebula

Star magnitudes

−1   0   1   2   3   4   5

STAR MOTION

N — S

Zenith

WEST

SOUTH

EAST

CORVUS

VIRGO

Spica

HYDRA

Horizon 20°N

Horizon 40°N

Horizon 60°N

CENTAURUS

5139

Alpha Centauri

LUPUS

Arcturus

BOOTES

CORONA BOREALIS

LIBRA

CIRCINUS

NORMA

TRIANGULUM AUSTRALE

ARA

SERPENS CAPUT

OPHIUCHUS

Antares

SCORPIUS

M6

M7

TELESCOPIUM

PAVO

HERCULES

Keystone M13

40°N

Epsilon Lyrae

Vega

LYRA

Albireo

20°N + 20°N

VULPECULA

SERPENS CAUDA

SCUTUM

M8

M22

Teapot

CORONA AUSTRALIS

SAGITTARIUS

INDUS

M27

SAGITTA

AQUILA

Altair

DELPHINUS

EQUULEUS

MICROSCOPIUM

PEGASUS

CAPRICORNUS

Ecliptic

AQUARIUS

PISCIS AUSTRINUS

WHOLE-SKY CHART

Southern Latitudes

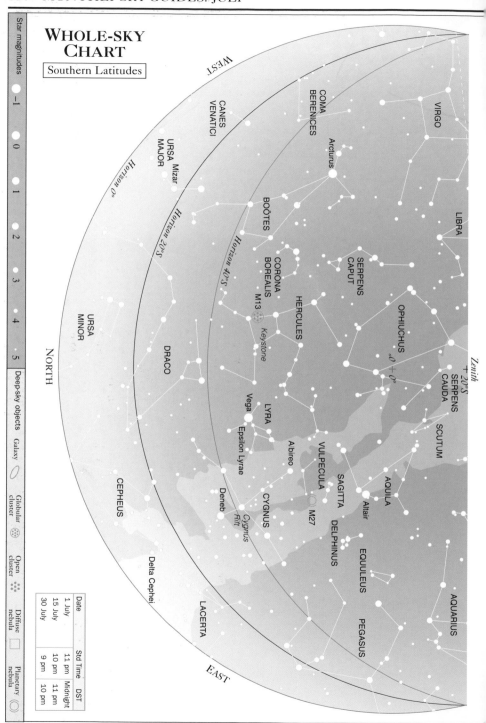

Star magnitudes

● −1 ● 0 ● 1 ● 2 ● 3 ● 4 ● 5

Deep-sky objects

Galaxy ⬭ Globular cluster ⊛ Open cluster ⁙ Diffuse nebula ▢ Planetary nebula ◎

WEST

NORTH

EAST

Horizon 0°

Horizon 20°S

Horizon 40°S

+ *20°S*

Zenith

+ *0°*

VIRGO

LIBRA

COMA BERENICES

CANES VENATICI

URSA MAJOR Mizar

Arcturus

BOÖTES

CORONA BOREALIS

SERPENS CAPUT

OPHIUCHUS

SERPENS CAUDA

SCUTUM

M13

HERCULES

Keystone

URSA MINOR

DRACO

LYRA

Vega

Epsilon Lyrae

Albireo

VULPECULA

M27

SAGITTA

AQUILA

Altair

DELPHINUS

EQUULEUS

AQUARIUS

CEPHEUS

Deneb

CYGNUS

Cygnus Rift

PEGASUS

Delta Cephei

LACERTA

Date	Std Time	DST
1 July	11 pm	Midnight
15 July	10 pm	11 pm
30 July	9 pm	10 pm

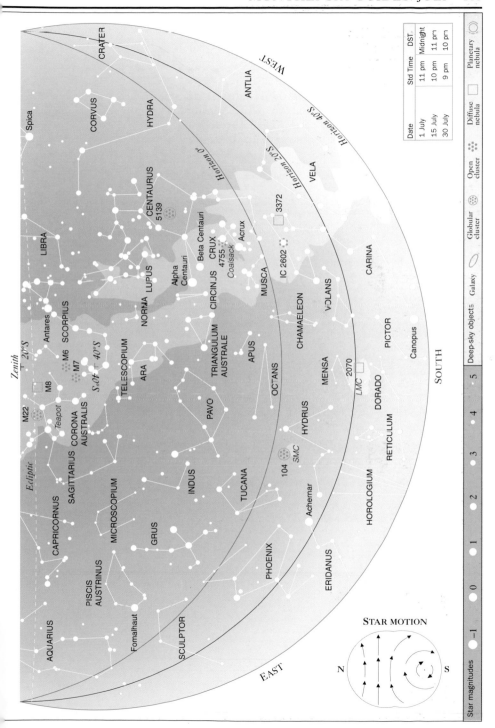

Date	Std Time	DST
1 July	11 pm	Midnight
15 July	10 pm	11 pm
30 July	9 pm	10 pm

Deep-sky objects

Galaxy · Globular cluster · Open cluster · Diffuse nebula · Planetary nebula

Star magnitudes

−1 · 0 · 1 · 2 · 3 · 4 · 5

STAR MOTION

WEST

SOUTH

EAST

Zenith

Ecliptic

20°S

40°S

60°S

Horizon 40°S

Horizon 20°S

Horizon 60°S

Spica
CRATER
CORVUS
HYDRA
ANTLIA
VELA
CARINA
LIBRA
CENTAURUS
5139
Beta Centauri
CRUX
Acrux
4755
Coalsack
Alpha Centauri
IC 2602
3372
MUSCA
PICTOR
Canopus
Antares
SCORPIUS
M6
M7
NORMA
LUPUS
CIRCINUS
TRIANGULUM AUSTRALE
VOLANS
CHAMAELEON
VELA
M8
M22
Teapot
CORONA AUSTRALIS
TELESCOPIUM
ARA
APUS
OCTANS
MENSA
2070
LMC
DORADO
RETICULUM
SAGITTARIUS
CAPRICORNUS
MICROSCOPIUM
PAVO
HYDRUS
INDUS
TUCANA
104
SMC
Achernar
HOROLOGIUM
GRUS
PISCIS AUSTRINUS
Fomalhaut
PHOENIX
ERIDANUS
AQUARIUS
SCULPTOR

N S

AUGUST

T HE BRIGHT STARS Altair, Deneb, and Vega form a prominent triangle that is well seen on August evenings from all but the most southerly latitudes. In the northern hemisphere, it is known as the Summer Triangle. Another major sight for northern observers is the Perseid meteor shower, visible in mid-month.

SUNRISE AND SUNSET ON 15 AUGUST		
Latitude	Sunrise	Sunset
60°N	04.10	19.50
40°N	05.10	17.00
20°N	05.40	18.30
0°	06.00	18.10
20°S	06.20	17.50
40°S	06.50	17.20

1 August Std time 🕐 DST 🕐   15 August Std time 🕐 DST 🕐   30 August Std time 🕐 DST 🕐

NORTHERN LATITUDES

• **LOOKING NORTH** The Plough (or Big Dipper) is in the northwest with Arcturus to its left. The bowl of the Little Dipper (in Ursa Minor) is to the left of Polaris, while to the right Cassiopeia appears like a back-to-front letter E. Perseus is rising lower down, with Pegasus and Andromeda further east.
• **LOOKING SOUTH** The stars of the Summer Triangle – Vega, Deneb, and Altair – are overhead. The Milky Way (see pp.188–89) runs southwest to northeast, and seems to divide in two in Cygnus. Ophiuchus and both parts of Serpens are in the west, with Sagittarius and Scorpius beneath them. Aquarius and Capricornus are in the southeast.

SOUTHERN LATITUDES

• **LOOKING NORTH** The bright stars Vega, Altair (in Aquila), and Deneb (in Cygnus) form a large triangle due north. The Milky Way (see pp.190–91), running northeastwards from near the zenith, seems to split in Cygnus. Ophiuchus and both parts of Serpens dominate the western sky, with Hercules just beneath them. In the northeast, the Great Square of Pegasus is rising.
• **LOOKING SOUTH** In the southeast, Achernar is rising, with Fomalhaut above it and slightly to the left. Higher up are Capricornus and Aquarius. Sagittarius is near the zenith, with Scorpius to its lower right. Centaurus and Crux (the Southern Cross) are setting in the southwest.

THE SUMMER TRIANGLE
Three stars in three separate constellations form a large isosceles triangle, which is a familiar feature in skies of northern summer and autumn, and southern winter and spring. The brightest of the three is Vega (top right) in Lyra, followed by Altair (bottom) in Aquila, and Deneb (top left) in Cygnus. The Cygnus Rift (see panel, right) runs through the triangle.

Star magnitudes   ●−1   ● 0   ● 1   • 2   • 3

LOOKING
SOUTH

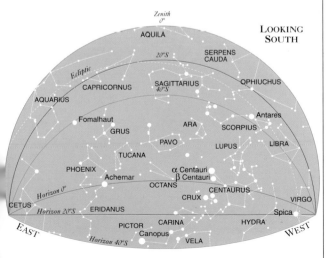

LOOKING
SOUTH

WHOLE-SKY CHARTS

AUGUST FEATURES

● **ALBIREO (CYGNUS).** This star, also known as Beta (β) Cygni, is one of the most celebrated doubles in the sky, on account of the coloration of its component stars and the ease with which they may be separated. The smallest of telescopes will show the stars; they appear amber and greenish, like two lamps in a celestial traffic light. See also p.88.

● **THE CYGNUS RIFT (CYGNUS).** This dark nebula, also known as the Northern Coalsack, divides the Milky Way into two. It can be traced with the naked eye from Cygnus, through Aquila, and into Ophiuchus, where it broadens out. See also p.88.

ALSO VISIBLE
● **Antares** (p.181)
● **Delta (δ) Cephei** (p.193)
● **Epsilon (ε) Lyrae** (p.181)
☐ **M8** (p.181)
⊛ **M13** (p.175)
⊛ **M22** (p.181)
◯ **M27** (p.193)
⊛ **NGC 104** (p.193)

AUGUST METEORS

THE PERSEIDS. Observers in the northern hemisphere have an opportunity this month to see the finest meteor shower of the year, the Perseids, which radiate from near the Double Cluster (NGC 869 and 884) in Perseus (see p.118). The meteors are bright, can flare up, and often leave trains. A peak of 75 or more meteors an hour is reached around 12 August, and activity can be seen for at least a week either side of this date.

WHOLE-SKY CHART

Northern Latitudes

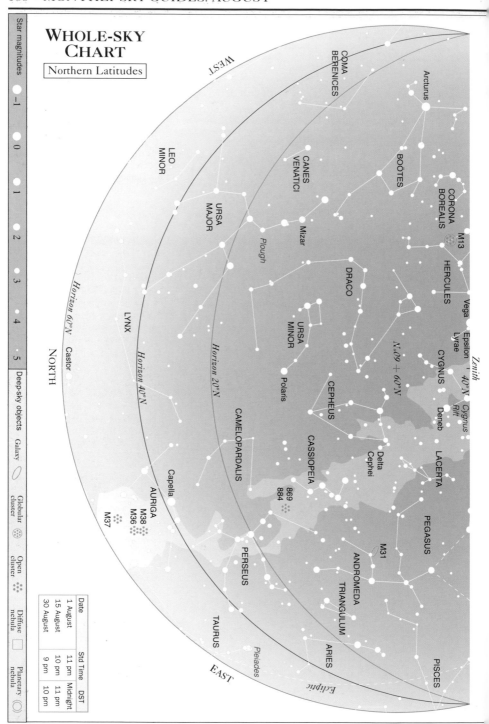

WEST

COMA BERENICES

Arcturus

LEO MINOR

BOÖTES

CORONA BOREALIS

CANES VENATICI

M13

HERCULES

URSA MAJOR

Mizar

Vega

Epsilon Lyrae

Lyrae

Cygnus Rift

Plough

DRACO

CYGNUS

Deneb

Zenith

40°N 40°N

N°09 + 60°N

LYNX

URSA MINOR

Horizon 60°N

Polaris

CEPHEUS

LACERTA

Castor

Horizon 40°N

Horizon 20°N

CAMELOPARDALIS

CASSIOPEIA

Delta Cephei

PEGASUS

Capella

869 884

M31

NORTH

AURIGA

M38
M36

ANDROMEDA

TRIANGULUM

M37

PERSEUS

ARIES

PISCES

TAURUS

Pleiades

Ecliptic

EAST

Date	Std Time	DST
1 August	11 pm	Midnight
15 August	10 pm	11 pm
30 August	9 pm	10 pm

Star magnitudes

−1 0 1 2 3 4 5

Deep-sky objects

Galaxy

Globular cluster

Open cluster

Diffuse nebula

Planetary nebula

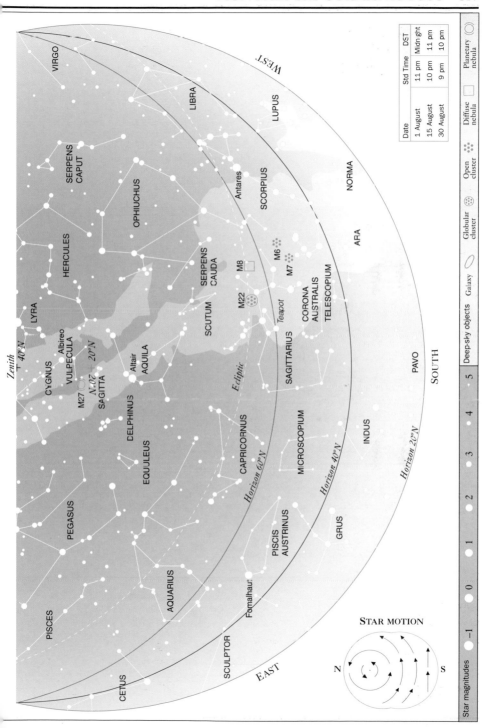

Date	Std Time	DST
1 August	11 pm	Midnight
15 August	10 pm	11 pm
30 August	9 pm	10 pm

Star magnitudes	−1	0	1	2	3	4	5	Deep-sky objects	Galaxy	Globular cluster	Open cluster	Diffuse nebula	Planetary nebula

STAR MOTION

N   S

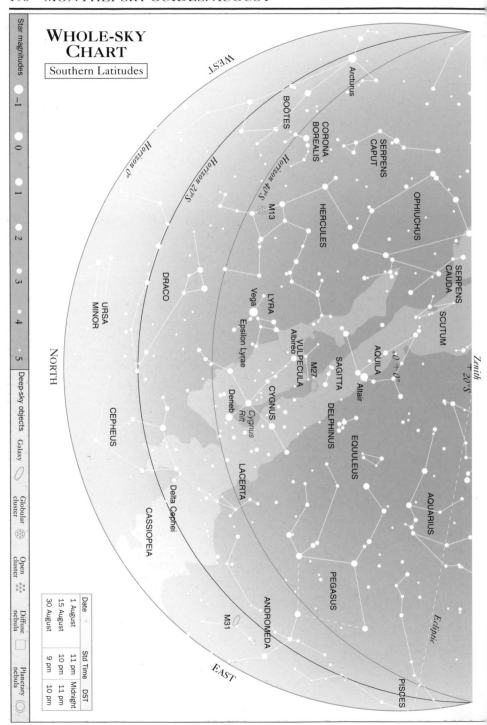

WHOLE-SKY CHART

Southern Latitudes

Star magnitudes

−1 0 1 2 3 4 5

Deep-sky objects

Galaxy

Globular cluster

Open cluster

Diffuse nebula

Planetary nebula

NORTH

WEST

EAST

Zenith

20°S

0° + 0°

Ecliptic

Horizon 0°
Horizon 20°S
Horizon 40°S

Arcturus

BOÖTES

CORONA BOREALIS

SERPENS CAPUT

M13

HERCULES

OPHIUCHUS

SERPENS CAUDA

SCUTUM

DRACO

URSA MINOR

Vega

LYRA

Epsilon Lyrae

Albireo

VULPECULA

M27

SAGITTA

AQUILA

Altair

CYGNUS

DELPHINUS

Deneb

Cygnus Rift

EQUULEUS

CEPHEUS

Delta Cephei

LACERTA

CASSIOPEIA

AQUARIUS

PEGASUS

M31

ANDROMEDA

PISCES

Date	Std Time	DST
1 August	11 pm	Midnight
15 August	10 pm	11 pm
30 August	9 pm	10 pm

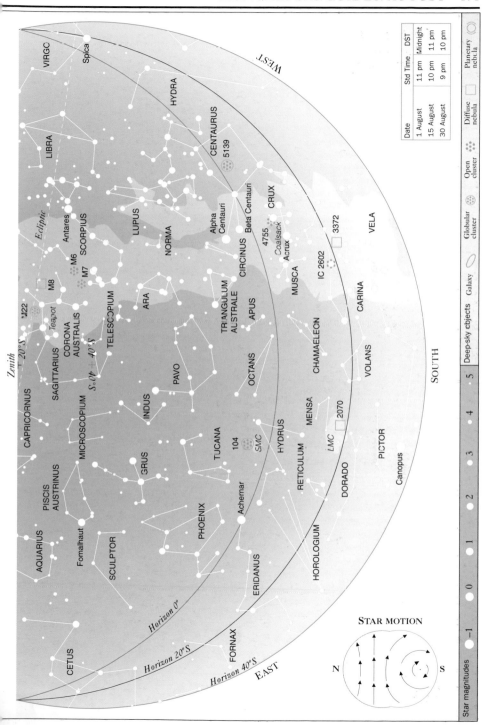

Date	Std Time	DST
1 August	11 pm	Midnight
15 August	10 pm	11 pm
30 August	9 pm	10 pm

Star magnitudes: −1, 0, 1, 2, 3, 4, 5

Deep-sky objects: Galaxy, Globular cluster, Open cluster, Diffuse nebula, Planetary nebula

STAR MOTION

N   S

SEPTEMBER

DAYS AND NIGHTS BECOME EQUAL in length as the equinox approaches, around 23 September, marking the start of northern autumn and southern spring. The Great Square of Pegasus is well placed for observers in northern latitudes, while in the southern hemisphere the brightest stars are in the western sky.

SUNRISE AND SUNSET ON 15 SEPTEMBER

Latitude	Sunrise	Sunset
60°N	05.30	18.20
40°N	05.40	18.10
20°N	05.50	18.00
0°	05.50	18.00
20°S	06.00	18.00
40°S	06.00	17.50

1 September Std time ⊕ DST ⊕ | 15 September Std time ⊕ DST ⊕ | 30 September Std time ⊕ DST ⊕

NORTHERN LATITUDES

• **LOOKING NORTH** The view to the north contains relatively few bright stars this month. Cepheus is due north, with Cassiopeia to its right. Andromeda and Pegasus are high in the eastern sky, while Perseus is rising in the northeast, followed by Auriga. Draco and Hercules are in the northwestern sky.

• **LOOKING SOUTH** Aquarius and Capricornus are centrally placed, with Fomalhaut below them. The Great Square of Pegasus, with Pisces to its lower left, dominates the view to the southeast. The Summer Triangle of Altair, Deneb, and Vega is almost overhead in the southwest, while Ophiuchus and Serpens Cauda set further west.

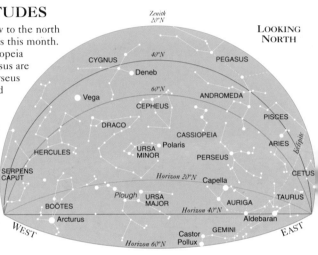

SOUTHERN LATITUDES

• **LOOKING NORTH** The large triangle formed by the bright stars Altair, Deneb, and Vega is prominent in the northwest. The Great Square of Pegasus dominates the northeastern sky, with Andromeda closer to the horizon and Pisces further east. Capricornus and Aquarius are almost overhead. Ophiuchus and Serpens Cauda are setting in the west.

• **LOOKING SOUTH** Achernar in Eridanus is prominent in the southeast, an otherwise fairly blank area of sky, with the Small Magellanic Cloud (SMC, see p.197) to its right. Fomalhaut is almost overhead. Scorpius is in the southwest, with Sagittarius above it.

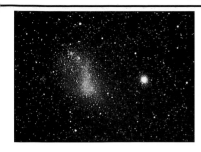

THE SMALL MAGELLANIC CLOUD (TUCANA)

This is the smaller, fainter, and more distant of two irregularly shaped small galaxies accompanying our own. To the naked eye, it looks like a cut-off part of the Milky Way. The cluster to its right is NGC 104 (see panel, right).

WHOLE-SKY CHARTS

SEPTEMBER FEATURES

● **DELTA (δ) CEPHEI.**
This is the prototype of the Cepheid variable stars that are used for finding distances in space. Delta Cephei's brightness rises and falls every 5 days as the star pulsates in size; at its peak, it is over twice as bright as when at its faintest. Changes in its brightness can be followed with the naked eye by comparing it with nearby stars of known magnitude. Delta Cephei is also an attractive double star, having a fainter companion that is visible with the smallest telescopes. See also p.80.

○ **M27 (VULPECULA).**
The easiest planetary nebula to see with binoculars lies in the often-overlooked constellation of Vulpecula, midway between the bright stars Deneb and Altair. Its popular name, the Dumb-bell Nebula, comes from its structure – more like a bow tie than a dumbbell – but this is visible only through a telescope. See also p.141.

⊛ **NGC 104 (TUCANA).**
Also known as 47 Tucanae, this is the second most prominent globular cluster in the entire sky – only Omega (ω) Centauri is brighter. To the naked eye, it resembles a hazy star. It appears in the sky near the Small Magellanic Cloud (SMC) but is actually within our own Galaxy. See also p.135.

ALSO VISIBLE
● **Albireo** (p.187)
● **Epsilon (ε) Lyrae** (p.181)
◕ **M31** (p.199)
⁙ **NGC 869 and NGC 884** (p.199)
● **The Cygnus Rift** (p.187)

Star magnitudes −1 0 1 2 3

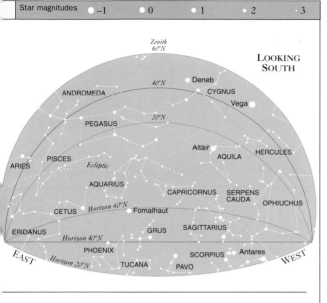

LOOKING SOUTH

Zenith 60°N

ANDROMEDA · Deneb · CYGNUS · Vega · 40°N · 20°N · PEGASUS · Altair · AQUILA · HERCULES · PISCES · ARIES · Ecliptic · AQUARIUS · CAPRICORNUS · SERPENS CAUDA · OPHIUCHUS · CETUS · Horizon 60°N · Fomalhaut · ERIDANUS · GRUS · SAGITTARIUS · Horizon 40°N · PHOENIX · SCORPIUS · Antares · EAST · Horizon 20°N · TUCANA · PAVO · WEST

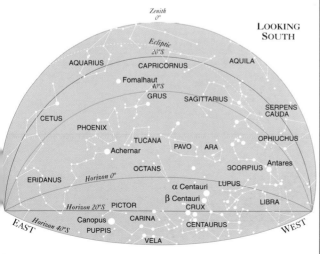

LOOKING SOUTH

Zenith 0°

AQUARIUS · CAPRICORNUS · AQUILA · Ecliptic 20°S · Fomalhaut · GRUS · SAGITTARIUS · 40°S · SERPENS CAUDA · CETUS · PHOENIX · TUCANA · PAVO · ARA · OPHIUCHUS · Achernar · OCTANS · SCORPIUS · Antares · ERIDANUS · Horizon 0° · α Centauri · LUPUS · β Centauri · CRUX · LIBRA · Horizon 20°S · PICTOR · Canopus · CARINA · CENTAURUS · EAST · Horizon 40°S · PUPPIS · VELA · WEST

WHOLE-SKY CHART

Northern Latitudes

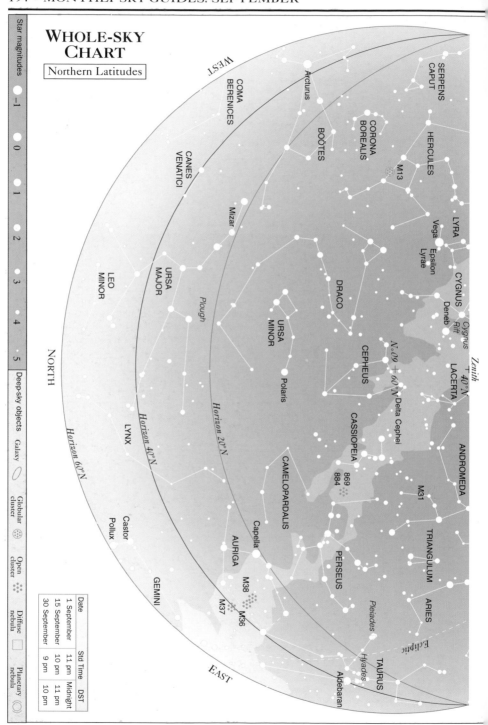

Star magnitudes

- -1
- 0
- 1
- 2
- 3
- 4
- 5

Deep-sky objects

- Galaxy
- Globular cluster
- Open cluster
- Diffuse nebula
- Planetary nebula

NORTH

WEST

EAST

Zenith

Serpens Caput
Coma Berenices
Arcturus
Corona Borealis
Boötes
Hercules
M13
Canes Venatici
Mizar
Vega
Epsilon Lyrae
Lyra
Cygnus
Deneb
Cygnus Rift
Lacerta
Draco
Leo Minor
Ursa Major
Plough
Ursa Minor
Cepheus
Delta Cephei
Polaris
Cassiopeia
Andromeda
M31
869
884
Camelopardalis
Triangulum
Lynx
Aries
Perseus
Castor
Pollux
Capella
Auriga
Pleiades
M38
M36
M37
Gemini
Hyades
Taurus
Aldebaran
Ecliptic

Horizon 20°N
Horizon 40°N
Horizon 60°N

Date	Std Time	DST
1 September	11 pm	Midnight
15 September	10 pm	11 pm
30 September	9 pm	10 pm

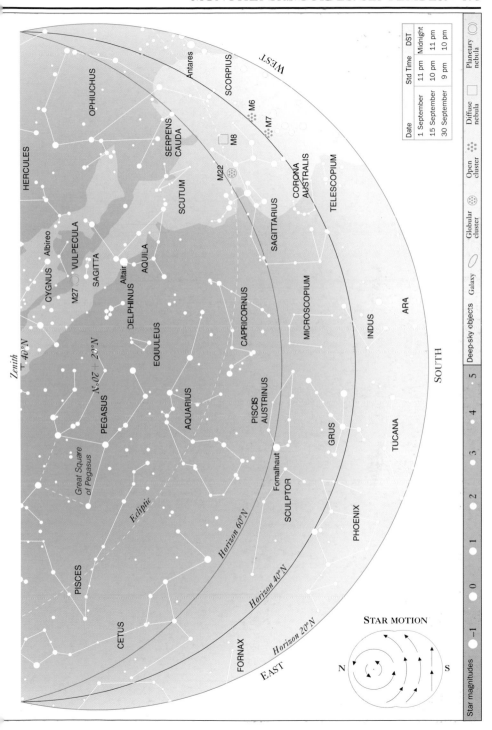

Date	Std Time	DST
1 September	11 pm	Midnight
15 September	10 pm	11 pm
30 September	9 pm	10 pm

WEST

Antares

SCORPIUS

M6

M7

M8

OPHIUCHUS

SERPENS
CAUDA

M22

CORONA
AUSTRALIS

TELESCOPIUM

HERCULES

SCUTUM

SAGITTARIUS

Albireo

CYGNUS

VULPECULA

M27

SAGITTA

Altair

AQUILA

DELPHINUS

MICROSCOPIUM

ARA

EQUULEUS

CAPRICORNUS

INDUS

Zenith

40°N

20°N

PEGASUS

AQUARIUS

PISCIS
AUSTRINUS

GRUS

TUCANA

SOUTH

Great Square
of Pegasus

Fomalhaut

SCULPTOR

Ecliptic

PHOENIX

PISCES

Horizon 60°N

CETUS

Horizon 40°N

FORNAX

Horizon 20°N

EAST

STAR MOTION

N   S

Deep-sky objects

Galaxy   Globular
cluster   Open
cluster   Diffuse
nebula   Planetary
nebula

Star magnitudes

−1   0   1   2   3   4   5

WHOLE-SKY CHART

Southern Latitudes

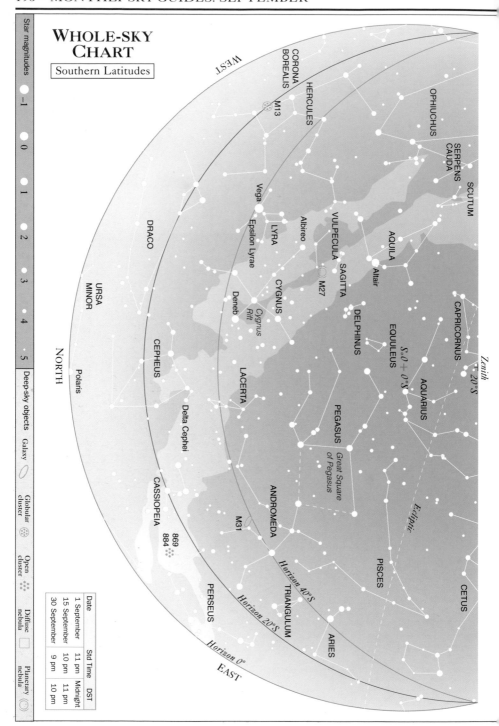

Star magnitudes							Deep-sky objects				
−1	0	1	2	3	4	5	Galaxy	Globular cluster	Open cluster	Diffuse nebula	Planetary nebula

NORTH

WEST

EAST

Date	Std Time	DST
1 September	11 pm	Midnight
15 September	10 pm	11 pm
30 September	9 pm	10 pm

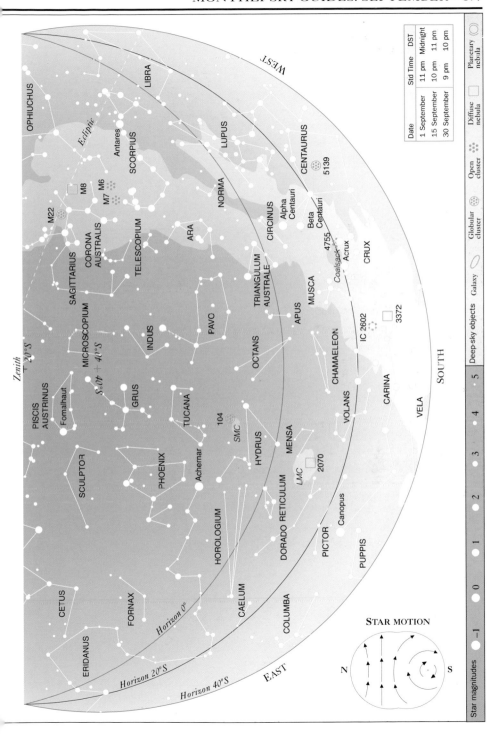

Date	Std Time	DST
1 September	11 pm	Midnight
15 September	10 pm	11 pm
30 September	9 pm	10 pm

WEST

OPHIUCHUS

LIBRA

Ecliptic

Antares

SCORPIUS

LUPUS

CENTAURUS

5139

M8 M6

M7

CORONA AUSTRALIS

NORMA

M22

SAGITTARIUS

TELESCOPIUM

ARA

CIRCINUS

Alpha Centauri

Beta Centauri

4755

Acrux

CRUX

Zenith

20°S

MICROSCOPIUM

APUS

MUSCA

Coalsack

TRIANGULUM AUSTRALE

PAVO

INDUS

OCTANS

CHAMAELEON

IC 2602

3372

S °0t + 40°S

PISCIS AUSTRINUS

Fomalhaut

GRUS

TUCANA

104

SMC

HYDRUS

MENSA

VOLANS

CARINA

VELA

SCULPTOR

PHOENIX

Achernar

LMC

2070

Canopus

PUPPIS

SOUTH

CETUS

FORNAX

HOROLOGIUM

DORADO RETICULUM

PICTOR

Horizon 0°

CAELUM

COLUMBA

ERIDANUS

Horizon 20°S

Horizon 40°S

EAST

STAR MOTION

N   S

Star magnitudes	–1	0	1	2	3	4	5	Deep-sky objects	Galaxy	Globular cluster	Open cluster	Diffuse nebula	Planetary nebula

OCTOBER

T HE ANDROMEDA GALAXY, M31, is almost overhead for observers in northern latitudes, although for those in the southern hemisphere it remains disappointingly low. There are few bright stars on display at this time of year, but the Great Square of Pegasus is easy to see from both hemispheres.

SUNRISE AND SUNSET ON 15 OCTOBER		
Latitude	Sunrise	Sunset
60°N	06.40	16.50
40°N	06.10	17.20
20°N	05.50	17.40
0°	05.40	17.50
20°S	05.30	18.00
40°S	05.10	18.20

1 October	Std time 🕐 DST 🕐	15 October	Std time 🕐 DST 🕐	30 October	Std time 🕐 DST 🕐

NORTHERN LATITUDES

• **LOOKING NORTH** The Milky Way arches overhead from west to east (see pp.200–201). Cassiopeia is high up, above and to the left of Perseus. Capella and the other stars of Auriga are rising in the northeast along with Taurus, a foretaste of winter. The Summer Triangle can still be seen in the west, with Altair lying in the southwestern sky (far right of Looking South map).
• **LOOKING SOUTH** High in the south, the Great Square of Pegasus is well placed, with Andromeda above and to its left, almost overhead. Pisces lies to the left of Pegasus, and Aquarius is to its lower right. Low in the south is Fomalhaut, with Cetus in the southeastern sky.

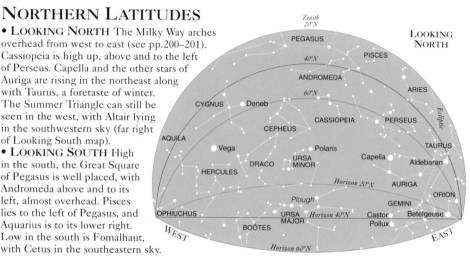

SOUTHERN LATITUDES

• **LOOKING NORTH** The Great Square of Pegasus is centrally placed, with Andromeda to its lower right. Pisces is above and to the right of Pegasus, with Aquarius above left, nearly overhead. Altair, Vega, and Deneb are setting in the northwest. Aldebaran and the other stars of Taurus are just starting to appear above the northeastern horizon.
• **LOOKING SOUTH** Achernar is high in the southeast with Canopus rising below it. The only other objects of note in this relatively blank area are the Large and Small Magellanic Clouds (LMC and SMC, see p.203). Low in the southwestern sky, Sagittarius is following Scorpius below the horizon.

THE GREAT SQUARE OF PEGASUS

The corners of this huge square are marked by three stars in Pegasus and one in Andromeda (top left). Despite the figure's considerable size (about 15 degrees to a side, large enough to enclose 900 full Moons), it contains few naked-eye stars.

Star magnitudes –1 0 1 2 3

LOOKING SOUTH

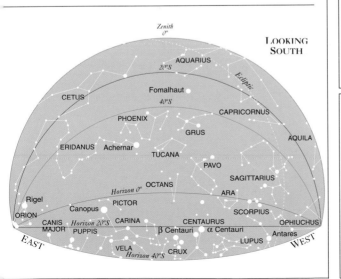

LOOKING SOUTH

WHOLE-SKY CHARTS

OCTOBER FEATURES

M31 (ANDROMEDA). The most distant object visible to the naked eye is a spiral galaxy similar to our home galaxy. Also called the Andromeda Galaxy, it can be seen with the naked eye in rural skies, but its full extent is better appreciated through binoculars. M31 is more than 2 million light years away, so the light by which we now see it left when mankind's ancestors still roamed the plains of Africa. See also p.64.

NGC 869 AND NGC 884 (PERSEUS). Two open clusters, known as the Double Cluster, mark the hand of Perseus. When seen with the naked eye, the pair resembles a knot that appears brighter than the surrounding Milky Way. They are easy to see through binoculars. See also p.118.

ALSO VISIBLE

- Albireo (p.187)
- Delta (δ) Cephei (p.193)
- M27 (p.193)
- NGC 104 (p.193)
- NGC 2070 (p.205)
- The Cygnus Rift (p.187)
- The Hyades and Pleiades (p.211)

OCTOBER METEORS

THE ORIONIDS. Radiating from northern Orion, near the border with Gemini, the Orionids reach a peak of about 25 meteors an hour around 21 October. As this area of sky does not rise until late, the shower is best viewed after midnight. The Orionids are fast moving but faint. Like the Eta Aquarids of May, they are caused by dust from Halley's Comet.

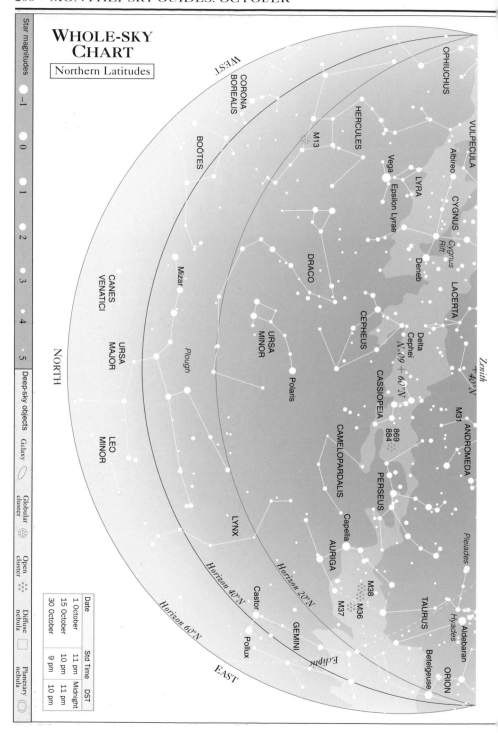

WHOLE-SKY CHART

Northern Latitudes

Star magnitudes

- −1
- 0
- 1
- 2
- 3
- 4
- 5

Deep-sky objects

Galaxy

Globular cluster

Open cluster

Diffuse nebula

Planetary nebula

NORTH

WEST

EAST

Zenith 40°N

Horizon 40°N

Horizon 20°N

Horizon 60°N

Ecliptic

OPHIUCHUS

CORONA BOREALIS

VULPECULA

BOÖTES

HERCULES

M13

Albireo

LYRA

CYGNUS

Vega

Epsilon Lyrae

Cygnus Rift

Deneb

LACERTA

DRACO

CEPHEUS

Delta Cephei

N°09 + 60°N

CASSIOPEIA

M31 ANDROMEDA

CANES VENATICI

Mizar

URSA MINOR

Polaris

869 884

PERSEUS

Plough

Pleiades

URSA MAJOR

CAMELOPARDALIS

Capella

AURIGA

M38

M36

M37

TAURUS

Hyades

Aldebaran

ORION

Betelgeuse

LEO MINOR

LYNX

Castor

Pollux

GEMINI

Date	Std Time	DST
1 October	11 pm	Midnight
15 October	10 pm	11 pm
30 October	9 pm	10 pm

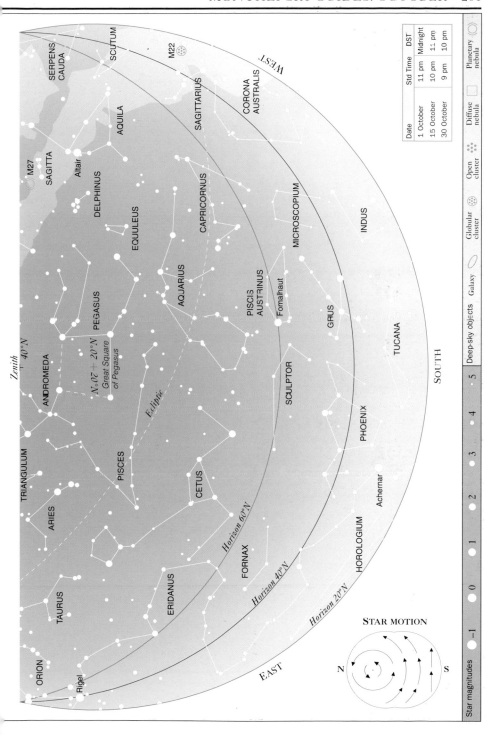

Date	Std Time	DST
1 October	11 pm	Midnight
15 October	10 pm	11 pm
30 October	9 pm	10 pm

SCUTUM
SERPENS CAUDA
M22
SAGITTARIUS
AQUILA
CORONA AUSTRALIS
WEST
SAGITTA
M27
Altair
DELPHINUS
EQUULEUS
CAPRICORNUS
MICROSCOPIUM
INDUS
Zenith
40°N
PEGASUS
N.°02 + 20°N
Great Square of Pegasus
ANDROMEDA
AQUARIUS
PISCIS AUSTRINUS
Fomalhaut
GRUS
TUCANA
Ecliptic
TRIANGULUM
ARIES
PISCES
SCULPTOR
PHOENIX
SOUTH
CETUS
Horizon 60°N
Achernar
TAURUS
ERIDANUS
FORNAX
Horizon 40°N
HOROLOGIUM
ORION
Rigel
Horizon 20°N
EAST

STAR MOTION
N
S

Star magnitudes   −1   0   1   2   3   4   5

Deep-sky objects   Galaxy   Globular cluster   Open cluster   Diffuse nebula   Planetary nebula

WHOLE-SKY CHART

Southern Latitudes

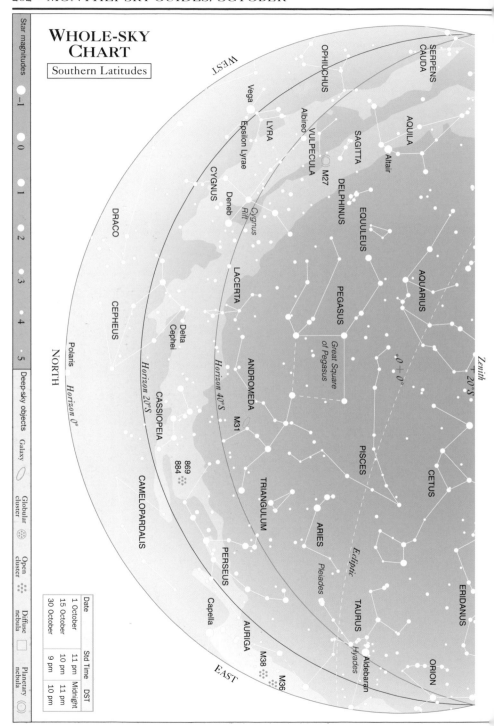

Star magnitudes

-1
0
1
2
3
4
5

Deep-sky objects

Galaxy

Globular cluster

Open cluster

Diffuse nebula

Planetary nebula

Date	Std Time	DST
1 October	11 pm	Midnight
15 October	10 pm	11 pm
30 October	9 pm	10 pm

WEST

OPHIUCHUS

SERPENS CAUDA

AQUILA

Altair

SAGITTA

Vega

LYRA

Albireo

VULPECULA

M27

DELPHINUS

Epsilon Lyrae

EQUULEUS

CYGNUS

AQUARIUS

Deneb

Cygnus Rift

PEGASUS

Great Square of Pegasus

DRACO

LACERTA

Horizon 40°S

PISCES

CEPHEUS

Delta Cephei

ANDROMEDA

M31

CETUS

Polaris

Horizon 0°

Horizon 20°S

CASSIOPEIA

869
884

TRIANGULUM

NORTH

CAMELOPARDALIS

PERSEUS

ARIES

Pleiades

ERIDANUS

Capella

AURIGA

TAURUS

Aldebaran

ORION

M38

M36

Hyades

Ecliptic

Zenith

20°S

0°

EAST

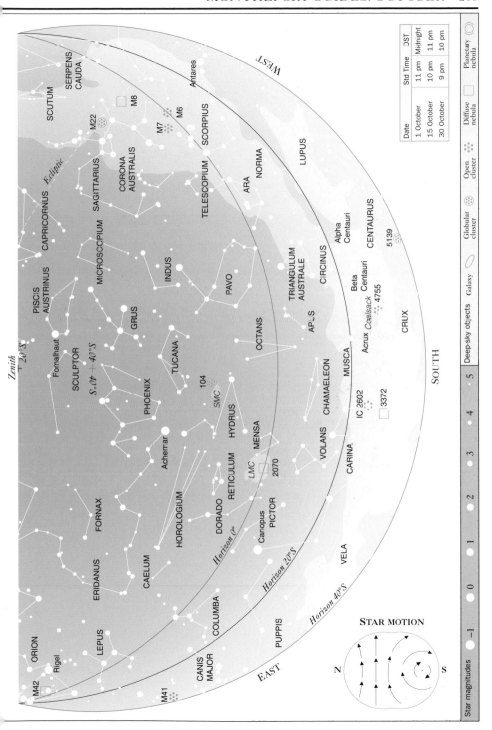

Date	Std Time	DST
1 October	11 pm	Midnight
15 October	10 pm	11 pm
30 October	9 pm	10 pm

Deep-sky objects

Galaxy | Globular cluster | Open cluster | Diffuse nebula | Planetary nebula

Star magnitudes

−1 0 1 2 3 4 5

STAR MOTION

N   S

NOVEMBER

A LL THE constellations named after characters in the story of Perseus and Andromeda are on view this month – Perseus and Andromeda themselves, Cassiopeia and Cepheus, her parents, and Cetus, the sea monster from which she was saved by Perseus. In northern latitudes, daylight-saving time is at an end.

SUNRISE AND SUNSET ON 15 NOVEMBER		
Latitude	Sunrise	Sunset
60°N	08.00	15.30
40°N	06.50	16.40
20°N	06.10	17.20
0°	05.40	17.50
20°S	05.10	18.20
40°S	04.40	18.50

1 November	Std time 🕐 DST 🕐	15 November	Std time 🕐 DST 🕐	30 November	Std time 🕐 DST 🕐

NORTHERN LATITUDES

• **LOOKING NORTH** The Milky Way (see pp.206–207) arches overhead from west to east. Perseus, Andromeda, and Cassiopeia are high up, with Cepheus beneath them. Auriga, with its brightest star Capella, is high in the northeast, with Gemini below it. The Summer Triangle of Vega, Deneb, and Altair is now low in the northwestern sky.
• **LOOKING SOUTH** Cetus lies due south, flanked higher up by Aries and Andromeda. Pisces, Pegasus, and Aquarius dominate the sky to the west. The stars of winter are rising in the east, among them Orion and Taurus, which contains red Aldebaran and the Hyades and Pleiades clusters (see p.207).

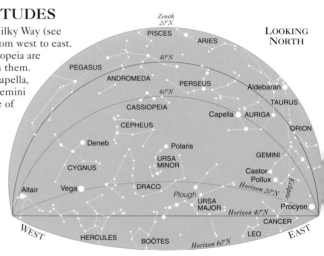

SOUTHERN LATITUDES

• **LOOKING NORTH** Cetus is almost over-head, with Pisces and Aries below it, while Perseus, Andromeda, and Cassiopeia are close to the northern horizon. Pegasus, with its Great Square, occupies most of the northwestern sky. In the northeast, Taurus is climbing into view, with Orion further east, a sign of approaching summer.
• **LOOKING SOUTH** Achernar is due south, with the Large and Small Magellanic Clouds (LMC and SMC, see p.209) below it. There are few noticeable stars near the zenith, but Sirius and Canopus, the two brightest stars in the sky, stand out in the east and south-east. Fomalhaut is high in the west.

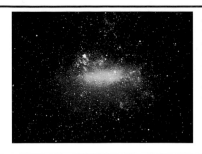

THE LARGE
MAGELLANIC CLOUD
Lying mostly in Dorado,
this is the larger, brighter,
and closer of two small
galaxies that accompany
our own. It appears to the
eye as a long, hazy patch
like a detached part of
the Milky Way, while
binoculars show a host of
star clusters and nebulae.

WHOLE-SKY CHARTS

NOVEMBER FEATURES

☐ **NGC 2070 (DORADO).**
The most prominent object
in the Large Magellanic
Cloud is a diffuse nebula
visible to the naked eye
and through binoculars. It
is popularly known as the
Tarantula Nebula because
of its spidery shape, which
is particularly noticeable on
photographs. It is about 50
times larger than the famous
Orion Nebula (M42) in our
own Galaxy. See also p.91.

ALSO VISIBLE
◝M31 (p.199)
❉ M36, M37, and M38 (p.211)
❉ M41 (p.151)
☐ M42 (p.145)
❉ NGC 869 and NGC 884 (p.199)
❉ NGC 2244 (p.151)
● The Hyades and Pleiades (p.211)

Star magnitudes ● −1 ● 0 ● 1 ● 2 · 3

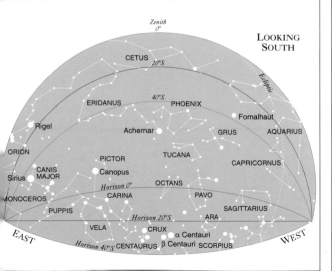

Zenith
60°N

LOOKING
SOUTH

PERSEUS
40°N ANDROMEDA

ARIES
20°N

AURIGA PEGASUS
TAURUS PISCES
Aldebaran

ORION CETUS
Betelgeuse
Rigel AQUARIUS
MONOCEROS *Horizon 60°N*
ERIDANUS Fomalhaut

Horizon 40°N CAPRICORNUS
CANIS PHOENIX
Sirius MAJOR GRUS
EAST Achernar *WEST*
TUCANA *Horizon 20°N*

Zenith
0°

LOOKING
SOUTH

CETUS
20°S

ERIDANUS *40°S* PHOENIX

Rigel Fomalhaut
Achernar GRUS AQUARIUS

ORION
PICTOR TUCANA
CANIS CAPRICORNUS
Sirius MAJOR Canopus
Horizon 0° OCTANS
MONOCEROS CARINA PAVO
PUPPIS SAGITTARIUS
Horizon 20°S ARA
VELA CRUX
EAST α Centauri *WEST*
Horizon 40°S CENTAURUS β Centauri SCORPIUS

NOVEMBER METEORS

THE TAURIDS. Starting in
late October and continuing
for a month or more, the
Taurids reach a sustained
peak in the first week of
November. Activity is no
more than 10 an hour, from
just south of the Pleiades,
but Taurid meteors are
striking because they move
slowly and are often bright.
THE LEONIDS. This shower
radiates from the head of Leo
around 17 November. Activity
is normally only about 10 an
hour at best, but it can surge
sharply at 33-year intervals
when the parent comet,
Tempel– Tuttle, returns to
the Sun. A Leonid storm
occurred in 1966, and there
were high rates of activity
from 1998 to 2002.

WHOLE-SKY CHART

Northern Latitudes

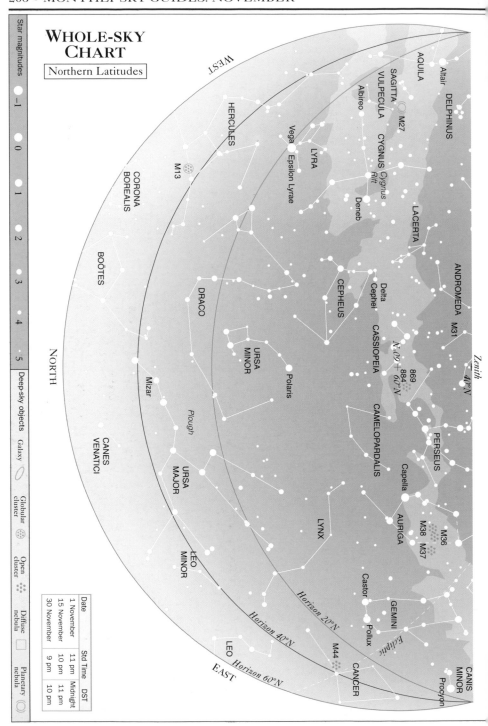

Star magnitudes

●	−1
●	0
●	1
●	2
●	3
•	4
·	5

Deep-sky objects

Galaxy	⬭
Globular cluster	⬡
Open cluster	⁙
Diffuse nebula	☐
Planetary nebula	◎

NORTH

WEST

EAST

NORTH

Zenith

40°N

Date	Std Time	DST
1 November	11 pm	Midnight
15 November	10 pm	11 pm
30 November	9 pm	10 pm

AQUILA
Altair
DELPHINUS
SAGITTA
VULPECULA
M27
Albireo
CYGNUS
Cygnus Rift
LACERTA
HERCULES
Vega
LYRA
Epsilon Lyrae
Deneb
ANDROMEDA
M31
CORONA BOREALIS
M13
CEPHEUS
Delta Cephei
CASSIOPEIA
869
884
PERSEUS
BOÖTES
DRACO
URSA MINOR
Polaris
CAMELOPARDALIS
Capella
AURIGA
Mizar
Plough
M38
M36
M37
CANES VENATICI
URSA MAJOR
LYNX
Castor
GEMINI
Pollux
LEO MINOR
Ecliptic
M44
CANCER
Procyon
CANIS MINOR
Horizon 20°N
Horizon 40°N
Horizon 60°N

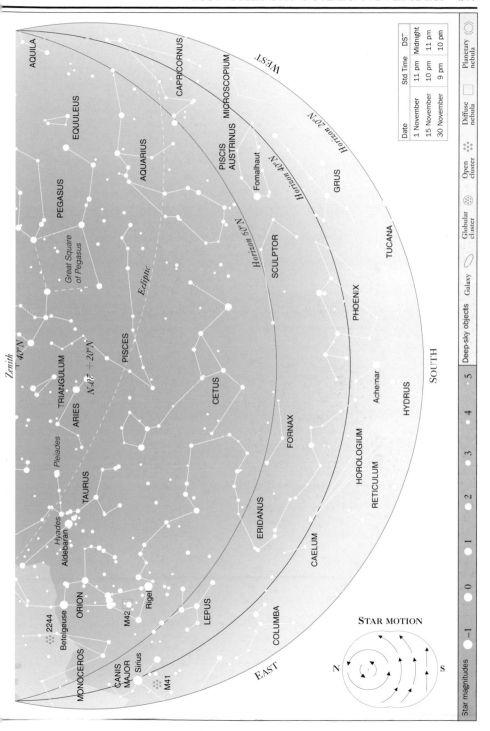

STAR MOTION

Star magnitudes

Date	Std Time	DST
1 November	11 pm	Midnight
15 November	10 pm	11 pm
30 November	9 pm	10 pm

Deep-sky objects | Galaxy | Globular cluster | Open cluster | Diffuse nebula | Planetary nebula

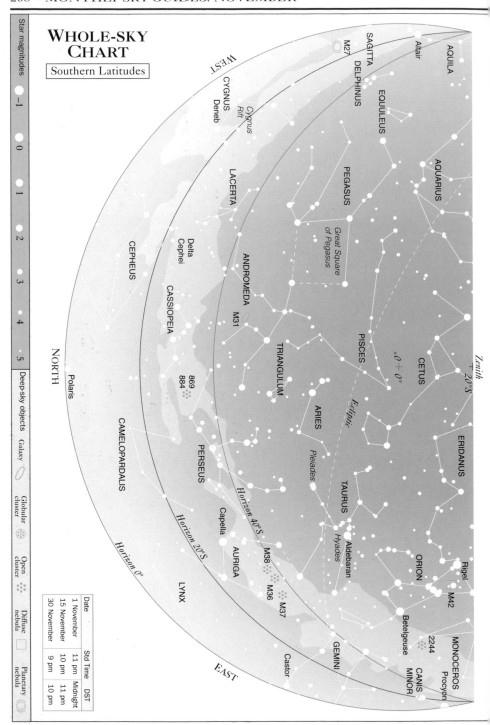

WHOLE-SKY CHART

Southern Latitudes

Star magnitudes

−1	0	1	2	3	4	5	Deep-sky objects

Galaxy	Globular cluster	Open cluster	Diffuse nebula	Planetary nebula

Date	Std Time	DST
1 November	11 pm	Midnight
15 November	10 pm	11 pm
30 November	9 pm	10 pm

WEST

NORTH

EAST

Zenith

AQUILA
Altair
SAGITTA
DELPHINUS
M27
CYGNUS
Deneb
Cygnus Rift
EQUULEUS
AQUARIUS
PEGASUS
Great Square of Pegasus
LACERTA
CEPHEUS
Delta Cephei
CASSIOPEIA
Polaris
CAMELOPARDALIS
ANDROMEDA
M31
869 884
PERSEUS
Capella
AURIGA
LYNX
TRIANGULUM
PISCES
CETUS
ARIES
Pleiades
TAURUS
Hyades
Aldebaran
M38
M36
M37
GEMINI
Castor
ORION
Betelgeuse
CANIS MINOR
Procyon
MONOCEROS
2244
ERIDANUS
Rigel
M42
+20°S
0°+0°
Ecliptic
Horizon 40°S
Horizon 20°S
Horizon 0°

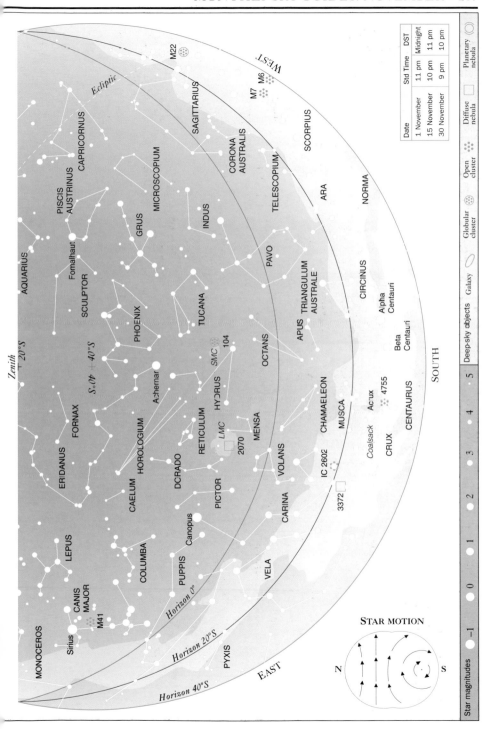

Date	Std Time	DST
1 November	11 pm	Midnight
15 November	10 pm	11 pm
30 November	9 pm	10 pm

Diffuse nebula · Planetary nebula · Open cluster · Globular cluster · Galaxy · Deep-sky objects

SOUTH

Star magnitudes: −1 0 1 2 3 4 5

STAR MOTION

N — S

DECEMBER

N IGHTS ARE AT THEIR LONGEST and days at their shortest in the northern hemisphere, and vice versa in the south. Much of the sky as it appears in the far south is occupied by constellations that were never seen by the astronomers of ancient Greece. A bright meteor shower radiates from Gemini in mid-month.

SUNRISE AND SUNSET ON 15 DECEMBER		
Latitude	Sunrise	Sunset
60°N	09.00	14.50
40°N	07.10	16.40
20°N	06.30	17.20
0°	05.50	18.00
20°S	05.20	18.40
40°S	04.30	19.20

1 December Std time 🕐 DST 🕐 | 15 December Std time 🕐 DST 🕐 | 30 December Std time 🕐 DST 🕐

NORTHERN LATITUDES

• **LOOKING NORTH** Perseus is almost overhead with Capella and the other stars of Auriga to its right. Gemini is further east, with Cancer rising beneath it. On the northeastern horizon, Regulus leads the stars of Leo into view. In the northwest are Cassiopeia and Cepheus, with Deneb closer to the horizon.
• **LOOKING SOUTH** Taurus is high in the south, ideally placed for observing the Pleiades and Hyades clusters (see p.213). Eridanus is beneath it, while to its lower left Orion is still rising, followed by brilliant Sirius and Procyon. Cetus can be seen in the southwestern sky, with Pisces and Pegasus visible progressively further to the west.

SOUTHERN LATITUDES

• **LOOKING NORTH** Eridanus, the celestial river, meanders overhead. Taurus is below it, with the Hyades and Pleiades (see p.214) ideally placed and Orion high to its right. Auriga and Perseus are near the northern horizon, with Gemini in the northeast. In the northwest, the Great Square of Pegasus is setting, followed by Pisces.
• **LOOKING SOUTH** Achernar and Canopus lie to the right and left of centre. In between them, slightly lower down, are the Large and Small Magellanic Clouds (LMC and SMC, see p.215). Sirius is high in the eastern sky, and Vela and Puppis are rising in the southeast. Fomalhaut is setting in the southwest.

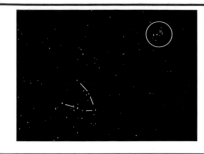

THE HYADES AND PLEIADES (TAURUS)

The stars of Taurus depict the top half of a bull's body. The large, V-shaped Hyades cluster (to lower left) outlines the face, and the red star Aldebaran represents one eye. The Pleiades cluster (top right) lies on the bull's back. See also panel, right.

Star magnitudes ● −1 ● 0 ● 1 • 2 · 3

Zenith
60°N

LOOKING
SOUTH

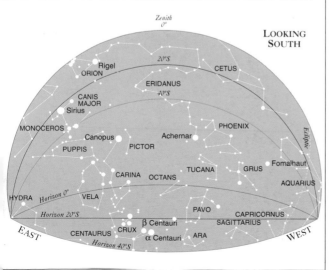

Zenith
0°

LOOKING
SOUTH

WHOLE-SKY CHARTS

DECEMBER FEATURES

❖ **M36, M37, AND M38 (AURIGA).** In the Milky Way star fields of Auriga, a crooked line of three open clusters can be seen through wide-field binoculars. M37 is the largest of them, while M36, in the middle of the line, is the smallest but also the easiest to resolve into individual stars with a small telescope. See also p.69.

● **THE HYADES (TAURUS).** This large, bright open cluster, the closest such cluster to Earth, contains more than a dozen stars visible to the naked eye. See also pp.132–33.

● **THE PLEIADES (TAURUS).** At first glance, this open cluster appears as a hazy cloud, but a closer look reveals several individual stars. Although the cluster is also called the Seven Sisters, normal eyesight shows only about six stars. People with exceptional vision can see several more, and binoculars bring dozens of stars into view. See also pp.132–33.

ALSO VISIBLE
❖ **M41** (p.151)
☐ **M42** (p.145)
❖ **M44** (p.157)
☐ **NGC 2070** (p.205)
❖ **NGC 2244** (p.151)

DECEMBER METEORS

THE GEMINIDS. The second-best shower of the year radiates from near Castor, in Gemini, reaching a maximum on 13 December, when as many as 100 bright meteors an hour may be seen. Lower rates of activity occur for several days either side of the maximum.

WHOLE-SKY CHART

Northern Latitudes

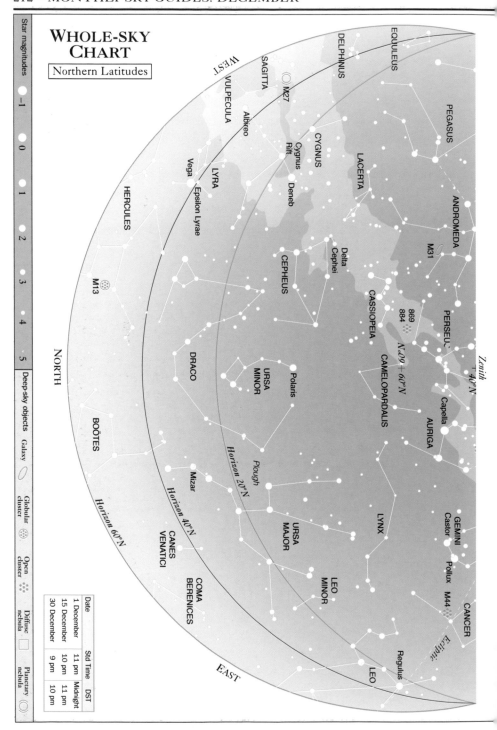

Star magnitudes
-1 0 1 2 3 4 5

Deep-sky objects   Galaxy   Globular cluster   Open cluster   Diffuse nebula   Planetary nebula

NORTH

WEST

EAST

Zenith 40°N

Date	Std Time	DST
1 December	11 pm	Midnight
15 December	10 pm	11 pm
30 December	9 pm	10 pm

Horizon 20°N
Horizon 40°N
Horizon 60°N

Ecliptic

EQUULEUS
DELPHINUS
SAGITTA
VULPECULA
M27
Albireo
Cygnus Rift
CYGNUS
Deneb
LACERTA
PEGASUS
ANDROMEDA
M31
PERSEUS
Capella
869 884
N.Q9 + 60°N
CASSIOPEIA
CEPHEUS
Delta Cephei
Vega
LYRA
Epsilon Lyrae
HERCULES
M13
DRACO
URSA MINOR
Polaris
CAMELOPARDALIS
AURIGA
BOÖTES
Mizar
Plough
Horizon 20°N
URSA MAJOR
LYNX
GEMINI
Castor
Pollux
M44
CANCER
LEO MINOR
CANES VENATICI
COMA BERENICES
Regulus
LEO

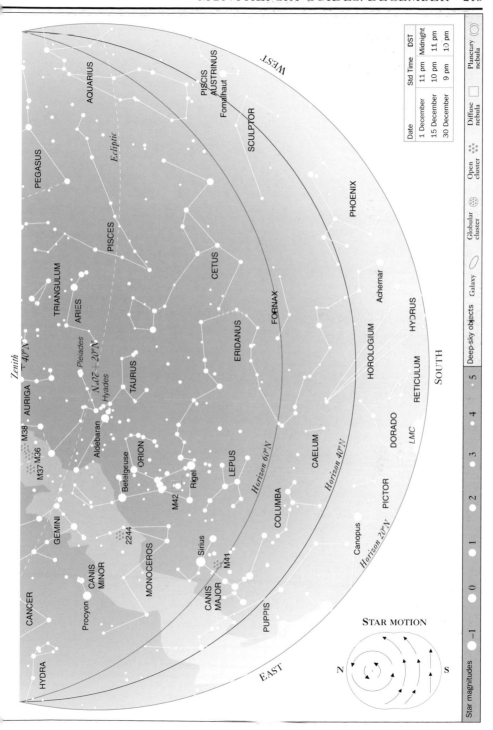

Date	Std Time	DST
1 December	11 pm	Midnight
15 December	10 pm	11 pm
30 December	9 pm	10 pm

Star magnitudes

−1 0 1 2 3 4 5

Deep-sky objects

Galaxy

Globular cluster

Open cluster

Diffuse nebula

Planetary nebula

STAR MOTION

N   S

WEST

SOUTH

EAST

Zenith

Ecliptic

AQUARIUS

PISCIS AUSTRINUS
Fomalhaut

SCULPTOR

PHOENIX

Achernar

HYDRUS

RETICULUM

HOROLOGIUM

DORADO

LMC

CAELUM

PICTOR

Canopus

PUPPIS

COLUMBA

PEGASUS

PISCES

TRIANGULUM

ARIES

Pleiades
Hyades

TAURUS
Aldebaran

ORION
Betelgeuse
Rigel
M42

LEPUS

CETUS

ERIDANUS

FORNAX

Horizon 60°N

Horizon 40°N

Horizon 20°N

+ 40°N

+ 20°N

AURIGA
M38
M37 M36

GEMINI

CANCER

HYDRA

CANIS MINOR
Procyon

MONOCEROS

2244

Sirius
M41

CANIS MAJOR

WHOLE-SKY CHART

Southern Latitudes

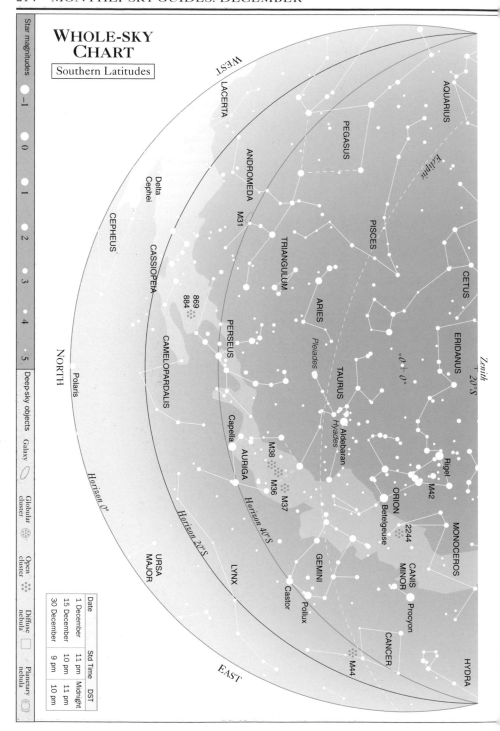

Star magnitudes

-1
0
1
2
3
4
5

Deep-sky objects

Galaxy

Globular cluster

Open cluster

Diffuse nebula

Planetary nebula

Date	Std Time	DST
1 December	11 pm	Midnight
15 December	10 pm	11 pm
30 December	9 pm	10 pm

NORTH

WEST

EAST

LACERTA

PEGASUS

AQUARIUS

ANDROMEDA

Delta Cephei

CEPHEUS

CASSIOPEIA

M31

TRIANGULUM

PISCES

CETUS

ERIDANUS

Ecliptic

Zenith 20°S

0° +0°

PERSEUS

ARIES

869 884

CAMELOPARDALIS

TAURUS

Pleiades

Aldebaran Hyades

Rigel

M42

ORION

Betelgeuse

2244

MONOCEROS

Polaris

Capella

AURIGA

M38

M36

M37

Horizon 40°S

Horizon 20°S

Horizon 0°

CANIS MINOR

GEMINI

Castor

Pollux

Procyon

URSA MAJOR

LYNX

CANCER

M44

HYDRA

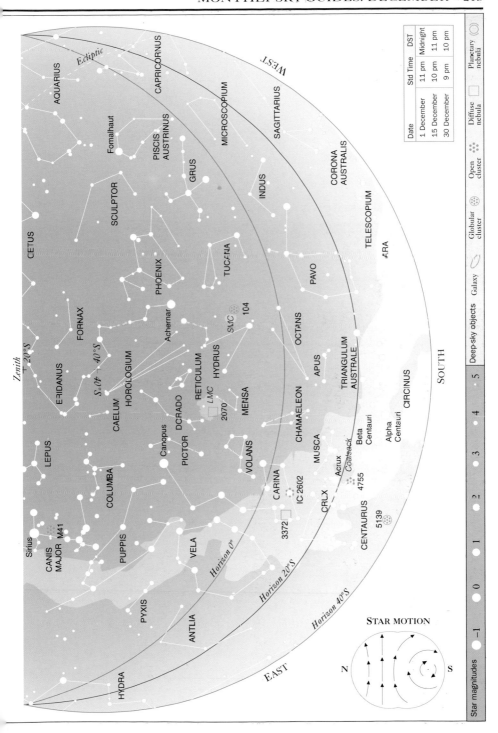

Date	Std Time	DST
1 December	11 pm	Midnight
15 December	10 pm	11 pm
30 December	9 pm	10 pm

STAR MOTION

Star magnitudes −1 0 1 2 3 4 5

Deep-sky objects Galaxy Globular cluster Open cluster Diffuse nebula Planetary nebula

GLOSSARY

WITH THE EXCEPTION of words in regular use, words that are defined elsewhere in the glossary appear in **bold** type.

• **ABSOLUTE MAGNITUDE**
A measure of the true luminosity of an object, defined as how bright it would appear if it were at a standard distance from the Earth, chosen to be 32.6 **light years**.

• **APERTURE**
The diameter of the light-collecting lens or mirror of an astronomical instrument.

• **APPARENT MAGNITUDE**
The brightness of an object as seen from the Earth. It is affected by the object's distance from us.

• **ASTERISM**
A pattern formed by stars in one or more **constellations**. Examples are the Plough (or Big Dipper), which is part of Ursa Major, and the Great Square of Pegasus, formed by stars in both Pegasus and Andromeda.

• **ASTEROID**
A small, rocky body, also called a minor planet, orbiting the Sun.

• **AXIS**
An imaginary line about which a celestial object rotates.

• **BINARY STAR**
A pair of stars linked by gravity, orbiting around a common centre of mass. See also **Eclipsing binary**, **Spectroscopic binary**.

• **BLACK HOLE**
A volume of space in which gravity is so great that nothing can escape, not even light, although objects can fall in. Black holes are thought to form when massive stars collapse.

• **CELESTIAL OBJECT**
An object in space, such as a star, planet, or **galaxy**, that appears in the Earth's sky.

• **CELESTIAL EQUATOR**
The celestial equivalent of the Earth's equator, lying on the **celestial sphere** directly over the Earth's equator.

• **CELESTIAL POLES**
The celestial equivalent of the Earth's poles, around which the **celestial sphere** appears to turn each day.

• **CELESTIAL SPHERE**
An imaginary sphere of infinite size around the Earth, on which celestial objects appear to lie. See also pp.16–17.

• **CEPHEID VARIABLE**
A type of **variable star** that pulsates regularly in size, every few days or weeks, with a period that is linked to its average luminosity.

• **CHARGE-COUPLED DEVICE (CCD)**
A light-sensitive silicon chip used in place of photographic film to record images of celestial objects.

• **CIRCUMPOLAR STAR**
A star that is above the horizon all night, as seen from a particular location on the Earth. Instead of rising and setting, the star appears to circle one of the celestial poles.

• **COMET**
A ball of frozen gas and dust on a long orbit around the Sun.

• **CONJUNCTION**
An occasion when two bodies in the **Solar System** (usually the Sun and a planet) line up as seen from the Earth. See also **Inferior conjunction**, **Superior conjunction**.

• **CONSTELLATION**
An area of sky, originally a star pattern, but now defined as the area within boundaries set by the International Astronomical Union.

• **DECLINATION (DEC.)**
The angle between an object and the **celestial equator**. Declination is the equivalent of latitude on the Earth. It is measured at right angles to the celestial equator, from 0° on the equator itself to 90° north or south at the **celestial poles**.

• **DEEP-SKY OBJECT**
A term applied to star clusters, **nebulae**, and **galaxies**.

• **DIFFUSE NEBULA**
A bright cloud of gas, illuminated by stars within it.

• **DOUBLE STAR**
Two stars that look close together as seen from the Earth. See also **Binary star**, **Optical double star**.

• **ECLIPSE**
An occasion when one celestial object cuts off some or all of the light from another.

• **ECLIPSING BINARY**
A pair of stars in orbit around each other, in which one star periodically passes in front of the other as seen from the Earth, cutting off its light.

• **ECLIPTIC**
The plane of the Earth's orbit around the Sun, projected on to the **celestial sphere**. The Sun appears to move along the ecliptic, but this is in fact due to the Earth's motion around the Sun.

• **ELONGATION**
The angle between a planet and the Sun, or between a moon and a planet, as seen from the Earth.

• **EQUINOX**
The occasion when the Sun lies on the **celestial equator**. This occurs twice a year, around 21 March and 23 September. At an equinox, day and night are roughly equal in length everywhere on the Earth.

• **GALAXY**
A mass of stars, numbering from millions to billions, all linked by gravity. Galaxies range from about a thousand light years to hundreds of thousands of light years across.

• **GIANT STAR**
A star that has become bigger and brighter in the late stages of its development.

• **GLOBULAR CLUSTER**
A ball-shaped group of stars, about 100 light years across, with tens of thousands to hundreds of thousands of members. Such clusters contain some of the oldest stars known.

• **INFERIOR CONJUNCTION**
The occasion when either Mercury or Venus lies between the Sun and the Earth.

• **LIGHT YEAR**
A unit of distance. It is the distance a beam of light covers in a calendar year, or 9,460,700,000,000 km (5,878,600,000,000 miles).

• **LOCAL GROUP**
The cluster of about 30 **galaxies** that includes our own.

• **LUMINOSITY**
The inherent brightness of a light-producing celestial object.

• **MAGNITUDE**
The brightness of a celestial object, measured on a numerical scale on which bright objects are given low

or negative values and faint objects have high values. The brightest stars are termed first magnitude, fainter ones second magnitude, and so on. In general usage, an object described as being of, for example, fourth magnitude has a magnitude between 3.5 and 4.49. *See also* **Absolute magnitude, Apparent magnitude.** *See also* p.18.

• **METEOR**
A streak of light in the sky, caused by a small particle burning up in the Earth's atmosphere.

• **METEORITE**
A fragment of an **asteroid** that has fallen to the surface of a planet or its satellite.

• **MILKY WAY**
The hazy band that can be seen in the sky on dark nights, composed of billions of distant stars in our own **Galaxy**. It is also a popular name for our Galaxy as a whole.

• **MIRA VARIABLE**
A red **giant** or **supergiant star** that pulsates in size over a period of months or years, varying in brightness by as much as 11 **magnitudes.**

• **NEBULA**
A cloud of gas and dust, usually found in the spiral arms of a **galaxy.** *See also* **Planetary nebula, Diffuse nebula.**

• **NEUTRON STAR**
A small and highly dense star consisting of the atomic particles known as neutrons, and thought to be the remains of a massive star that has exploded as a **supernova.**

• **NOVA**
A star that erupts temporarily in brightness by many thousands of times. Novae occur in close **binary stars,** one member of which is a **white dwarf.** Gas flows from the companion star on to the white dwarf, causing a small explosion which leads to the brightening.

• **OPEN CLUSTER**
An irregularly shaped group of dozens or hundreds of relatively young stars, usually found in the spiral arms of a **galaxy.**

• **OPPOSITION**
The occasion when a body in the **Solar System** appears opposite the Sun, as seen from the Earth, and is hence visible all night.

• **OPTICAL DOUBLE STAR**
Two stars that appear close to one

another in the sky but in fact lie at different distances from the Earth.

• **ORBIT**
The path of an object that is moving through space under the gravitational influence of another body of greater mass.

• **PARALLAX**
The change in position of an object when seen from two different locations. How much the object's position changes depends on its distance and the separation of the observing locations. Nearby stars show a slight parallax shift as the Earth orbits the Sun, from which their distances can be calculated.

• **PHASE**
A fraction of the illuminated disc of a planet or moon, as seen from the Earth.

• **PLANET**
A relatively large object that orbits a star and does not emit light.

• **PLANETARY NEBULA**
A shell of gas thrown off by a star late in its development.

• **RADIANT**
The point from which the **meteors** in a shower appear to diverge.

• **REFLECTING TELESCOPE**
A telescope in which light is collected and focused by a mirror.

• **REFRACTING TELESCOPE**
A telescope in which light is collected and focused by a lens.

• **RETROGRADE MOTION**
Movement from east to west (or clockwise as seen from above an object's north pole). This is opposite to the general direction of motion in the **Solar System.**

• **RIGHT ASCENSION (RA)**
A coordinate on the **celestial sphere,** the equivalent of longitude on Earth. It is measured in hours (one hour being equivalent to 15 degrees) from the point where the Sun crosses the **celestial equator** every March (the vernal equinox).

• **SOLAR SYSTEM**
The Sun and the various bodies in orbit around it. These include the nine planets and their moons, as well as **asteroids, comets,** and smaller pieces of debris.

• **SOLSTICE**
The occasion when the Sun reaches its furthest point either north or south of the **celestial equator.** This happens around

21 June, the longest day in the northern hemisphere, and 22 December, the longest day in the southern hemisphere.

• **SPECTROSCOPIC BINARY**
A pair of stars so close together that they cannot be separated with any telescope. The fact that the star is a **binary** is revealed only when its light is studied with a spectroscope.

• **STAR**
A ball of gas that generates heat and light as a result of nuclear reactions at its core.

• **SUPERGIANT STAR**
A star at least ten times as massive as the Sun, and which has become bigger and brighter in the late stages of its development. Supergiants can be hundreds of times the diameter of the Sun, and tens of thousands of times as bright.

• **SUPERIOR CONJUNCTION**
The occasion when Mercury or Venus lies on the far side of the Sun, as seen from the Earth.

• **SUPERNOVA**
An explosion in which, for a few weeks or months, a star brightens by millions of times. Only the most massive stars become supernovae.

• **UNIVERSE**
Everything that exists, including all matter, space, and time.

• **VARIABLE STAR**
Any star that appears to change in brightness. This is usually due to pulsations in the size of the star, but some variables are actually close **binary stars** in which one star periodically **eclipses** the other. *See also* **Cepheid variable, Mira variable.**

• **WHITE DWARF**
A small, dense star with a mass similar to that of the Sun, but only about 1 per cent of the Sun's diameter.

• **ZENITH**
The point in the sky directly above an observer.

• **ZODIAC**
The band of sky either side of the **ecliptic** through which the Sun and planets move. Although there are 12 **constellations** of the zodiac dating from ancient times, more recent changes in constellation boundaries also mean that the Sun and planets also pass through a 13th constellation, Ophiuchus.

INDEX

ACKNOWLEDGMENTS

THE AUTHOR AND PUBLISHER would like to thank the following people for their invaluable help: Robin Scagell for advice on photography; the staff at Her Majesty's Nautical Almanac Office, Cambridge (particularly Steve Bell, David Harper, Catherine Hohenkerk, and Andrew Sinclair) for their work on the star charts and planet location diagrams; and John Woodruff for proof-reading and indexing.

DORLING KINDERSLEY would also like to thank: Broadhurst, Clarkson and Fuller Ltd (63 Farringdon Road, London) for supplying telescopes; Lynne Marie Stockman for reference material for the inset chart of the Pleiades on p.133; Nick Stevens for the photographs used in the illustration of moon phases on p.40; Giles Sparrow for checking the constellation figure artworks; and Lesley Riley for editorial assistance.

ILLUSTRATION CREDITS
All star charts and planet-location diagrams plotted by Her Majesty's Nautical Almanac Office, Royal Greenwich Observatory. Solar System locator illustrations by Rob Campbell. Illustrations of the internal structure of the planets and the rings and moons of the gas planets by Luciano Corbella. Tilt, rotation, and orbit illustrations and pie-charts of atmospheric composition by Martin Cropper. Constellation figure illustrations by Gavin Dunn.
  Other illustrations are by the following artists/organisations: Julian Baum 14 (b), 26 (all), 29 (c), 32 (c), 38, 41 (c), 42 (cl & cr), 46 (c), 50 (c), 51, 54 (c), 56 (c), 58 (c), 59 (t), 60 (t), 61. Richard Bonson 12 (c), 13 (all), 14 (t & c), 19 (bl), 23 (all). Rob Campbell 12 (b), 27 (c). Luciano Corbella 9 (b), 19 (br), 34 (cl), 44 (cr). DK Cartography/Planetary Visions Ltd (London) 36 (c). DK Cartography 142 (t). John Egan 16 (all), 17 (all), 53, 60 (bl). Helen Taylor 15 (tr, bl, & br), 18 (b), 20 (b), 21 (all), 33 (c), 36 (b), 39 (c), 40 (t), 43 (c), 44 (cl), 47 (t), 59 (c). King and King 28 (all), 40 (b), 62.

PHOTOGRAPHY CREDITS
The following pictures were provided by Galaxy Picture Library: Robin Scagell 12, 17, 22 (all), 27 (clb), 30 (tr), 33 (tr), 43 (tc & tr), 47 (cl), 51 (tr), 60, 64, 67 (both), 68, 69, 70, 72, 78, 81, 85, 86 (tr & bl), 87 (all), 88 (both), 90 (cr), 93, 95, 96, 97, 99, 103, 105, 108, 121, 124, 126, 133, 137, 138 (both), 145, 157, 163, 169, 175, 187, 199, 211, jacket back flap; Stan Armstrong 28 (tr, cr & tc); Howard Brown-Greaves 28 (c); Adrian Catterall 108 (br); Stephen Fielding 129; Chris Floyd 127 (br); Bob Garner 43 (c), 47, 51 (cr); Gordon Garradd 30 (tl), 74, 76, 77, 79, 91, 94, 106, 114, 116, 122, 127 (bl), 134, 139, 151; Maurice Gavin 33 (c), 41 (b), 47 (cr), 51 (c), 107; Y. Hirose 40; Eric Hutton 115 (tl inset); JPL 31 (r), 35 (all), 45 (all), 48, 49 (all); Chris Livingstone 205, 193; Rob McNaught 181; Brian Manning 90 (br); Michael Maunder 28; Stan Moore 111; Bob Mizon 141; NASA 53 (br), 311 (Calvin J. Hamilton), 41 (l), 53 (cl), 57; Terry Platt 137 (tr); Pedro Re 99 (tr), 100, 113, 117, 130, 140; Royal Observatory, Edinburgh and Anglo-Australian Observatory (©) 1982 10 (both); Trevor Searle & Phil Hodgins 137 (bl); Charles Smith 22 (br); Michael Stecker 13, 64, 66, 73, 77, 89 (tr), 110, 115, 115 (br), 118, 125 (all), 127 (tl), 128, 131, front cover (br); Nick Szymanek/Ian King 83, 89 (bl), 120, 132, 137 (br); STScI 10, 59, 131 (tr); US Geological Survey 39.
Pictures from other sources: Anglo-Australian Observatory: 9 (all), 13 (c), 135. Corbis: Roger Ressmeyer 8–9 (t). Andy Crawford 20 (all), 21, 22 (cl), 23 (all), 24 (all), 143. Dave King 22 (cr). Science Photo Library: NASA/GSFC 37; Hale Observatory 27 (tr); Frank Zullo 2.

Jacket design by Sharon Spencer

KEY TO PICTURE CREDITS
a=above, c=centre, b=below, l=left, r=right, t=top